THE SOCIO-ECONOMICS OF CONVERSION FROM WAR TO PEACE

Studies in Socio-Economics

MORALITY, RATIONALITY, AND EFFICIENCY
NEW PERSPECTIVES ON SOCIO-ECONOMICS
Richard M. Coughlin, editor

SOCIO-ECONOMICS
TOWARD A NEW SYNTHESIS
Amitai Etzioni and Paul R. Lawrence, editors

INSTITUTIONAL CHANGE
THEORY AND EMPIRICAL FINDINGS
Sven-Erik Sjöstrand, editor

THE MORAL PHILOSOPHY OF MANAGEMENT
FROM QUESNAY TO KEYNES
Pierre Guillet de Monthoux

THE SOCIO-ECONOMICS OF CRIME AND JUSTICE
Brian Forst, editor

ECONOMY, ENVIRONMENT, AND TECHNOLOGY
A SOCIOECONOMIC APPROACH
Beat Bürgenmeier, editor

THE SOCIO-ECONOMICS OF CONVERSION
FROM WAR TO PEACE
Lloyd J. Dumas, editor

THE SOCIO-ECONOMICS OF CONVERSION FROM WAR TO PEACE

EDITOR
Lloyd J. Dumas

M.E. Sharpe
Armonk, New York
London, England

Library of Congress Cataloging-in-Publication Data

The socio-economics of conversion from war to peace / Lloyd J. Dumas, editor
p.   cm.
Includes index.
ISBN 1-56324-528-0.   ISBN 1-56324-529-9 (pbk.)
1. Economic conversion—United States.
2. Economic conversion.
I. Dumas, Lloyd J.
HC110.D4S53   1995
338.973—dc20
94-48186
CIP

Printed in the United States of America

The paper used in this publication meets the minimum requirements of
American National Standard for Information Sciences—
Permanence of Paper for Printed Library Materials,
ANSI Z 39.48-1984.

∞

BM (c)   10   9   8   7   6   5   4   3   2   1
BM (p)   10   9   8   7   6   5   4   3   2   1

Contents

List of Tables

Preface

Conversion: A Study in Transition

The idea that people will, in times of peace, convert their swords into plowshares is indeed a very old one. It evokes hopes of large amounts of resources being released for peaceful use, enriching people rather than killing them. And neoclassical economists have little trouble with expecting resources to be "reallocated" as the demand for military goods declines and for consumer goods to reach new highs. The facts are much more complicated. The sector of the economy involved in arms production and sales draws largely on government funds and thus is driven significantly by political considerations, and is not governed by market considerations (although there is some competition among the arms dealers of various nations). Thus, for instance, Electric Boat keeps producing nuclear submarines despite the fact that the Pentagon declares that it does not need any more. It gets the $2 billion (take or leave a few hundred million, mainly take) because of political connections of the corporation and the labor unions involved, not any discernible military or peace-time need.

This case is unfortunately not an exception. Much arms production is driven not by the demands of the marketplace, but by the demands of political actors: politicians who fear unemployment in their jurisdictions; corporations that find that it is easier to lobby for continued arms production—with PAC contributions and "grassroots" pressure—than it is to face competition in the civilian sectors; and international arms traders who bribe their way to fuel arms races by supplying both sides with ever deadlier and costlier weapons, "up-grading" the old ones as if they were passenger cars. And hired intellectuals produce rationales to justify continued high levels of military commitments in peace time:

"Who knows what the future will bring?" they write, "You can never be too careful," etc., ad nauseam.

All too quickly conversion gets redefined as not necessarily meaning conversion but as producing some goods in another place, for example Russians trying to make tractors in tank factories but continuing to operate those as part of the army's industrial base, or some other such rather limited adjustment.

The first task of socio-economics is to detail the varying major factors—most of which are not purely economic—that slow down the conversion process. The second and more difficult task is to develop politics that will reduce these hurdles and allow us to overcome them. Many scores of billions that are now at best wasted, at worst used for war, are at stake. Even more important, many very talented and hardworking people could be redirected to pursuits that are socially useful if we could find the ways. The book before us addresses both of these crucial issues. Much work remains to be done.

Amitai Etzioni
November 1994

Introduction

We are rapidly approaching the end of a century and of a millennium. Such times naturally call forth reevaluations of the past and visions of the future. It has been a millennium disgraced by innumerable wars and capped by a century that has few rivals in the sheer magnitude of human cruelty. The twentieth century has seen two world wars and hundreds of wars on less than global scale, repeated attempts at genocide that have resulted in the deaths of millions, and the development of weapons arsenals so fearsome as to threaten the end of human society, if not the extinction of the species. It has also been a time of unprecedented advance in democracy, of spectacular achievements in the technical capacity for extending and improving the material conditions of human life, of breaking the bonds that for all of human history had held us to the surface of the planet on which we were born. Now, in the last decade of that century, of that millennium, we turn toward the future and ask what lies ahead.

There are few issues in which the choices that lie before us and the power to shape our own future are highlighted more sharply than that of economic conversion. This issue presents us with a problem, but more than that, it presents us with an opportunity. Conversion inherently requires us to think about how to leave the past behind and how to find the future. It inevitably raises the question of what shape the future should take. And that is an extremely powerful question.

The question "Convert to what?" not only raises detailed, practical issues of finding alternative civilian products and blueprinting the retooling of factories and retraining of workers it also raises broader issues of the nature of the economy and society in which we wish to live. If product planning and programs of retooling and retraining are dictated from above, they are unlikely to generate the kind of enthusiasm and support they might have if they were developed with the active participation of the workers (and perhaps communities, as well) most directly affected by the transition. For this and other reasons, more participatory approaches to conversion are much more likely to succeed, even in the narrow sense, than those that are imposed. They also tend to empower people. If conversion is handled properly, it may just give ordinary people the revolutionary idea that they can control their own lives, the revolutionary idea that is, after all, the cornerstone of democracy.

The long Cold War has seriously damaged the economy, and our decision to finance much of it through borrowing has mortgaged the future. Conversion offers us the possibility of repairing the damage and paying off the mortgage. The military sector is the only domestic source, available in less than a generation, of enough high-quality technical talent to rebuild the competitiveness of U.S. industry. It is also a source of enormous capital resources. Properly done, conversion can trigger an industrial renaissance in this country unlike anything seen since the Industrial Revolution itself.

Capturing the full benefits of conversion requires the development and implementation of effective policy. Developing and implementing effective policy necessarily begins with a thorough understanding of both the nature of the problems presented by conversion and the enormous opportunities it offers.

Part I explores the issues that underlie the process of conversion. In the first chapter, I explain why persistent high levels of military spending are so peculiarly debilitating to an economy, and hence why conversion is so important to repairing the economic damage of the long Cold War. I then present a political economist's view of the nature of the conversion problem, highlighting by inference the critical elements of cost-effective conversion. In chapter 2, Dana L. Dunn considers how the wealth of knowledge developed by sociologists might be brought to bear on the conversion problem. Dunn's work begins to fill an important deficit in the conversion literature, which to date has largely ignored valuable sociological insights into human behavior. George Mehring then carries this broadening of perspectives farther by looking at the conversion process from the viewpoint of organizational behavior. Mehring emphasizes the value of strategic learning in achieving the flexibility that is so important to the smooth transition of an organization from military-oriented to civilian-oriented activity.

Part II focuses on the American experience of conversion and related structural adjustment. Domenick Bertelli analyzes the efforts of military contractors to shift gears and enter civilian markets, arguing that the record is not nearly as bleak as is ordinarily supposed. While efforts to date have certainly fallen far short of what might be hoped, Bertelli finds reason for optimism. In chapter 5, Elizabeth Mueller zeroes in on retraining, one of the single most important elements of effective conversion. She compares the track record of federal training programs as they have been applied to displaced military industry workers in two very different regions—rural Flemington, New Jersey, and urban St. Louis, Missouri. Mueller concludes that there is much left to be done, including better integration of training programs with other federal adjustment programs for the military sector. Taking an activist's view, Fred Rose looks in chapter 6 at why it has been so difficult to create politically effective coalitions between organized labor and peace groups, both of which share a strong interest in successful conversion that seems to make them natural allies. Although he believes these problems can be overcome, Rose argues that much of the difficulty lies in very different perspectives on organizing that arise from the different socioeconomic backgrounds of the majority of participants in the labor and peace movements.

The explicit linkage between public policy and conversion is the focus of part III. Gregory Bischak argues the necessity of building "job bridges" to carry us over the gap between the short-term problems of conversion and its long-term benefits. Such bridges are more than a stopgap measure; they substantially reduce the pressure to continue useless military projects or encourage international arms sales. Jim Raffel considers the history of legislative efforts on conversion. While useful, these efforts have not been all that successful in passing legislation that is sufficiently comprehensive and well designed to work. Although the nation still lacks a coherent and effective conversion strategy, Raffel suggests that the reform agenda put forth by an interesting coalition of labor, peace, religious, and social justice groups contains the seeds of a better framework. In chapter 9, Jonathan Feldman evaluates the potential contribution of economics-based public choice theory to understanding behavior in the arena of military spending. He focuses especially on the evidence concerning one of its key assumptions—that an essentially autonomous public gets what it wants in the "political marketplace." Feldman concludes that there is so much government manipulation of public attitudes in this arena that public preferences are anything but autonomous here.

With all of the remarkable changes that have occurred in the previously socialist countries of Eastern Europe and the former Soviet Union, the ordinary problems of military–civilian conversion are greatly complicated by vast, underlying structural economic and political shifts. In part IV, Michael Oden and John Ullmann look at these issues. Oden considers how the previous, politically driven patterns of location of military industry in this region of the world have created very different regional economic impacts as military spending has not merely declined, but collapsed. Considering the nature of the conversion and restructuring problem in Russia (where the problem is most severe), Oden points to some scattered success stories and argues that strategies for improving enterprise performance in a low-investment environment are key to broadening the success of conversion. Ullmann emphasizes the importance of applying a criterion of economic viability rather than simple technical feasibility in choosing civilian alternative product lines. He points out that this represents a fundamental shift in orientation in an industrial sector so long accustomed to control by central planners. Productive investment in equipment, facilities, and human resources is indispensable to effective conversion in the former Communist economies. Looking to the West's attitudes toward aid, along with the East's priorities, Ullmann warns that

> the choice is not between making new investments and spending money on the one hand, and not making them and saving money on the other. The choice is between turning the former Communist countries into functioning societies that can take part in the world economy, and having them as permanent international relief clients that stumble from one crisis to another and constitute a potentially disastrous threat to world peace.

I strongly concur in that warning. Crippled economies and chaotic political environments are not conducive to intelligent public decision making and have more than once led to the ascendance of dangerous leaders who have wreaked havoc within their borders and beyond.

There are considerable differences in perspective, philosophy, and approach among the contributors to this book. While there are many areas of commonality, there are some sharp disagreements. What binds them together is a strongly shared belief that conversion is an imperative of our time, that it can be properly understood only by a multidisciplinary approach, and that "getting it right" will have a very positive impact on the quality of life and the character of society in the twenty-first century.

Part I
The Underlying Issues

Lloyd J. Dumas

Finding the Future: The Role of Economic Conversion in Shaping the Twenty-first Century

Expenditure, Investment, and Military Spending

After more than a decade of rapidly increasing federal budget deficits under administrations claiming to be fiscally conservative, it is no wonder that by the mid-1990s, the general public had become suspicious of deficit-reduction proposals. To avoid further antagonizing the public in this environment of skepticism and mistrust, Democrats and Republicans outdid themselves (and each other) in proposing budget cuts intended to show their determination to limit tax increases. Having more than quadrupled the national debt between 1980 and 1992, the United States clearly could not indefinitely continue to run up the national MasterCard bill. So there was tremendous pressure from all sides to narrow the gap between federal revenues and outlays, and at least to slow the rate of increase in the national burden of debt.

In all of this, two critical matters seem to have been lost: (1) the key economic difference between expenditure and investment; and (2) the enormous excess in the military budget.

In general, there is little or no distinction in government budgeting between expenditures and investments. A dollar of outlay is a dollar of outlay. Yet, from an economic point of view, expenditures and investments are entirely different. Expenditures are outlays that exchange money (or other resources) for goods and services that accomplish a particular present goal. After the money has been paid out and the goods and services received, the transaction is over. Investments, however, are outlays of current resources made in the hope and expectation of generating a future return. That is, investments are undertaken not to achieve an immediate goal, but to increase the resources available to the investor in the future.

This distinction is an important part of the difference between an economist's or enlightened businessperson's approach to dealing with red ink, and that of an accountant. To an accountant, overcoming deficits—whether in budgets, trade, or balance of payments—calls for reducing outflows and increasing inflows. It does not really matter which outflows are reduced or which inflows are increased. A businessperson or an economist, on the other hand, might recommend *increasing* outflows *in the form of investments* in order to generate much larger future inflows that will turn the deficit into surplus. For example, a retail business that is losing money might be best advised to increase its outlays on advertising in order to build its customer base, rather than simply cutting staff. As the saying goes, "You have to spend money to make money"—that is, as long as the "spending" is in the form of investment.

During the long Cold War, the military budget was the largest single category of federal expenditure on goods and services. For nearly half a century, with the armed might of a rival military superpower as a foil, the budget supported a large military establishment, serviced by an unparalleled system of laboratories and industrial facilities. The military budget is an expenditure, not an investment. As such, it had a particular though vaguely defined goal, to provide for the nation's security. Now the Cold War is over, the Soviet Union is no more, and the United States is the only global military superpower.

Although much has been made of the threats of international terrorism and Third World conflict by those who seek to maintain as large a military as possible, these threats, such as they are, were no less serious before the demise of the Soviet Union. The "Soviet threat" was indisputably the main driver and rationale for those huge Cold War budgets, and it no longer exists. Thus, apart from the issue of whether there was ever any justification for the huge military budgets that characterized the Cold War, it is inconceivable that the continuation of military spending at anywhere near that level is justifiable today. Furthermore, many large and expensive military systems, from the MX missile to the B1 (and B2) bomber to the Trident submarine, have absolutely no relevance to dealing with Third World conflict or international terrorism.

Arguments for an even-handed approach to budget reduction, balanced between military spending and domestic programs, are simplistic and make no sense. They are appealing because they have the appearance of fairness. But fairness is not the issue. Fairness may be an appropriate criterion for judging what levels of support make sense for programs of income transfer that benefit one or another segment of the population, but it is wholly inappropriate in the case of mission-oriented programs such as education, roadbuilding, or the military. Within the bounds of affordability, levels of support for the military should be based on what is needed to achieve the mission of securing the nation against real and significant external military threats. According to such a criterion, disproportionately large cuts in the military budget are entirely sensible and justifiable. That is not a matter of ideology, it is a matter of common sense.

This situation does not call for 5 or 10 percent cuts in military spending. A military budget no larger than half, and probably more like a quarter to a third of the Cold War average, properly spent, will give us a military force strong enough to provide as much security as military forces are capable of providing in the present and foreseeable future. In any case, by some estimates more than half the United States' Cold War military budget was designed to defend other nations with standards of living comparable to our own, against a threat that no longer exists. Why then, even with all the pressures to cut the federal budget deficit, are we so reluctant to recognize the enormity of excess in present military expenditures and to do what so obviously needs doing?

This is a classic case of a set of vested interests resisting every attempt to move decisively into the future. These interests have become so intertwined with the existing political and socioeconomic structure that it is extremely difficult to disentangle them. Like a tumor that has attached itself to the body's vital organs, it cannot be safely removed by simply chopping it away. It must be detached with the care and precision of a skilled surgeon's knife. Rough across-the-board policies will not work. Generalized macroeconomic stimulation is not the answer. Achieving the real benefits of the long-promised peace dividend is not merely a matter of changing some programs or shifting piles of money around, it is a matter of fundamental structural change. It requires a well-thought-out, careful structural approach.

Economic conversion is just such a careful structural approach. Conversion reaches into the economy and redirects human and capital resources from military to civilian-oriented activity. It involves the retraining and reorientation of work forces and the restructuring of organizations and facilities that have been serving the military sector so that they can *efficiently* produce civilian goods and services. It is a way of reassuring the individuals, companies, and communities whose income, profits, and economic base are currently locked into the military system that the realization of the dream of peacefully ending the Cold War need not be the beginning of an economic nightmare for them. It is a way of removing obstacles to change, of helping them let go.

But it can be much more than that. Economic conversion can play a critical role in directing key economic resources to the kinds of investment that are so important to rebuilding the competitiveness of U.S. industry and generating real economic growth that can help put an end to our trade and budget deficits. To fully understand why conversion is at the fulcrum of this important change of direction, it is first necessary to understand why the military budgets of the Cold War were so peculiarly damaging to our economic well-being.

Military Spending and Economic Decay

The predominant view among economists is that money value is the arbiter of economic value. As a reflection of this, the most commonly used measure of the total economic output of a society, the gross national product (GNP) (or its close relative, the gross domestic product—GDP), includes only goods and services for which money has been paid. That goods and services produced without money exchange (for example, within the household) can be useful is not denied. But they are clearly not considered part of the "economy," and are therefore not counted as part of economic output. On the other hand, all goods and services (that are legal) for which money has been paid are part of economic output, whatever their function or purpose. If the economy is defined as the system of production and exchange of goods and services for money, then money value *is* the appropriate arbiter of economic value. This is not, however, the most useful or insightful way to define economic activity.

It is more productive to define the economy as that part of the society whose central function is to provide material well-being. It generates and distributes both the goods and services that directly satisfy material needs (i.e., consumer goods, such as televisions and furniture) and the means required to supply them (i.e., producer goods, such as metal-cutting machines and industrial furnaces). This definition of the economy means that money value is no longer the same as economic value. The proper criterion of economic value becomes the extent to which a good or service contributes to material well-being. A bookcase made at home is just as much a part of economic output as a comparable bookcase bought from a furniture store. Whether or not it has money value, any activity that results in such a good or service contributes to the economy's goal of improving material well-being. Therefore, it makes sense to call that activity economically "contributive."

On the other hand, not all goods and services with money value add to the material standard of living. Some goods and services are created to satisfy other human wants and needs. Churches are not constructed and bibles printed to provide material well-being, but to help fulfill the need for spiritual guidance; courthouses and law books are not aimed at increasing the material wealth of society, but at providing political order and control; battle tanks and missiles do not themselves add to the material standard of living, they are produced to enhance physical security. Though these goods may carry a very hefty money price, and may be very useful for the purposes they serve, they do not directly contribute to the central purpose of the economy and so do not have any *economic* value. It is logical, then, to classify activities that result in goods or services that do not have economic value as economically "noncontributive."[1]

Although noncontributive activities are without *economic value*, to the extent that they use productive resources they do have *economic cost*, in terms of opportunities foregone. In other words, the economic cost of a noncontributive activity is measured by the economic value that could have been created by using the same labor, machinery, and equipment to produce goods and services that have economic value.

Economically productive resources that are used for noncontributive activity can be said to be "diverted" to other than economic purposes. An economy in which significant amounts of critical economic resources have been persistently diverted to noncontributive activities will tend to experience a long-term decline in its productive competence—that is, in its ability to produce efficiently.[2] And declining productive competence will lead to a deteriorating standard of living in the long run.

There is no question that the production of military goods and services is noncontributive activity. Whatever else may be said for such products, they do not add to the present standard of living as consumer goods do, or to the economy's capacity to produce standard-of-living goods and services in the future, as producer goods do. Military-oriented activity may be only one of many forms of noncontributive activity, but it is one of the largest and most important in the world today. And the voracious appetite of modern military sectors for both capital and engineers and scientists creates a particularly damaging kind of resource diversion. Why is the diversion of technologists and capital so damaging?

The majority of the population earns the largest part of its money income in the form of wages and salaries. Ongoing increases in wages and salaries that outrun inflation are thus key to producing sustained, broad-based improvement in the standard of living. But, since wages and salaries are the largest part of cost for most producers, increases in labor costs will squeeze profits, creating strong cost-push pressure for price increases. Unless some way is found to offset this pressure, widespread increases in product prices will be reflected in a rising rate of inflation. This will wear away the purchasing power of higher wages, undermining the rise in living standards. Furthermore, over time rising prices will make domestic producers less competitive with foreign producers who are still able to offset costs. As a result, markets will be lost, forcing layoffs and causing rising unemployment. Not, on the whole, a very upbeat picture.

The ability to offset cost-push pressures depends crucially on the rise of productivity. Although many things affect the rate of productivity increase, more than anything else, rising productivity depends on improving the techniques of production and the quantity and quality of capital available to workers. Improvements in the techniques of production come primarily from research and development (R&D) aimed at discovering and applying new civilian-oriented technology. Regardless of the amount of money spent, without a great enough quantity and quality of engineers and scientists available to perform the work, such R&D will not be successful. Money does not create technological progress, engineers and scientists do. However, if enough capital is not available, it may be difficult to provide the required research facilities, or to widely deploy the results of successful R&D to the factory floor throughout industry.

A persistent, large-scale diversion of engineers and scientists and/or capital to economically noncontributive military activity will unavoidably reduce their availability to contributive civilian activity. The stream of civilian-oriented, productivity-enhancing technological innovation will slow down, causing the rate of productivity growth to drop. Reduced productivity growth will, in turn, undermine the ability of domestic producers to offset the rising cost of labor, or for that matter, of any other input to production and supply. If wages and salaries continue to rise, the result will be cost-push inflation that will wear away the purchasing power of the nominally higher pay. If higher prices cannot be sustained in the face of foreign competition, there will be direct downward pressure on wages and salaries. If protectionist measures dull the edge of foreign competition, higher prices will penalize domestic consumers. In all three cases, the standard of living will decline; only the distribution of the loss and the mechanism by which the decline is transmitted will differ.

How large has the diversion of technological and capital resources been in the service of the arms race? For decades now, about 30 percent of the nation's engineers and scientists (full-time equivalent) have been engaged in military R&D. Because pay has been higher and access to state-of-the-art facilities and equipment better in that arena, the military has tended to attract a disproportionate number of the "best and the brightest" technologists. Thus, although the quantitative diversion of engineers and scientists is large enough, adjusted for quality, the "brain drain" is even larger.[3] Concerning capital diversion, as of 1990 the total book value of physical capital directly owned by the Department of Defense (DoD) (including plant equipment, structures, weapons, and related equipment and supplies) was more than 80 percent of the total book value of capital equipment and structures in all U.S. manufacturing facilities combined![4]

The standard of living in the United States has been declining since the mid-1970s. The failure of American industrial competitiveness has been highlighted by the replacement of more than three-quarters of a century of continuous trade surpluses (1894–1970) by decades of trade deficits. Hundreds of thousands of high-paying manufacturing jobs have been lost, while job creation has focused on "MacJobs"—low-paying, no-future jobs in the downscale part of the service sector. And all this alongside a national orgy of borrowing that quadrupled the national debt and transformed the United States from the world's largest net creditor internationally to the world's largest net debtor. Had the huge amount of capital borrowed just since 1980 been used for contributive investment and combined with the talents of otherwise diverted engineers and scientists, the United States would have undergone an industrial renaissance. Instead, such resources were lavished on largely noncontributive activity, and all we have to show for all that debt is protracted economic decline.

One clear implication of this analysis is that not all parts of the military budget have equal economic meaning. Roughly half the military budget has traditionally been operations and maintenance expense, including the salaries and benefits of those in the armed services. Although these outlays involve a great deal of money, they have relatively little economic impact. *The main economic action lies in procurement and R&D expenditures, because those are the outlays that draw engineers and scientists, industrial capital, and other productive economic resources into the military sector.* Compared with cutbacks in military procurement and R&D, troop reductions and base closings thus do very little to release the economic resources critical to industrial renewal. Yet the military spending cuts to date have been concentrated mainly on operations and maintenance.

Conversion and Reconversion

Economic conversion is key to economic renewal for two related reasons. First, it provides a means for efficiently reconnecting labor and capital resources released from the noncontributive military sector to contributive work in the civilian economy. It is, after all, not what diverted resources are doing (noncontributive activity), but what they are *not* doing (contributive activity) that causes economic decay. *Shrinking the military sector will do nothing to repair the economic damage of the arms race unless the released resources are reconnected to contributive civilian activity.* In economic terms, nothing will have been accomplished if those people and facilities are released from the military sector and become unemployed. Second, conversion can help reduce the natural resistance of entrenched vested interests to this restructuring by reassuring them that in fact reconnection, rather than unemployment, lies at the end of the road.

At the end of the World War II, the United States faced a great challenge. A large fraction of the nation's output had to be moved from military to civilian production. With a combination of private sector and federal, state, and local government planning, the challenge was met with flying colors. Some 30 percent of U.S. output was transferred in one year without the unemployment rate ever rising above 3 percent.[5] This experience made it clear that it is possible to redirect enormous amounts of productive resources from military to civilian activity without intolerable economic disruption. But it is an experience that must be interpreted with care.

First of all, rationing during the war combined with high incomes to create considerable pent-up demand for all manner of consumer products. When rationing ended with the war, there was a ready-made, unsatisfied market for a wide variety of goods to which war producers could turn. There was little foreign competition to challenge American producers, since every major industrial nation except the United States had been severely damaged by the war. Even more important, the companies that supplied the military during the war were basically civilian companies that shifted to military production for a few years from their normal business of making civilian products. All of their workers, including managers, engineers, and scientists, knew how to operate in a civilian commercial market environment. That is what they had spent most of their working lives doing. Though modifications had been made during the war, most production facilities and equipment had originally been designed and configured for efficient civilian production. For these firms and their work forces, this was a "reconversion"—that is, they were going back to business as usual.

The situation today is quite different. There is no deep well of unsatisfied pent-up demand, and there is fierce foreign competition. Decades, rather than a few years, of high military expenditures have drained the U.S. economy and put many domestic producers far behind their overseas rivals. It is no coincidence that the two most successful industrial economies in competition with the United States have been the two industrialized nations prevented by the World War II terms of surrender from building massive military forces—Germany and Japan.

Today there are generations of managers, engineers, scientists, and production and maintenance workers whose employment experience includes little or nothing but military-oriented work. Many present-day military-industrial firms have never operated in civilian commercial markets. Even those that are large-scale manufacturers of both military and civilian products (e.g., Boeing and Rockwell International) typically have operationally insulated military and civilian divisions functioning as separate, wholly owned subsidiaries reporting to the same overall top management.

Furthermore, during World War II, both the means of production and the technologies used in designing and manufacturing military goods were still fairly similar to those in the civilian economy. Over the past half century, the physical plant, machinery, and technologies involved in military and civilian manufacturing have sharply diverged. The technologies embodied in the designs of the products themselves are even more different. For the major military producers, moving into civilian commercial markets is most assuredly not returning to "business as usual." It is movement into new and unexplored territory. It is conversion, not reconversion.

That makes the process more difficult. But with some care and advanced planning, there is little question that it can be successful.

The Nature of the Conversion Problem

The United States' military sector does not operate by market principles. It is the closest thing to centrally planned socialism in the United States. The nature, quantity, and price of output are not determined by impersonal market forces. They are set by the interaction of the Pentagon's central planners and the managers of military industry. The vast majority of Department of Defense business is negotiated rather than awarded through a serious and enforced competitive bidding process. In practice, virtually all major military contracts operate as if they were "cost-plus"—with producers reimbursed for whatever they have spent, "plus" a guaranteed profit. Under such a contract, the manufacturer bears virtually no risk and can increase revenues without hurting profits by high-cost, inefficient operation. In a competitive commercial marketplace, this kind of inefficient operation would cause serious, if not fatal, problems for the company. In the sheltered and subsidized world of the centrally planned military sector, it is a recipe for growth and success.[6]

Much of the capital of the military sector is owned by the government. Some military-oriented production and maintenance facilities are wholly government-owned and completely government-operated

(GOGO). Many more are government-owned but operated by private military contractors (GOCO). As of the mid-1980s, there were more than fifty GOGO and more than sixty GOCO military-serving manufacturing and maintenance facilities entirely owned by the federal government.[7] In addition, a great deal of government-owned industrial equipment is used in privately owned and operated plants by military contractors.

Military industrial firms serve a well-funded customer willing to cover whatever costs they might incur. They therefore have a tremendous advantage over market-oriented firms in bidding for resources. Civilian commercial firms must be concerned with the cost of everything they buy. They are not guaranteed reimbursement of costs plus a profit in advance by their customers. Backed by an essentially cost-plus procurement system, military firms can pay as much as they need to pay to make sure they get the inputs they want, whether those are exotic metals or engineers. As a result, the military sector is able to divert resources from the civilian economy almost as easily as if they were diverted by government decree (which is how the same thing was accomplished in planned economies, like that of the former Soviet Union).

While the military sector is relatively insensitive to cost, it is very much driven by performance. Military firms are contracted to design and deliver products that are capable of high levels of performance under extraordinarily hostile operating conditions. Although they do not always succeed, they are pressed hard to squeeze every ounce of performance out of products that can operate under varied and extreme conditions of vibration, shock, temperature, humidity, dirt, and so on. The cost-insensitive, performance-driven world of the military sector affects both the capital and the labor it uses. Some capital is so specialized to military-serving use that it has no sensible civilian alternative use; other capital may technically be usable for civilian purposes, but has a cost-capability tradeoff that makes it inappropriate for a market-oriented firm.

More important, long years of training and experience in the peculiar world of the military sector can create a labor force with a trained incapacity to function effectively in a civilian commercial environment. Except possibly for wage expectations, this is not that much of a problem for most factory-floor workers or lower-level administrative and clerical personnel. But managers, engineers, and scientists are generally so greatly affected that they are not readily reemployable in the civilian, market-oriented sector without significant reshaping. They need to be taught some new skills (retraining) and just as important, taught to look at what they do from the entirely different perspective of a cost-sensitive operating environment (reorientation).

Managers, for example, are used to operating in a one-customer world of guaranteed profit, where the critical skills are maintaining capability with little regard to cost, meeting the bureaucratic requirements of the armed forces procurement regulations, and lobbying effectively for contracts. This has little in common with the critical civilian commercial sector skills of minimizing cost, serving many and varied customers, and navigating in the constantly changing commercial marketplace where nothing is guaranteed. Military sector engineers are able to use the most exotic materials and must specify the most exacting tolerances to meet stringent military performance requirements. For the most part, these engineers will not even be aware of just how dramatically tight tolerances and exotic materials can increase the cost of manufacturing and maintenance. They do not know because they have not had to know. But unless they come to understand the cost implications of their work and learn to take them seriously, they will be of very little use to any civilian firm that might hire them.

Policies for Successful Conversion

Given a thorough understanding of the endpoints of conversion—the very different operating environments of the military and of the civilian sectors—policies can be designed to carry workers and facilities successfully through this difficult transition. For technical reasons, some things must be done regardless of the particular shape the conversion process takes. It is abundantly clear, for example, that any sensible conversion process must take seriously the need both to retrain and to reorient managers, engineers, and scientists. But other things are greatly affected by whether conversion is internal or external to the firm.

"Internal" conversion involves the transition of work force, facilities, and equipment within a formerly military-oriented firm that is shifting to servicing a civilian market. "External" conversion involves the transition of workers, facilities, and equipment that are released by a military-oriented firm and so must find reemployment elsewhere.

Internal conversion has much to recommend it. It minimizes disruption of the lives of workers and their families, since it aims at keeping as much of the work force intact as is economically sensible. It minimizes disruption of the surrounding community as well by maintaining the tax base and the geographic patterns of living, spending, and commuting. And working within the familiar context of an existing firm and workplace means that less on-the-job adjustment is required on the part of the affected work force. On the other hand, some external conversion is unavoidable.

Even if all military contractors were committed to planning for internal conversion, some part of their work force would have to be externally converted. The engineering intensity and management staff size common in military industry are simply unsupportable in any economically viable, unsubsidized civilian firm. One of the most striking anecdotal illustrations is the B1 bomber plant in El Segundo, California, which at the height of its operation had 14,000 workers, including 5,000 production workers, 5,000 engineers, and 4,000 managers. What civilian manufacturer, low tech or high tech, would need or could support one engineer and almost one manager per production worker? Efficiency inevitably requires some paring of the work force. External conversion is therefore needed both to reshape the engineers and managers laid off from converting military enterprises and to reconnect them to other civilian firms.

Furthermore, no matter how carefully internal conversion is planned, some of the plans will not work well. There are many reasons, some of which have more to do with the uncertainties of life in the world of business than with the quality of planning. External conversion will be required to find new civilian opportunities for the workers (and perhaps the facilities as well) associated with the plans that failed. But the plain fact is, the main reason external conversion will be required is that many military contractors, especially major contractors, are extremely resistant to any form of internal conversion planning. They intend to fight for every bit of military business that remains and to "downsize" (a euphemism for laying off workers and shrinking the company) when they lose military contracts. For many years, these firms successfully used "job blackmail" (threats to lay off large numbers of workers) to coerce the Congress into funding military programs that, in some cases, even the Pentagon did not want. And old habits die hard.

Some argue that external conversion is preferable because it is easier to get off on the right foot in a new enterprise than it is to completely reshape patterns within an existing company. There is something to be said for this point of view. It *is* more difficult to change patterns of behavior when much of the surrounding physical and sociological environment remains the same. Yet business enterprises that are healthy and vital must retain the flexibility to reshape themselves when business conditions change. There are few ways to get deeper into trouble in business, especially in the long term, than to get caught in a changing game without recognizing that the game is changing. For military industrial firms, like it or not, the game is most assuredly changing. For the firms as well as their employees and the surrounding community, then, there is much to recommend internal conversion.

One of the great technical advantages of internal conversion has to do with reshaping the labor force. Job retraining programs are far more effective if they are targeted to specific job opportunities. With internal conversion, the nature of the job any given worker will be doing after conversion is known nearly as well as the nature of his or her present job. Whether we are dealing with scientists, engineers, production workers, clerical/administrative workers, or managers, it is much easier to develop a successful program for whatever retraining and/or reorientation might be required with this knowledge in hand. Knowing what position the trainee will be filling is such an advantage that it must also be taken seriously in external conversion. Mechanisms need to be developed for connecting workers to future employment before retraining begins, if at all possible. For example, the government might sign retraining contracts with potential civilian employers. The government would agree to pay for or heavily subsidize a program of retraining that is tailored to the needs of the employer, provided the employer agrees to hire (and retain for a specified minimum period) the trainee upon successful completion of the program.

Both public and private sectors have key roles to play in converting the economy. There are things they should do, and just as important, there are things they should not do. It is very helpful to have the coordination and assistance that the federal government can provide, but if the conversion process is not highly decentralized, it has very little chance of working well. The search for productive and profitable civilian activities to replace the previous military mission, and the plans for the reshaping of capital and labor they imply, must be tailored to the details of each particular facility and workplace. This is one case where a one-size-fits-all approach virtually guarantees that nothing will fit anyone. It is a mistake for the federal government to try to blueprint facility and work-force conversion. There is no good substitute for a high degree of decentralization in the detailed planning and plan implementation process. Even close oversight of microlevel conversion by the federal government is a poor idea. It is unlikely to improve the effectiveness of conversion plans and highly likely to be inefficient and expensive. Although this is more obviously true of internal conversion, it is important for external conversion as well.

A more appropriate role for the federal government is to use its leverage as customer to pressure military industry to begin planning for internal conversion without further delay. This could easily be accomplished by following the precedent of other federal legislation, such as equal employment opportunity laws, that set requirements for eligibility for federal contracts. One low-cost approach is to require military contractors to set up independently funded labor–management "alternative use committees" (AUCs) as a condition of eligibility for any future federal contract, military or civilian. There is no airtight guarantee that this planning will be taken seriously and done well. But with independent funding and the combination of competing and common interests of labor and management in the conversion process at work, the probability of triggering effective internal conversion is certainly much higher.

It may also be time to resurrect, in updated form, one of the most successful federal investment programs in the nation's history, the World War II vintage GI Bill of Rights. Under the provisions of the GI Bill, millions of individuals who had served in the armed forces received training and educational benefits to help them improve their earning capacity and employment opportunities. According to former Senator Ralph Yarborough, who chaired a committee that evaluated the performance of the program, the GI Bill was an investment with an enormous rate of return. The extra federal taxes collected out of the higher incomes earned because of the training amounted to some thirty times the program's cost to the taxpayer. And this does not even begin to consider the plethora of other benefits to the economy and society that attend a better-trained and better-educated work force and citizenry. A new GI Bill for all workers in the military sector would make a great deal of sense in facilitating conversion today. I see no reason why this approach could not eventually be broadened to cover all displaced workers. However, it is important to recognize that workers undergoing conversion (particularly engineers, scientists, and managers) do have special problems. Even more important, *the successful conversion of these workers, especially of engineers and scientists, holds the key to the kind of industrial renewal that can and will brighten the economic prospects of the entire labor force.*

With all the differences between the reconversion problem that followed World War II and the conversion problem today, the basic division of responsibility that succeeded then still makes sense. The public sector—federal, state, and local—took care of education and training, and planned public works projects to create productive jobs building the nation's infrastructure. But the private sector did all of the microlevel corporate planning.

Alternatives to Conversion

Conversion is only one of three policy approaches that deal with the economic transition to lower levels of military expenditure. It is the most thoroughgoing approach, reaching into the structure of economy to redirect human and capital resources from military to civilian activity. But it is also the most complex and most difficult.

Diversification is one alternative approach. It seeks to minimize the economic stress of transition by reducing economic dependence on the flow of military dollars. It has for years been the preferred strategy of those military-dependent firms in the United States that have paid attention to the possibility that the volume of their military contracts might someday fall. By operating parallel civilian product divisions within their own firms or acquiring other civilian producers, they can protect the company's financial position against the possible loss of military business. When major military firms have tried to diversify by producing civilian products in their military divisions without the kind of retraining and restructuring that is at the heart of conversion, the results have routinely been disastrous for both the companies and their customers. There are quite a few examples of failures of this particular type of diversification.

The prime contractor on the Bay Area Rapid Transit (BART) system in San Francisco was Rohr, a military aerospace company. BART was years late getting into service and greatly overran its initial cost estimates. Boeing Vertol, the military helicopter division of Boeing Aircraft, took a considerable financial loss producing light rail transit vehicles (streetcars) for the city of Boston because of unreimbursed cost overruns. The vehicles broke down so frequently and sometimes so completely that they could not be repaired on site. They had to be shipped back to the factory. Vought Corporation, the military aerospace division of LTV, manufactured an automated "people mover" called Airtrans for Dallas/Ft. Worth Airport in the 1970s. Twenty years later, the system still did not meet all of its original specifications. Its overruns and project delays led to a flurry of lawsuits between Vought and the airport authority.

Ironically, the dismal record of this type of diversification has often been cited as proof that internal conversion does not work. But this is not conversion. In fact, given the striking differences between the operating environments in the military and civilian commercial sectors discussed earlier, it is completely predictable that this type of diversification is doomed from the beginning. These experiences demonstrate the importance of heeding the caveats of internal conversion. It is dishonest to use these cases as examples of the failure of conversion. And to use them as an excuse for not facing the need to take this transition seriously is unconscionable.

Community economic adjustment is another alternative approach. It involves government providing financial and technical assistance to military-dependent cities and towns to help them overcome the problems created by base closings, loss of business by local military contractors, or the need to reintegrate large numbers of discharged military personnel into the local economy. For decades, community economic adjustment has been the Pentagon's policy of choice for quieting the uproar that attends the announcement of military base closings. Typically, the Department of Defense has not provided much financial aid under this program. It has instead offered limited technical assistance and served as a liaison for the communities with other federal agencies.

Properly implemented diversification and well-funded economic adjustment programs can provide some help in mitigating the financial stresses that military-dependent companies and communities face as military budgets are cut back. Unfortunately, neither of these policies does much to help displaced military sector workers modify and redirect their skills for civilian employment. Only conversion seeks to recoup the largest part of the huge investment society has made in the skills of the workers and in the facilities and equipment of the military sector. It takes seriously the possibility of reusing military-serving facilities and equipment, but only where such reuse makes economic sense. And most important, conversion refuses to accept the personal cruelty and social foolishness of writing off a generation of military sector workers because their current skills and orientation need reshaping to fit changing labor needs. Diversification and community economic adjustment programs are much more ready to abandon and move on.

Conversion and the Twenty-First Century

Times of transition are always difficult. They call on us to break old familiar patterns that have come to feel comfortable. Effort is required where habit and routine once carried us through. It takes some courage to face up to the need for change, even when it is clear that the patterns of the past are no longer tenable. It takes some creativity and determination to recast our lives in ways that are not just different, but better.

We are living in an era of profound change. That can be frightening, but it can also be liberating. Where the structures of the past have crumbled, there is the opportunity to create new and better structures for the future. And it is easier to build bridges when walls come down.

In the last decades of the twentieth century, structures have crumbled and walls have come down all over the world. That we are passing through a time of profound change is undeniable. What we do—or fail to do—now will change the shape of the century to come. The enormous, worldwide preemption of productive resources for military purposes over the past fifty years says a great deal about the world we have created and the priorities we have established. If we have courage, foresight, and determination, we can break with the deadly, fear-driven legacy of this tortured century. We can find a more productive, life-enhancing way to use our talents and capabilities. Conversion, properly understood and implemented, can help us work our way through the myriad of details needed to build a practical path to a world that is both more prosperous and more humane.

Notes

1. See Lloyd J. Dumas, *The Overburdened Economy: Uncovering the Causes of Chronic Unemployment, Inflation and National Decline* (Berkeley: University of California Press, 1986).
2. Ibid., pp. 147–83.
3. Ibid., pp. 209–11.
4. The book value of capital owned by the Department of Defense is from Department of Defense, *Real and Personal Property* (September 30, 1990). The book value of capital in U.S. manufacturing as a whole is from Bureau of Economic Analysis, U.S. Department of Commerce, *Survey of Current Business* (January 1992), p. 113.
5. Kenneth E. Boulding, in Foreword to Lloyd J. Dumas (ed.), *The Political Economy of Arms Reduction: Reversing Economic Decay* (Boulder, CO: The American Association for the Advancement of Science and Westview Press, 1982), p. xiii.
6. See Lloyd J. Dumas, "Payment functions and the productive efficiency of military industrial firms," *Journal of Economic Issues* (June 1976): 454–74.
7. Lloyd J. Dumas, "Commanding resources: The military sector and capital formation," in Dwight R. Lee (ed.), *Taxation and the Deficit Economy: Fiscal Policy and Capital Formation in the United States* (San Francisco: Pacific Research Institute, 1986), table 12–1, p. 336.

2

DANA L. DUNN

Sociological Dimensions of Economic Conversion

Sociological insights into the meaning of work enhance purely economic perspectives and can inform the process of converting firms from military to civilian production. For sociologists, work is far more than the means to an economic end. In many respects, we are our work—work defines individuals in modern society.[1] If this seems an overstatement, consider what we mean when we ask a new acquaintance, "What do you do?" We do not mean "What kind of hobbies do you have?" or "Where do you like to go on vacation?" or "How much television do you watch?" We mean "What kind of work do you do?" The answer to this simple question conveys a myriad of information, including economic status, social standing (class), and level of education.[2] It is often assumed that occupation is also an indicator of interests, abilities, political views, and even personality traits. In other words, asking "What do you do?" is shorthand for "Who are you?" "How do you fit in?" Others react to us on the basis of their assumptions about our work. Sooner or later this impacts our self-concept, our perception of who we are. Sociologists conclude that work contributes to feelings of self-esteem. [3]

Work affects self-esteem primarily in two ways. First, work contributes to feelings of efficacy and provides individuals with a sense of self-mastery and mastery over their environment. Second, work is a means of producing something of value to others, of making a contribution to one's fellow human beings. This second contribution of work to self-esteem is externally derived—an indicator of others' estimate of our worth. If others value our work and judge it to be meaningful, our self-esteem is enhanced. If others fail to value what we produce, our self-esteem suffers a blow.[4]

Work has another important social meaning. Social thinkers dating back at least as far as Karl Marx have noted that the workplace is an important source of social relationships.[5] Sociologists view the workplace as a social system comprised of two primary components, a system of technical relationships and a system of social relationships.[6] In modern society, the workplace is commonly an arena for forming friendships and other social ties. Marx argued that workers who are deprived of the opportunity for positive social relations on the job suffer from alienation, a distortion of human nature.[7]

These social functions and meanings of work must be considered in the effective design of programs to convert military firms to civilian production. It is necessary to know what work means to an individual in order to assess how she or he will respond to a change in work. Sociology can help determine the most effective way to accomplish economic conversion, and especially to motivate workers to be cooperative and enthusiastic about the workplace transition. Sociological insights also add to understanding of the potential benefits of conversion to both workers and employing organizations. There is a well-developed sociological literature addressing issues of worker satisfaction, motivation, and productivity; however, insights from this sociology of work literature have been largely neglected in writings on economic conversion.[8] Perhaps this is because economic conversion has only recently begun to receive the attention it deserves. Certainly scholars, primarily economists and engineers, as well as social activists have done much important work to lay the foundation for conversion. But, because economic institutions are social constructions and economic change is social change, sociologists can build on that foundation.[9]

The first section of this chapter presents an overview of theories and research on work organizations and structuring work, along with their implications for worker satisfaction and productivity. The structure of technical and human systems of production and their effects on workers will be linked to the process of economic conversion. Attention is then focused on the nature of what workers produce and possible effects on work outcomes. Next, effective methods of introducing change into the workplace are presented, drawing in particular from studies of worker participation. Differences between military and civilian firms in terms of organizational culture are also discussed, as is the need to incorporate culture change into the conversion process. The concluding section suggests directions for future research.

Theories of Organizations and Structuring Work

Classical theories of the sociology of work were heavily influenced by the research and writings of Frederick W. Taylor, the founder of scientific management.[10] Around the turn of the twentieth century, which was a period of rapid industrial growth, work organizations were faced with the problem of bringing large numbers of relatively inexperienced workers together to staff modern factories.[11] Taylor's scientific management was designed to control and measure work output so as to eliminate inefficiency and increase productivity.[12] A key element of the scientific management model was the separation of planning and actual physical work activities—thinking and doing. Under scientific management, management plans and monitors the labor process and the "shop floor" workers perform the actual physical work.[13] Jobs are minutely subdivided such that narrow, quickly learned work tasks can be assigned to semiskilled and unskilled blue-collar workers.[14] Management's task was to specify the division of labor, and to prescribe and monitor quantity, quality, and time standards for each task.

This "scientific" design of the work process was accompanied by financial incentives to workers who met and/or exceeded standards. In the short run, the scientific management model appeared to be a successful means of improving worker output and organizational profits. But the appropriation of thinking from the workers, the extreme specialization of work tasks, and the strict control over the conduct of their work eventually led to worker dissatisfaction and ill feelings between management and workers.[15] Scientific management principles slowly began to lose favor as it became apparent that workers desired more from their work than economic incentive—they desired a voice in the design of more varied and interesting work.[16] A more humanistic approach to work developed in response to the shortcomings of scientific management.[17] The human relations in industry movement was spurred by research conducted in the late 1920s through the early 1940s by Elton Mayo in the Western Electric Company's Hawthorne plant.[18] Mayo and colleagues concluded, after a lengthy series of studies, that the workplace was a social system wherein the culture and conditions of workers affected their attitude toward work and subsequently their output. The "economic being" model was slowly supplanted by a new model that emphasized that workers were people and had social needs.[19] The emerging human relations and human resources schools shifted management's emphasis from reward and punishment to subjective states of workers as the primary shapers of behavior.[20] Management practices that were more sensitive to worker's needs, more varied, challenging, and interesting work tasks, and worker input into the design of work began to be heralded as the key to maximizing productivity and profits.

The changing nature of workers themselves has also contributed to shifting orientations toward structuring work. Over the course of the first half of the twentieth century, the skill and education level of the work force increased. This increase was felt in terms of both higher educational attainment by production workers and a shifting mix of occupations toward those requiring more skill and education. As a result, repressive, authoritarian means of control became less tolerable. This change complemented a broader social trend occurring in many social institutions—the family, schools, the military. Further, the population's increasing material standard of living reduced the motivating potential of financial incentives.[21] These trends have continued, perhaps even escalated, over recent decades,[22] with the result that skilled and educated workers today not only desire but increasingly require work that is intrinsically motivating.

Implications for Economic Conversion

The many lessons learned during the scientific management and human relations/human resources eras have important implications for the process of economic conversion. Sociological findings regarding the effects of financial incentive, design of work tasks, style of management, and most important, worker attitudes suggest that both workers and work organizations may derive benefits from the conversion from military to civilian production. For workers, the benefits are largely, though not solely, intrinsic. The opportunity to enhance self-esteem through work and to self-actualize is viewed as a primary motivator under the humanistic perspective, and, as I will argue, such rewards are more likely to be present in firms producing civilian products. For work organizations faced with the loss of defense contracts, conversion can provide a means of generating necessary profits, and perhaps even a widening of the profit margin through the efforts of a more motivated and more satisfied work force.

It is well established that military firms, which are less sensitive to considerations of cost than civilian firms, often pay wages above the market rate.[23] Higher than average wages in military producing firms are typically viewed as incentives for workers to produce high-quality products, and are sometimes viewed as an obstacle to converting to civilian production. However, experience with scientific management job design principles suggests that financial incentives, while important, play only a limited role in motivating workers. Furthermore, "carrot and stick" techniques of motivating workers are particularly ill-suited for encouraging the creativity, enthusiasm, and application of intelligence to work required of highly skilled technical workers (e.g., technicians, engineers).[24] Studies in the humanist tradition suggest that such workers are more likely to be motivated by work that is properly designed and supervised—varied, challenging, and interesting work tasks and considerate, nonauthoritarian forms of leadership.[25] Because highly skilled defense workers are likely to be concerned with much more than maximum economic gain, the lower wages associated with civilian production do not necessarily present a daunting obstacle to converting. This is particularly true when wage reductions resulting from conversion can be offset by positive factors such as the greater employment stability associated with civilian production.[26] The wage cuts and concessions during the 1980s are evidence that workers will accept lower wages as an alternative to unemployment.

Scientists, technicians, engineers, and managers employed in military firms are required to emphasize quality and high performance; thus, they are highly specialized. The technical complexity of the product, detailed reporting requirements and federal regulations, and secrecy requirements also contribute to extreme specialization among defense workers.[27] Specialization, a primary job design principle of scientific management, has been shown in numerous studies to be associated with boredom, dissatisfaction, a lack of work motivation, and declines in productivity.[28] Converting to civilian product lines can eliminate pressures for the extreme fragmentation of work tasks. With far greater opportunities for job enrichment (job enlargement and job rotation), civilian firms have the potential to reap the rewards of greater worker motivation and productivity that result from a more satisfied work force.

The separation of planning and doing, the hallmark of scientific management (and a key reason it was not successful over the long term), is also an important element of the division of labor in defense production. Separating the planning, design, and construction functions of weapons system production has performed a variety of functions including diffusing the responsibility for creating devastating weapons, including weapons of mass destruction. This strict division of labor helps defense workers go about their tasks with little if any feeling of moral conflict.[29] The division of labor in defense contracting firms is associated with a hierarchy of authority that restricts worker input into decision making.

The high-performance demands associated with military products also limit worker participation in decision making by requiring defense workers to become expert at a narrow range of tasks, thus preventing them from developing the kind of comprehensive understanding of the production process required for informed decision making. Detailed military specifications for defense products further circumscribe worker decision making. The Hawthorne studies led researchers to suggest a link between the extent to which workers participate in decision making about their work and levels of satisfaction and productivity. Subsequent research supports the existence of this link.[30] Secrecy, extreme performance, and other defense production requirements that exaggerate the division of labor and restrict worker decision making are less common in civilian production, suggesting that conversion can be associated with significant increases in worker participation and higher levels of worker satisfaction and productivity.

The sociologist Max Weber developed an "ideal type" model of bureaucratic organizations which contains among its elements the characteristics of defense production described above: extreme specialization, a strict division of labor, and a hierarchy of authority.[31] Weber was ambivalent about the effects of bureaucracy.[32] In a sense, Weber saw bureaucracy as a "necessary evil"—necessary from the standpoint of organizational efficiency, and evil because it is "disenchanting" and represents a threat to individual liberty. In other words, Weber thought that the efficiency resulting from bureaucratic forms of organization was bought at a cost. The success of alternative forms of organizations such as worker collectives and worker-owned and -managed companies suggests that the costs associated with bureaucratization are not

always offset by the benefits of this form of organizational structure.[33] Defense contracting firms, constrained by the nature of what
they produce and their unique market, are forced to emulate the bureaucratic model and suffer the associated ill effects of worker disenchantment. Converting to civilian-oriented product lines provides the
opportunity to emulate alternative organizational forms that are associated with higher rates of worker satisfaction and output.

Economic Conversion: A Strategy for Reducing Worker Alienation

Karl Marx argued that the structure and organization of work in nine-
teenth-century Great Britain produced worker alienation and dissatisfaction. For Marx, this alienation consisted of four basic components:
loss of control over and isolation from the product, loss of control over
the production process, isolation from fellow workers, and the lack of
opportunity to develop personal potential.[34] Theorists adopting a humanist approach to the design of work, such as Maslow, Argyris, and
Herzeberg, acknowledge Marx's components of alienation and suggest
that they result in a dissatisfied work force.[35] Each of the four components of alienation described by Marx is more likely to exist for workers in military than in civilian firms.

Defense workers are isolated from the product of their labor in that
they do not directly use or consume it, nor do they typically see it
being used. This separation from the product means that defense workers are less likely to feel the sense of pride and accomplishment in their
work that results from contact with the finished product. They often try
to compensate for this by convincing themselves that they are engaged
in the important work of "defending the nation," a line of thinking that
has become vastly harder to justify with the ending of the global Cold
War. I will return to this issue shortly. In addition, the fact that military
goods do not directly contribute to the material standard of living has
led to their classification as distractive—the resources used in their
production are wasted from the point of view of the economy.[36]

Furthermore, defense workers producing nuclear weapons and associated delivery systems are involved in the production of weapons
systems that most people hope and expect will never be put to use. The
defense policy of the last half-century has emphasized nuclear deter-
rence; thus, it is not intended that these destructive weapons will ever

be employed—they exist primarily for the purpose of discouraging the enemy from attacking. Under ideal circumstances, then, the exacting work of highly skilled defense workers will never be "put to the test." Such workers are denied the sense of accomplishment that can be derived from seeing the product perform. On the other hand, the belief that the products they are producing will never be used is often key to coming to terms with the morality of helping to create weapons of such horrifying destructive capability.

Not only do defense workers have no control over the product, they often do not even have a good sense of what they are producing. The extreme degree of specialization in defense production (described earlier), combined with high levels of secrecy, serves intentionally to obscure understanding of the final product. The defense worker's failure to fully understand the product and its intended functioning is also helpful in enabling him or her calmly to create weapons—even weapons of mass destruction—without a feeling of moral revulsion.[37] While this type of obfuscation may be necessary in defense production to inhibit worker resistance on moral grounds, it clearly serves to sever the connection between the worker and the product of his or her labor, contributing to feelings of alienation.

As discussed earlier, defense workers have especially limited control over the production process. Because of the specialization and strict division of work inherent in military production, defense workers are likely to be more alienated from the production process than nondefense workers. They are also often more isolated from their fellow workers for the same reasons. Secrecy requirements in defense production, in addition to their other effects, contribute to feelings of alienation from coworkers outside their own departments of the firm. Finally, defense workers are alienated from their own human potential. Marx argues that the first three components of alienation—separation from the product, the production process, and one's fellow workers—cause workers to become less human. He suggests that they are reduced in their work to animals or machines, and as such are less able to self-actualize, to express their human potential.[38]

Contemporary researchers have expanded upon Marx's writings on alienation by addressing the subjective experience of alienation.[39] Seeman, for example, argues that workers experience alienation in the form of feelings of powerlessness, self-estrangement, meaninglessness, isolation, and normlessness. The impact of such subjective states upon work performance seems obvious. To the extent that military production processes embody structural features that give rise to these subjective states in workers, it can be argued that economic conversion can be a means of improving workers' levels of satisfaction, and helping them to develop their full human potential more completely.

The Nature of the Product and Effects on Workers

There are many aspects of the product of workers' labor (beyond the separation and isolation described by Marx) that may affect their attitudes and behaviors. Work enhances self-esteem when it makes a positive contribution to humanity that is recognized and valued by others. For example, imagine the feelings of pride associated with producing a drug or safety device that is known to save many lives. On the other hand, imagine the feelings associated with producing a device that is designed to kill millions, a weapon of mass destruction. Interestingly, the socialization (training) processes that prepare defense workers for their jobs and the ongoing culture of defense contracting firms, combined with workers' self-interest and ability to rationalize, often result in a positive "slant" on military weapons as products.[40]

Just as soldiers are resocialized to accept killing as normal, and even desirable, defense workers are resocialized to view their role in the production of weapons as positive and socially contributive. Various techniques are used to accomplish this resocialization.[41] The social construction of the other (in sociological parlance, the "outgroup") as "the enemy," followed by depersonalization, dehumanization, and/or objectification, serve to eliminate any feelings of guilt that might otherwise arise.[42] The screening process for obtaining security clearance is another important element of resocialization for select defense workers. Nash, a former intelligence analyst with the Department of Defense, states,

> I . . . had the impression that being cleared had its rewards. These were personal and had to do with being confronted by a screening process, passing the test, and then enjoying final acceptance. Being cleared represented a flattering experience sharpened by the quality of selectivity, not unlike the feeling accompanying acceptance by a fraternity or country club. You knew you were chosen. Being included confirmed that you had been found worthy.[43]

The awarding of security clearance conveys a special status on the defense worker and helps to legitimate his or her role in the production of weapons.

The resocialization of defense workers is further reinforced by the above-market wages they receive. Because the financial security of workers in defense firms results from their role in the production of weapons, they are very motivated to perceive a need for such weapons. As Markusen and Harris state, "To question such weapons and policies may be tantamount to questioning their own integrity."[44] York, a former high-level official in the Department of Defense, describes the mindset of participants in the defense industry:

> They derive their incomes, their profits, or their consultants' fees from [defense employment]. But much more important than money as a motivating force are the individuals' own psychic and spiritual needs; the majority of the key individual promoters of the arms race derive a very large part of their self-esteem from their participation in what they believe to be an essential—even a holy—cause.[45]

Financial and intrinsic rewards become intertwined when defense workers view their above market salaries as compensation for important, productive work.

Successful resocialization of defense workers hinges, to some extent, on the public's perception of their work. Taxpayer support of defense production legitimates the work of employees in defense contracting firms.[46] The aura of secrecy surrounding defense contractors and their employees buffers the workers from the public and reduces the likelihood of public scrutiny or criticism of defense industry work. Such factors combine to enable defense workers to view their work and their product as any other worker might: they derive not only their income, but also their self-esteem and self-definition from their work role.

The fact that defense firms and their client, the Department of Defense, invest in the resocialization of defense workers is an indication of their concern that workers would otherwise experience ethical discomfort as a result of the nature of the product, and that this ethical conflict could impact levels of motivation and productivity. During the past decade, a variety of factors suggest that the potential for ethical dilemmas among defense workers has increased. First, as the domestic economic crisis has intensified, workers' attitudes toward military spending have changed. A 1983 survey of AFL-CIO union leaders found that 60 percent of those polled would not support any increase in military spending. In addition, the majority of American union members express endorsement of a nuclear weapons freeze.[47] Workers who are less supportive of military spending will exhibit less patriotic commitment to producing weapons, and will be susceptible to moral conflict over the nature of the product.

A second factor that may increase the level of ethical discomfort for defense industry employees is related to a broad social trend—society's expectations with regard to business have changed and expanded over recent years.[48] Widespread reports of corporate misbehavior, ranging from worker exploitation and consumer deception to environmental pollution and the actual injury of the public through hazardous products or work environments, have made citizens increasingly aware of the potential of business to harm society. As a result, the public is beginning to demand that organizations refrain from harming society and actively contribute to the public good. Work organizations are being asked to exercise moral judgment in decision making—to have a conscience. This new emphasis on the social responsibility of business has focused attention on the impact of the output, the goods and services, produced by firms. Increased public scrutiny of the output of defense firms may lead to less public support for their activities and render resocialization of defense employees for participation in defense work less effective than it has been in the past.

Society's changing expectations with regard to business are also reflected in the movement toward socially responsible investing. Socially conscious investment strategies are employed to influence the behavior of corporate organizations. They can boost the availability of investment capital to nonmilitary firms, giving them an advantage relative to military contractors. The fact that socially conscious investment funds (the bulk of which avoid investment in military companies) contain over $500 billion suggests the potential impact of this type of selective investment.[49]

Recent changes in the arena of international relations have reduced public support for high levels of defense production. The breakup of the Soviet Union and the disintegration of the Warsaw Pact have resulted in a decreased perception of threat, and less willingness to view citizens of the resulting nations as "the enemy." Without the threat of some kind of "evil empire" to justify one's role in producing weapons, commitment to defense work eventually will wane. As this occurs, defense workers are more likely to be negatively affected by the nature of their product.

Finally, the increasing success of a social movement, the peace movement, in educating the public about the dangers of nuclear war and the economic ill effects of defense production make it increasingly difficult for defense contractors to isolate their employees from such messages. Urged by activists to engage in self-reflection, a number of participants in defense work have chosen to resolve their moral dilemma by leaving the military sector and "going public" with their stories.[50] The voice of experience is a powerful one, and it can have a strong influence on those who are still employed in defense work. Admittedly, one response of defense contractors and employees will be a posturing—an intensification of efforts to justify and to rationalize one's role in the production of weapons. But declining public support will slowly erode the defense mechanisms of workers in the military sector and, as this occurs, worker motivation will suffer.

Economic conversion creates the opportunity to change the nature of the product so as to make the output of firms more compatible with the new emphasis on corporate social responsibility. Conversion involves the application of science and technology to economic and social development. Examples of socially useful products that have been suggested as civilian product alternatives for converted military firms include renewable sources of energy, innovations in health care, food products, and communication networks.[51] Converting to socially useful production eliminates the need to resocialize workers because intrinsic motivation is inherent due to the nature of the product. The benefit to workers is obvious and is likely to spill over to the firm in the form of heightened employee commitment and productivity.

Unemployment and the Remedy of Economic Conversion

Given Marx's definition of alienation, unemployment might be considered the ultimate alienating experience. Unemployed individuals lose their connection to fellow human beings when they lose the opportunity to engage in productive work. Social scientists have studied the effects of unemployment on individual workers and their families, as well as communities with high rates of unemployment. The established effects of unemployment extend well beyond the loss of income and include negative effects on the physical and mental health of workers and their families (e.g., stress-related diseases, suicides, homicides) and "ripple effects" in the community, such as increased demand for public assistance, decreased retail purchases, and increases in the rates of both property and violent crime.[52] One of the most significant benefits of economic conversion is the prevention of the widespread unemployment of defense workers.[53] The instability in defense industry employment, combined with a shrinking military budget, means that failure to plan for conversion will result in the dislocation of large numbers of defense workers in the coming years.

Using national data covering a thirty-year period (1940–73), Brenner statistically estimated the impact of unemployment on various forms of social trauma. He found that a 1 percent increase in unemployment, sustained over a period of six years, was associated with 37,000 total deaths, 20,000 cardiovascular deaths, 920 suicides, 650 homicides, 4,000 mental hospital admissions, 500 deaths from cirrhosis of the liver, and 3,300 state prison admissions. These high social costs of unemployment extend to virtually all segments of the population; thus, for this reason alone, actors at all levels of the social hierarchy have a vested interest in pursuing economic conversion.[54]

Over the last several decades, deindustrialization has led to widespread structural unemployment as manufacturing plants have closed their doors in response to decreased demand for their products. Further, technology has automated a number of jobs out of existence; still other jobs have been exported to other nations. Some workers displaced by these events have been able to reconnect with new employment. That being the case, why can't defense workers do the same when the loss of military contracts results in layoffs? The optimistic answer is that some defense workers *will* find new employment. The realistic answer forces us to consider the nature of the new jobs being filled by displaced workers. Underemployment is the norm for these workers as they accept lower-wage positions in the service economy that do not fully utilize their skills and abilities. While the United States produced more new jobs than most of the rest of the industrialized nations combined during the 1980s, most of those jobs are relatively low-wage, service sector jobs requiring little skill or training, and having very little future opportunity.[55] Underemployed workers are particularly likely to experience high levels of alienation because they are not challenged by their routine jobs and have limited control over their work. Conversion, once again, is a practical remedy for the problem of underemployment for defense workers. Proper conversion planning involves assessing the skills and abilities of the existing work force, and developing new product lines in accordance with the nature of the human capital present in the firm.

Accomplishing Economic Conversion: The Sociology of Workplace Transition

Sociology can do more than provide evidence of the potential benefits of economic conversion; it also can provide direction for accomplishing the workplace transition. Industry studies conducted during the human relations era are among the first to analyze the most effective means of introducing change into the workplace. A classic study by Coch and French illustrates the potentially profound impact of the way in which change is introduced.[56] Coch and French were called in to consult with management in a pajama factory staffed by women workers. Factory management reported high rates of labor turnover and a slowing of productivity rates shortly after the introduction of new methods of production.

Coch and French attributed these problems to worker resistance, and devised a study to explore methods of reducing the turnover and productivity problems associated with changes in the production process. Female pajama factory workers were divided into four groups, each to be exposed to a different method of introducing change. The first group, the no participation group, was simply informed of the change by management officials. The second group, the participation through representation group, was called to a meeting where a management representative explained the need to change production methods. A question and answer session followed the presentation. The two groups then chose representatives who were to be trained in the new methods, and the new piece rate was set by a time study of these workers. Following the time study, a second meeting was called to explain the piece rate, and then other group members were trained in the new method.

The final two groups were total participation groups. Once again, members met as a group to hear a presentation on the need for change. For the total participation groups, however, all members worked under the new method and were allowed to make suggestions, and each member participated in the time study. The no participation group exhibited the greatest turnover and productivity problems after the introduction of change. The participation through representation group was much quicker to recover productivity after the change, and experienced no turnover problems. The two total participation groups also recovered quickly and eventually *exceeded* previous levels of productivity and exhibited no turnover after the change. Marked differences in satisfaction were also noted across the groups, with the no participation group reporting far higher levels of job dissatisfaction.[57] Coch and French concluded that allowing workers to contribute input to the decision to introduce change into the workplace was the key to their acceptance and cooperation.

Coch and French's research paved the way for a series of studies on the effect on employee motivation of styles of management and worker participation in decision making. The majority of these studies suggest that when workers have input into decisions that directly affect their work and working conditions, they are more satisfied and more productive.[58] Worker participation in management can take a number of forms, ranging from worker-owned and -controlled organizations (maximum participation) to suggestion boxes (minimum participation).

In most cases, not all of a company's decisions are turned over to the workers. Managers continue to run the company and to coordinate all of the organization's major functions. Workers have input into the decision-making process in accordance with their knowledge and skills, particularly when decisions directly affect their job and working conditions. Research has shown that workers must feel that the organization is sincere when soliciting employee input in order to "avoid having workers feel that participative management is merely a refined Tayloristic technique for improving productivity at their expense."[59]

As discussed earlier, a number of constraints prevent defense firms from implementing participatory management; thus, they are unable to reap the potential benefits. Converting to civilian product lines not only removes the obstacles to participatory management, but also creates a special need for increased employee involvement in decision making during the transition period. Because workers are more committed to making changes in which they have had a voice, involving defense workers early in the conversion planning process is important.

One stellar example of defense workers' involvement in conversion planning is the British Lucas Aerospace "corporate plan."[60] Faced with job cutbacks and layoffs, Lucas employees formed a shop stewards' committee representing employees from every unit in the organization to develop proposals for alternative products. The resulting "corporate plan" included only socially useful products that could be produced using existing equipment and workers. Unfortunately, management resistance to the plan was strong, and the apparently viable plan was never implemented. Nonetheless, the Lucas case provides a valuable model for economic conversion. The fact that the workers were centrally involved in planning for the important workplace transition, combined with the emphasis on socially useful alternative products, would have resulted in strong worker motivation. Further, for many workers the Lucas plan was a realistic means of avoiding the trauma of unemployment.

Developing a range of alternative products is a critical first step in the economic conversion process. It must be followed by the retraining and reorientation of all workers in order for the workplace transition to be successful.[61] Retraining involves teaching employees new skills when required; it is a rather straightforward process. Reorientation, by contrast, involves more subtle forms of resocialization that prepare the former defense employee for work in a "civilian" environment; this may be somewhat more complex. As noted earlier, workers are resocialized after they accept employment with defense contracting firms. Because the organizational structure, culture, and job demands in civilian producing firms differ markedly from those in military contracting firms, this resocialization must be undone—workers must be resocialized yet again.

Economic Conversion, Organizational Culture Change, and Employee Resocialization

Organizations have cultures just as societies do. Organizational culture consists of shared values, beliefs, assumptions, perceptions, norms, artifacts, and behavioral rituals.[62] Advocates of the new organizational culture perspective on work organizations argue that in order to function effectively, workers must have knowledge of the culture of their workplace. This cultural knowledge is transmitted through workplace socialization, both formally (by official representatives of the organization) and informally (through peers). The culture of organizations is determined in part by the products they produce and by the client or market for those products. Because economic conversion calls for new product lines and new markets, it involves changes in the organizational culture and requires the resocialization of employees.

Perhaps the most striking culture contrast between civilian and defense producing firms results from the greater financial risk in civilian producing firms.[63] In defense firms, once a military contract is secured, cost-plus pricing more or less guarantees the rate of profit. Because of high levels of government sponsorship, military research and development also involves relatively little financial risk. Civilian firms differ in that there is a high level of uncertainty regarding these matters. Deal and Kennedy suggest that the amount of risk taking or uncertainty present in an organization is one of the most important influences on corporate culture[64]; thus, economic conversion results in significant culture change. Defense employees must be resocialized to work effectively in a higher-risk environment prior to undertaking civilian production. They must be prepared for the different work atmosphere, norms, and patterns of behavior common in such environments.

Additional factors are likely to contribute to significant organizational culture differences between military and civilian producing firms are summarized below.

Characteristics Creating Organizational Culture Contrasts

Defense contracting firm	*Civilian firm*
• High levels of secrecy	• Limited secrecy
• Limited attention to cost minimization	• Heavy emphasis on cost
• Excessive regulations (military specifications)	• Fewer regulations
• Extreme performance demands	• Less emphasis on performance
• Less stable employment	• More stable employment
• One or a few clients	• Potential for many clients

The organizational culture perspective is relatively new, and little systematic research has been done to examine precisely how the characteristics of firms listed above affect organizational culture. Research of this type would be very useful in designing resocialization programs associated with conversion.

Directions for Future Research on the Sociology of Conversion

Economic institutions are created and altered by human actors who are in turn affected by the institutions they have created. Because the discipline of sociology focuses on these social processes, it has practical application to economic conversion. Sociology sensitizes conversion planners to the meaning of work for the individual, providing direction for the design of satisfying alternative work. With its focus on the interplay between human actors and social structure, sociology is an excellent vehicle for examining the effects of job design, methods of managing, and the product itself on both workers and their employing organizations. While the existing stock of sociological knowledge is helpful in planning and implementing economic conversion, much more research is needed. Defense contracting firms undergoing conversion provide an exciting laboratory for the sociologist. Systematic study of conversion as a workplace transition may give rise to a new era in the sociological understanding of work.

Economic conversion is well suited for longitudinal research designs, and many methods of data collection are appropriate, including surveys, direct observation, and experimental design. Some defense contracting firms, faced with reductions in military contracts, are currently experimenting with a range of new products. Associated changes in production methods, worker resocialization, styles of management, the division of labor, and organizational culture accompany the shift to new product lines. These organizational changes can be conceptualized as either independent or dependent variables in sociological studies. For example, what is the effect of the manufacture of socially useful products on worker self-esteem, work satisfaction, and productivity? Or, how does the transition to civilian production affect the division of labor and organizational culture? Past research in industrial sociology suggests hypotheses and provides guidance for research design; studies of economic conversion can serve as the empirical testing ground for sociological theory.

Scholarly issues aside, economic conversion is a high-priority social issue. In an attempt to ensure peace, we have continually prepared for war. This preparation for war can become a self-fulfilling prophecy. In the absence of conversion, we need weapons contracts to provide jobs for defense workers. In order to produce the weapons, we must fund a massive defense budget or radically increase arms sales around the world. In order to justify such allocation of resources, we need a threatening enemy. Defense workers also require this socially constructed enemy in order to rationalize their work. With all the necessary ingredients in place, how long can war be avoided?

The sociologist Robert Merton notes that bureaucratic structures are prone to goal displacement.[65] This dysfunction occurs because the employees of bureaucratic organizations, with their complex rules, regulations, and procedures, become so focused on the details of internal operations that they lose sight of the original goal. Those who staff the organization and whose livelihoods depend on its continued existence become more concerned with preserving the organization and their own future within it than with the original goal. Defense contracting firms provide an excellent example of bureaucratic goal displacement; the original goal of promoting peace (by preparing for war) is displaced by the need to provide continued employment for workers and profits for the organization. Economic conversion supplies new goals (socially useful products) for defense firms, and moves us a great deal closer to the more peaceful world that we seek.

Notes

1. R. Blauner, *Alienation and Freedom: The Factory Worker and His Industry* (Chicago: University of Chicago Press, 1964); see also J. O'Toole, E. Hansot, W. Herman, N. Herrick, E. Libow, B. Lusignan, H. Richman, H. Sheppard, B. Stephansky, and J. Wright, *Work in America* (Cambridge, MA: MIT Press, 1973); as well as R.M. Pavalko, *Sociology of Occupations and Professions* (Itasca, IL: Peacock, 1988).

2. R.A. Hedley, *Making a Living: Technology and Change* (New York: HarperCollins, 1992).

3. E.C. Hughes, *Men and Their Work* (Glencoe, IL: Free Press, 1958).

4. Blauner, *Alienation and Freedom*; O'Toole et al., *Work in America*. See also: R. Coles, "On the meaning of work," *The Atlantic* (October 1971); E.F. Schumacher, *Good Work* (New York: Harper and Row, 1979); and P. Thompson, *The Nature of Work: An Introduction to Debates on the Labour Process* (London: Macmillan, 1979).

5. K. Marx, *Das Kapital*, vol. 1. (Hamburg: Otto Meissner, 1958 [1867]). See also M. Seeman, "On the meaning of alienation," *American Sociological Review*, *24*, 6 (1959): 783–91.

6. Thompson, *The Nature of Work*.

7. Marx, *Das Kapital*, vol. 1. See also K. Marx, *The Economic and Philosophic Manuscripts of 1844*, ed. by Dirk J. Struik (New York: International Publishers, 1932).

8. L.J. Dumas, "Economic conversion: The critical link," in L.J. Dumas (ed.), *Making Peace Possible: The Promise of Economic Conversion* Oxford: Pergamon Press, 1989), pp. 1–15.

9. M. Granovetter and R. Swedberg, *The Sociology of Economic Life* (Boulder, CO: Westview Press, 1992).

10. Thompson, *The Nature of Work*. See also C. Tausky, *Work Organizations: Major Theoretical Perspectives* (Itasca, IL: Peacock, 1978).

11. P. Goldman and D.R. Van Houten, "Bureaucracy and domination: Managerial strategy in turn-of-the-century American industry," in F. Hearn (ed.), *The Transformation of Industrial Organization: Management, Labor and Society in the United States* (Belmont, CA: Wadsworth, 1988), pp. 46–66. For a detailed discussion of the role of the military in industrial development in the United States from the Industrial Revolution through the era of scientific management, see David Noble, "Command performance: A perspective on the social and economic consequences of military enterprise," in Merritt Roe Smith (ed.), *Military Enterprise and Technological Change: Perspectives on the American Experience* (Cambridge, MA: MIT Press, 1985). Noble argues that certain requirements of military industry (e.g., uniformity, predictability) presaged scientific management.

12. F.W. Taylor, *Scientific Management* (New York: Harper and Row, 1947).

13. Tausky, *Work Organizations*; Thompson, *The Nature of Work*.

14. C. Gill, *Work, Unemployment and the New Technology* (Oxford: Basil Blackwell, 1985). See also R.A. Rothman, *Working: Sociological Perspectives* (Englewood Cliffs, NJ: Prentice-Hall, 1987).

15. Tausky, *Work Organizations*.

16. J. Simmons and W. Mares, *Working Together: Employee Participation in Action* (New York: New York University Press, 1985).

17. R.L. Ford, *Work, Organization and Power* (Boston: Allyn and Bacon, 1988). See also T.J. Watson, *Sociology, Work and Industry* (London: Routledge and Kegan Paul, 1980).

18. Tausky, *Work Organizations*; Thompson, *The Nature of Work*.

19. Ford, *Work, Organization and Power*.

20. Tausky, *Work Organizations*.

21. Ibid.

22. H.L. Sheppard and N.Q. Herrick, *Where Have All the Robots Gone? Worker Dissatisfaction in the 1970s* (New York: Free Press, 1972). See also R.E. Walton, "Alienation and innovation in the workplace," in W.M. Hoffman and J.M. Moore (eds.), *Business Ethics* (New York: McGraw-Hill, 1984), pp. 261–63.

23. L.J. Dumas, "The conversion of military economy: The United States," in L.J. Dumas (ed.), *The Political Economy of Arms Reduction: Reversing Economic Decay* (Boulder, CO: Westview, 1982), pp. 27–68. See also J.S. Gansler, *Affording Defense* (Cambridge, MA: MIT Press, 1989), as well as J. Tirman, *The Militarization of High Technology* (Cambridge, MA: Ballinger, 1984).

24. E.O. Wright, *Class Structure and Income Inequality* (Ph.D. dissertation, University of California, Berkeley, 1976).

25. Tausky, *Work Organizations*.

26. Gansler, *Affording Defense*.

27. Ibid. See also C. Sanger, "The West and the rest: Conversion and third world development," in S. Gordon and D. McFadden (eds.), *Economic Conversion: Revitalizing America's Economy* (Cambridge, MA: Harper and Row, 1984), pp. 47–60.

28. O'Toole et al., *Work in America*. See also R. Hodson and T.A. Sullivan, *The Social Organization of Work* (Belmont, CA: Prentice-Hall, 1990), as well as C. Tausky and E.L. Parke, "Job enrichment, need theory and reinforcement the-

ory," in R. Dubin (ed.), *Handbook of Work, Organization, and Society* (Chicago: Rand McNally, 1976), pp. 531–66.

29. H.C. Kelman and V.L. Hamilton, *Crimes of Obedience* (New Haven, CT: Yale University Press, 1989). See also L. Peattie, "Normalizing the unthinkable," in J.B. Harris and E. Markusen (eds.), *Nuclear Weapons and the Threat of Nuclear War* (New York: Harcourt, Brace, Jovanovich, 1986), pp. 385–93.

30. O'Toole et al., *Work in America*; Simmons and Mares, *Working Together*. See P. Blumberg, *Industrial Democracy: The Sociology of Participation* (New York: Schocken, 1968). See also L. Coch and J.R.P. French, Jr., "Overcoming resistance to change," *Human Relations*, 1:512–32, as well as D. Zwerdling, *Workplace Democracy: A Guide to Workplace Ownership, Participation, and Self-Management Experiments in the United States and Europe* (New York: Harper Colophon, 1978).

31. M. Weber, *From Max Weber*, ed. by H. Gerth and C. Wright Mills (New York: Oxford University Press, 1958). See also M. Weber, *Economy and Society*, ed. by Gunther Roth and Claus Wittich (New York: Bedminster, 1960).

32. G.R. Ritzer and D. Walczak, *Working: Conflict and Change* (Englewood Cliffs, NJ: Prentice-Hall, 1986).

33. Zwerdling, *Workplace Democracy*.

34. Marx, *Das Kapital*.

35. Ford, *Work, Organization and Power*. See C. Argyris, *Understanding Organizational Behavior* (Homewood, IL: Dorsey, 1960). See also F. Herzeberg, *Work and the Nature of Man* (Cleveland: World, 1966) as well as A.G. Maslow, *Motivation and Personality* (New York: Harper Brothers, 1954).

36. L.J. Dumas, *The Overburdened Economy* (Berkeley: University of California Press, 1986).

37. M. Everett, *Breaking Ranks* (Philadelphia: New Society Publishers, 1989). H. Nash, "The bureaucratization of homicide," *Bulletin of the Atomic Scientists* (April 1980).

38. Ritzer and Walczak, *Working*.

39. Hodson and Sullivan, *The Social Organization of Work*.

40. Everett, *Breaking Ranks*; Nash, "The bureaucratization of homicide"; and Peattie, "Normalizing the unthinkable." See also E. Markusen and J.B. Harris, "Nuclearism and the erosion of democracy," in E. Markusen and J.B. Harris (eds.), *Nuclear Weapons and the Threat of Nuclear War* (San Diego: Harcourt, Brace, Jovanovich, 1986), pp. 366–84.

41. For a more detailed discussion of techniques used to accomplish resocialization, see E. Goffman, *Asylums: Essays on the Social Situation of Mental Patients and Other Inmates* (Chicago: Aldine, 1961). This book includes a discussion of strategies used to resocialize soldiers.

42. Markusen and Harris, "Nuclearism." See S. Keen, *Faces of the Enemy: Reflections of the Hostile Imagination* (San Francisco: Harper and Row, 1986). See also L. Kurtz and J. Turpin, "The social psychology of warfare," in L. Kurtz, *The Nuclear Cage: A Sociology of the Arms Race* (Englewood Cliffs, NJ: Prentice-Hall, 1988), as well as R.S. Moyer, "The enemy within," *Psychology Today*, *19* (January 1985): 31–35.

43. Nash, "The bureaucratization of homicide," p. 24.

44. Markusen and Harris, "Nuclearism," p. 366.

45. H. York, *Race to Oblivion* (New York: Simon and Schuster, 1970), p. 235.

46. Everett, *Breaking Ranks*.

47. G. Carroll, "How to get labor involved," in S. Gordon and D. McFadden (eds.), *Economic Conversion: Revitalizing America's Economy* (Cambridge, MA: Ballinger, 1984), pp. 219–36.

48. G.F. Cavanaugh, "Corporate values for the future," in W.M. Hoffman and J.M. Mills (eds.), *Business Ethics* (New York: McGraw-Hill), pp. 509–23.

49. C. Gorman, "Listen here, Mr. Big," *Time* (1989).

50. Everett, *Breaking Ranks*.

51. S. Gordon and D. McFadden (eds.), *Economic Conversion: Revitalizing America's Economy* (Cambridge, MA: Ballinger, 1984).

52. B. Bluestone and B. Harrison, "The impact of private disinvestment on workers and their communities," in L. Perman (ed.), *Work in Modern Society* (Dubuque, IA: Kendall/Hunt, 1986), pp. 51–55. See H. Brenner, "Estimating the social costs of national economic policy: Implications for mental and physical health and clinical aggression," a report prepared for the Joint Economic Committee, U.S. Congress (Washington, DC: U.S. Government Printing Office, 1976). See also S. Cobb. and S. Kasl, "Termination: The consequences of job loss," Public Health Service, Center for Disease Control, National Institute for Occupational Safety and health, U.S. Department of Health, Education, and Welfare (Washington, DC: June 1977), as well as D. Stillman, "The devastating impact of plant relocations," *Working Papers*, 5, 4 (July–August 1978).

53. Dumas, "The conversion of military economy," and *The Overburdened Economy*.

54. Brenner, "Estimating the social costs."

55. B. Bluestone and B. Harrison, "The great American job machine: The proliferation of low wage employment in the U.S. economy," in D.S. Eitzen and M. Baca Zinn (eds.), *The Reshaping of America* (Englewood Cliffs, NJ: Prentice-Hall, 1989), pp. 103–8.

56. Coch and French, "Overcoming resistance to change."

57. Ford, *Work, Organization and Power*, and Tausky, *Work Organizations*.

58. Simmons and Mares, *Working Together*; Zwerdling, *Workplace Democracy*. See also J. Rothschild and J.A. Whitt, *The Cooperative Workplace: Potentials and Dilemmas of Organizational Democracy and Participation* (Cambridge: Cambridge University Press, 1985).

59. O'Toole et al., *Work in America*, p. 105.

60. H. Wainwright and D. Elliot, *The Lucas Plan: A New Trade Unionism in the Making?* (London: Allison and Busby, 1982).

61. Dumas, *The Overburdened Economy*; Gansler, *Affording Defense*.

62. J.S. Ott, *The Organizational Culture Perspective* (Chicago: Dorsey Press, 1989).

63. Gansler, *Affording Defense*; Sanger, "The West and the rest."

64. T.E. Deal and A.A. Kennedy, *Corporate Cultures: The Rites and Rituals of Corporate Life* (Reading, MA: Addison-Wesley, 1982).

65. R.K. Merton, *Social Theory and Social Structure* (New York: Free Press, 1968).

3

GEORGE MEHRING

Restructuring the Organization: The Importance of Strategic Learning in Conversion

Paradoxical Flexibility

Imagine waking up and finding yourself in a strange and different land. Your clothing is out of place, you can't understand what the people around you are saying, and all of the landmarks that you have grown used to are gone. You have to survive in this new land, but more than just survive, you must learn to grow and participate in the life around you. For those who work in defense industries, conversion will be a lot like this.

Defense-based industries face the situation where their major market has substantially deteriorated, if not disappeared, and their entire way of doing business is under revision. What are the guideposts for the conversion of such systems? An even more fundamental question is to what should these organizations be converting? Answers cannot be found in the world outside of the converting system. It too is changing at a destabilizing rate. Converting organizations must identify and apply methods for redefining themselves. Also, the economy targeted by converting firms is not the economy that exists now, but that economy that will exist in the near future. Although firms cannot rely on the environment for direct guidance, they cannot operate without an ongoing review of the information that they can glean from their world. This information, taken in concert with the system's own efforts to redefine itself, has the potential to guide it into the future. At a time when many industries that grew to maturity during the Cold War must revisit their core purposes, goals, and modes of operating, "strategic learning" offers a new set of tools to understand issues associated with organizational governance and change.

The governance and direction of defense-based organizations facing conversion raise challenges to both the organizations and the individuals that compose them. These challenges must be met on their own ground, either personal or organizational. Typical methods for dealing with a crisis include managers setting goals and objectives, then allocating the organization's resources to meet them. But the tried and true methods of managing are not enough to meet the fundamental need for reorientation of entire industries. New models of organizations are necessary and new methods of governance are needed to direct them. Strategic learning is a new approach to directing such organizations. It integrates the discipline of strategic planning with new methods for organizational design and learning. This model also addresses the need for leadership development and the governance of the new organizational patterns. This chapter explores the complementary themes of transformation on both the personal and the organizational level as they relate to the defense conversion process.

Organizations in the conversion process must develop a language for understanding and communicating change. Many years ago, Kurt Lewin proposed a fundamental model for the change process that has found application in many cases of successful organizational change. Lewin's model consists of three phases: unfreezing, change, and refreezing. During the unfreezing stage, the organization is prepared for change by diagnosis of the problems it faces and identification of various solutions. These solutions are put into place during the change phase, and in the final phase they are frozen into place. The assumption in Lewin's model is that the new system is taking root in a stable environment. In the world economy, we now know that stability is a luxury of the past. There is no longer a place for refreezing. We have to look for other models that will permit organizations to initiate change and develop a permanent state of flexibility while retaining the essential skills and serving the core values that define the organization as a unique entity. This is paradoxical flexibility, whereby organizations are able to be consistently focused by core values, missions, and strategic intents, and yet they maintain the flexibility to adapt rapidly to, if not to anticipate, changing conditions in their operating environment.

The character of this chaotic environment was anticipated by Emery and Trist in 1965, who identified it as the turbulent field. This view presents a model of organizations conceptualized as components embedded in a field. This field represents the context or environment in which the various organizations operate and contains all relevant features of the organization's world. It is the source of all information and resources. In a turbulent field, the change energy that impacts upon any given component of the field can come not only from the actions of the other components but from the field itself. In impacting the target or focal organization, it has the potential to affect all other features of the field. In other words, the actual ground to which the system is anchored is capable of unpredictable and potentially destabilizing shifts. This model bears substantial correspondence to the operating environment in the defense sector. Organizations facing conversion in both the public and the private sectors are encountering an environment that no longer permits them the luxury of freezing a new structure or operating modality into place. There is simply too much novelty to cope with, without an internal capacity to deal with change and ambiguity.

The challenge that an organization in a turbulent field must face is to configure itself to anticipate, absorb, or adapt to multidimensional and nonlinear change while preserving those distinctive elements, capabilities, or features that identify a system as a discrete organization. To accomplish this balance, the organization must develop a range of strategies for the allocation of resources that takes into account proactive and quick reactive response to rapid and nonlinear environmental change.

Historically, the development of such strategies has been accomplished through a process of strategic planning, in which an organization develops a scheme for the allocation of resources to meet a variety of goals. Strategic plans, and their underlying assumptions about the nature of the business and the economy, are typically developed to cover periods of three to five years. The challenge for converting industries comes from confronting a turbulent field that is an unpredictable generator of novelty. Operational planning must neither be framed on too broad a time cycle, nor based upon assumptions that the turbulent field will behave in a linear manner. In these circumstances, change in the environment outpaces the organization's capacity to incorporate new factors into strategic planning and its dependent operational planning. Converting industries must develop the capacity to continually learn and adapt on a strategic level and to use this skill to replace the strategic planning function. In order to develop an organization that is capable of strategic learning, three areas must be addressed: the role of organizational leadership, organizational design and strategy, and the role of directive behavior or governance in both communicating the intent of the organization to its members and stakeholders and shaping the actions of the organization's members.

Crisis and Response: The Role of Leadership in Strategic Learning

> *I've been with Exxon for thirty-eight years, and the thing that has bothered me most is not the castigation, the difficulties or the long hours; it's been the embarrassment. I hate to be embarrassed, and I am.*
> Lawrence Rawl, Chairman, Exxon[1]

> *Where Exxon looks chiefly vulnerable is in leadership. Rawl and his team appear to lack the ability to understand people and to inspire them. . . . By going to Alaska and acquitting himself while in the spotlight, Rawl would have accomplished two purposes: He would have reassured the public that the people who run Exxon acknowledged their misdeed and would make amends. And he might have salvaged the pride that Exxon workers once had in their company. Says one manager: "Wherever I travel now, I feel like I have a target painted on my chest." Employees are confused, embarrassed and betrayed.*
> J. Nulty[2]

Not every corporation faced with a crisis has responded as non-adaptively as Exxon did during the *Valdez* disaster, Thiokol did with the space shuttle *Challenger*, or Union Carbide did at Bhopal, India, but there are many instances in which organizations, large and small, have created greater problems for themselves in the face of crisis. Ironically, the escalation of the organization's problems has been directly related to the organization's attempts to control the original crisis. Ultimately, this form of defensive behavior stems from a lack of connection on the part of the managers with a deeper sense of self. This results in a variety of actions that take them further away from a solution and into territory that is progressively more anxiety-provoking, causing even more defensive behavior. When enough examples of disastrous crisis management exist for given organizations, they may be considered "crisis-prone."[3] A review of the dynamics of crisis management found significantly similar management behavior and dynamics in a variety of crisis-prone organizations. Consistently, major disasters were the result of deep defects within the organization's structure and culture. These defects were the result of emotional, not cognitive limitations on the part of people in organizations. When a major crisis occurs, it triggers deep anxieties related to self-esteem, self-worth, and even one's basic identity in the staff of the organization. This existential threat unleashes powerful defensive reactions that may include the denial of the situation's gravity, which may in turn lead to other crises, setting off even more defensive reactions. People learn the value of these defensive routines in protecting themselves from anxiety and uncertainty.

Mitroff and Pauchant feel that two principal distinctions differentiate crisis-prone organizations from those that are able to perceive and deal with crises, and are therefore considered "crisis-prepared." The first feature addresses individual moral leadership or character; the second speaks to what is essentially the organizationally scaled correlate of the same dynamic and is variously referred to as corporate character, conscience, or culture. Managers in crisis-prone corporations attempt to protect both their own identity and that of the organization. For these managers to admit emotionally that their corporation could experience a major crisis, they must admit that both they and their organization are not "perfect" or "excellent." They are embedded in a system that cannot learn from its environment owing to the organization's cultural blindness.

Becoming a Leader: The Process of Transformation

> *Everyone has talent. What is rare is the courage to follow the*
> *talent to the dark place that it leads.*
> Erica Jong
> *Harper Book of Quotations*

Three separate concepts apply to the directing of the actions of organizations within the model of strategic learning. Two concepts apply to roles filled by individuals within the organization: *leader* and *manager*. The third term, *governance*, addresses the process that integrates these roles in the service of the organization. When an individual is referred to as a leader, we are referring to his or her engagement in a process that is interpersonally intensive. The concept of management refers to the control of a structurally intensive, systematized operation. Too often in the management literature, one of these roles is exalted at the expense of the other. However, when the integrating concept of governance is introduced, there is room for both roles within the organization. The question then changes from determining whether an individual is a "manager" or a "leader," to determining the appropriateness of a given role given the overall conditions and issues of governance facing the organization.

Are some people born to lead, or does some series of events transform them into leaders? The topic of leadership development has long been the focus of much interest among academics and practitioners. Two specific topics within this area are key to understanding the actions of a leader. The first topic addresses how and why an individual becomes a leader. The second topic deals with the actions of the individual once a psychic shift to leadership has occurred. Substantial evidence exists that the most crucial events in the development of top managers are the results of being exposed to challenging experiences, primarily those relevant to one's career or personal life. However, to be maximally effective, these developmental opportunities must also provide for some sort of feedback on the actions of the executive. These opportunities can be external. But it is equally important for the executive to reflect on his or her learning from the situation and to have the opportunity to test her or his hypothesis in the future.[4]

Leaders actually think differently than managers.[5] They differ in what they attend to, how they perceive and process information, how they interact with others, and how they work. This is due to the fact that managers and leaders have different personalities. Zaleznik feels that leaders grow through mastering personal conflict during their developmental years while individuals better characterized as managers "confront few experiences that generally cause people to turn inward." (Note here Zaleznik's choice of the word "confront." He does not imply that managers and leaders have essentially different sets of experience, but that they deal with experience differently.) Leaders' personalities have been developed through a different process than that of the manager. Managers tend to interpret life as a steady progression of essentially neutral to positive events, resulting in security at home, in school, in the community, and at work. Leaders have interpreted some of their life experiences as discontinuities. They have endured life events that managers might have treated as ordinary, but that leaders interpret as separate from the mainstream flow of life. The result of this feeling of estrangement is that the person has turned inward in a process of redefining his or her identity and has reemerged with a sense of self that was created by the person and not inherited from the environment. William James calls the person who has undergone this process *"twice born."*[6] But why doesn't everyone become a leader? It is improbable that anyone grows to adulthood without encountering some form of crisis or event that would cause him or her to question the nature of his or her identity. The variables here that would determine whether one would emerge from this process inclined toward leadership would be related to the pretraumatic personality. Significant factors in this process would include one's view of the self and the world, one's level of cognitive development, and one's capacity to internalize responsibility. All of these factors are deeply rooted within the human psyche.

Leadership is internally transparent; that is, an individual cannot legitimately identify her or his own behavior or attitudes as those of a leader. Leadership and its reciprocal, followership, are characteristics of interpersonal relationships. They are perceived qualities. A person cannot be a leader alone. A leader must have people that will follow the agenda or vision that she or he represents for them. The followers then define the actions of the leader as a function of the vision, and will only hold faith with the leader while she or he is perceived to be in service of the vision. When the leader strays from the vision, the followers will choose, on the basis of their values and experiences, whether to follow the leader and found a cult of personality or return to the original vision and either seek out or develop a new leader.

The Templates of Transformation

What, then, is the process of examination that the individual engages in that results in his or her emergence as a leader? Models of the transformation process that creates leaders both fill the world around us and dwell within us. We call the models around us stories and myths. The models that exist within us are called archetypes. Archetypes, identified by Carl Jung, are unconscious patterns that have evolved to provide ways for us to impose order and to interpret the world we experience. Archetypes are universal: everyone inherits the same basic archetypal structures. Archetypes are common across cultures and peoples. The experience of the energized archetypes is communicated through myths. A common archetype in classical and popular literature is that of the *hero*. We are all familiar with various myths that have arisen around this archetype. Using these myths as a tool to interpret our experience, we identify heroes through their actions in the world around us. The archetype acts as a magnet, collecting relevant information around itself and forming the information into a pattern that holds meaning for the individual. Jung called this pattern a *complex*. This complex is a way for the individual to explain his or her experience. The term *"inferiority complex"* has entered into the vernacular; what this originally meant, however, was that the individual's persona had gathered about it information that carried the theme of the person's inability to cope with the world. The individual uses this information to generate stories or myths about himself or herself that carry this message and further define his or her personality and subsequent actions around the concept of incapacity. In this way, the archetypes can communicate with our conscious experience and provide meaning to our experience.

Understanding the impact of archetypes is essential in the development of leaders and the conversions of industrial systems because they provide the maps for our psychic journeys. The leader's successful completion of these inward journeys is the analog for the successful completion of the conversion of any organizational system. The nascent leader must follow these maps on her or his journey of rediscovery. Campbell identified this process as the hero's journey, a process common in world mythology, from the *Odyssey* to *Star Wars*.[7] The components of the hero's journey are separation, initiation, and return. During the separation period, the voyager realizes that she or he does not belong with or fit into the current environment. This is essentially consistent with the reports of leaders interviewed by Zaleznik.[8] These people reported a sense of detachment, a sense that they just did not fit, whether in a family, social, or work situation. The next phase is that of the initiation. According to Campbell, the journeyer frequently is helped in the process of initiation by a guide of some sort. This guide is often represented as someone who is older and wiser than the journeyer and who provides assistance during the process of initiation. During this process, the initiate learns new skills or develops new knowledge to help him or her correct the original situation. During the period of return, these gifts are tested. This process can account for Zaleznik's finding that leaders and managers think differently. Leaders have derived more value from their experience, and they continue to add value to their overall coping skills by examining each new experience.

Even individuals with a strong tendency to act as a leader will not act in such a way all of the time. In any social setting, people can choose to accept one of five roles. One choice, withdrawal, removes them from participating in further interaction in that specific setting. The other four roles frame broadly set parameters on an individual's participation in the actions of the group. These four roles can be arrayed in a matrix. In general, individuals in the leadership role determine the agendas for a group, while the manager's role centers on execution. A follower acts in response to the leader's actions, being motivated primarily by similar values. The subordinate is motivated by the end goal of completing a task. This motivation may not be based upon the individual's values, in that the subordinate has accepted the subjective environment as part of the general environment in which the task is embedded. The labels for each of the roles should be perceived only as labels, free of positive or negative associations. Each of the roles is necessary, each has no intrinsic "goodness" or "badness." The appropriateness of the actor's choice in a given situation is the key element in determining whether a role is appropriate given the environment of the moment and the orientation of the organization. The challenge for converting industries is to make this perception and the requisite adjustments.

Historically, the culture of defense-related industries has been strongly dominated by engineering, particularly with a systems orientation. These organizations must now develop a clear stream of outwardly aware and inwardly focused leaders. As these leaders develop, they will face a significant challenge in sharing their perceptions of the emerging economy with the existing managerially oriented cultures.

The new leaders' challenge can be framed as a function of communication dynamics. As long as the exchange between positions remains oriented vertically in the matrix, communication—and the assumptions upon which the communication is based—will remain coherent and consistent. If diagonal channels or horizontal channels are initiated, the potential for misunderstanding rapidly escalates, based on the lack of shared values and assumptions between the roles. The leader–follower channel tends to be process-intensive, where the manager–subordinate channel is oriented to the maintenance of structural elements. Given that these vertically related roles share similar underlying attributes—specifically, those that differentiate between the leader and manager roles— other attributes can also be assumed to shared. The only real difference between leaders and followers or managers and subordinates has to do with their perceived positions in the group, not their behavior.

One of these shared attributes is the fact that leaders think differently from managers. The specific nature of the added value of the leaders' learning seems to be similar to the concept of double-loop learning. Double-loop learning is an extension of single-loop learning.[9] Single-loop learning is a three-phase process based on an ability to detect and correct error in relation to a given set of operating norms. This process works by the process of an individual (1) scanning the environment, (2) comparing the information with operating norms, searching for mismatches of data or errors, and (3) initiating appropriate action if indicated.

Single-loop learning serves the structural element. This form of learning cannot initiate change except in relation to, and limited by, the structure in which it is embedded. A thermostat is a classic illustration of a single-loop system. It can only "decide" whether a room's temperature is at the point where a heater needs to be turned on. The structure of the system permits only that much freedom.

Double-loop learning depends on the learner's ability to question the relevance of operating norms before making a final decision on initiating action. The values governing the situation are considered before action is undertaken. While this system serves structural elements well, it can initiate change outside of the limits of the system when those limits are inadequate to meet the needs framed by the values. If double-loop learning is applied to the above example of a thermostat, someone in the room will notice that it is getting warm outside and that the heat is no longer needed. The thermostat for the heater will then be turned off and the air conditioner switched on.

Managers tend to be very skilled at single-loop learning. They are capable of running an organization well as long as the need for fundamental change does not emerge as an environmental factor. Individuals acting out of the "managers' mindset" can typically deal with change if it can be addressed by incremental adjustments to existing features of the organization. People who are acting as leaders are needed to move organizations through times of change when the fundamental assumptions that have been in play cease to be valid. These individuals have already been through this questioning process internally; they now have the ability to apply the skills that they learned in a broader context. In Campbell's pattern of transformation, they can act as the guide for the organization's heroic journey. It is clear that a major task of the leader is to apply double-loop learning. A framework for understanding this application process can be found in the research of Kouzes and Posner,[10] which indicates that the primary task of the leader is to challenge the process. This does not necessarily mean that the leader must be the innovator of a new idea but that he or she recognizes the value of the concept and pushes for its inclusion. This same research identified other key behaviors of leaders, including inspiring a shared vision, enabling others to act, modeling the way, and encouraging the heart.

Upon reflection, one realizes that all these actions reside within the domain of the mature personality. A person facing significant threats from anxiety, in the form of an organizational crisis, may find it very difficult to call upon the internal resources necessary to support the actions that are perceived by others as leadership. A person who has endured and successfully coped with significant turmoil would have learned the skills and confidence to deal with this level of threat. Coping with early crises would better prepare a leader to handle subsequent ones as long as she or he maintained the capacity for double-loop learning. If one dropped back into a single-loop model, it would be difficult to address a crisis that was more severe than any other one had faced to date, for one would not be able to step out of the current frame and develop perspective on the crisis. Without this level of perspective, one is unable to address fundamental issues about the nature of the crisis and one's response to it. Given this, one would tend to develop incremental solutions to the crisis, and one's actions would most likely not be judged the actions of a leader.

**Frameworks for Growth and Learning:
Organizational Design and Strategy**

To have any hope of being effective, strategy must be congruent with the essential design of the organization. In the process of strategic planning, the resources of the organization are focused on defining a strategy for a given period of time and under certain conditions or assumptions. These resources are focused, via a series of goals, upon features believed to be significant in gaining or maintaining competitive advantage. Strategic goals can address both qualitative and quantitative aspects of organizational performance. These goals should be as specific as possible in that progress toward their completion can be observed and measured. Optimally, the goals of strategy cannot be driven solely by short-term outcomes, financial performance, productivity, or the use of strategic resources. Practically, an organization will get what it measures. *An organization that tracks personnel as cost centers will be more likely to reduce staff in a fiscal crunch than one that manages strategic human resources as an asset.*

The role of strategic learning for the enterprise must be to create and maintain *a sustainable entity* that fulfills its mission and whose structure, practice, and polices are congruent with the vision that drives the organization. The concept of a sustainable organization encompasses all of those realms and more, and finds that the concepts of behavioral ecology become as relevant to the corporation as the concepts of economics. Implicit in the concept of the sustainable organization is the view that the organization is embedded in an environment with which it shares significant interaction. The products and byproducts of the organization's activity are perceived by various stakeholders that in turn assign values to them. The various publics of the organization, internal and external, may key in on different features, or assign opposing values to the same feature. The task of the sustainable organization is to manage these perceptions or the reactions of the stakeholders through information gathering, review of operating assumptions, and projection of resources in meaningful response. A sustainable organization is one that explores and identifies its boundaries and the features that define the boundaries from both sides of the line of demarcation (what the organization looks like to the world and what the world looks like to the organization). The boundaries of competing and conflicting entities must be identified and examined for points of similarity and differentiation. The internal boundaries of the organization, the descriptors that the participants in the organization, must also be examined. These are the elements that define the scope of products and services that the organization provides, the norms for behavior, and the specific attitudes and competencies that the participants value.

When strategy is aimed at the development of a sustainable organization, it also commits the members of the organization to create an organization capable of learning. From the perspective of sustainability, strategic planning becomes an exercise in organizational ecology. The various forces that drive, stress, and restrain an organization are balanced through the alignment of the organization's strategic resources over time. The paths for alignment of strategic resources can initially be identified by the identification, evaluation, and prioritization of relevant features in the internal and external environment. After the internal and external boundaries are identified and understood, the exchange of energy and material with the environment must be tracked. Some of these resources can be categorized as financial capital, supplies, and information. Human capital and knowledge are as vital to the learning organization as capital equipment was to smokestack industries.

The next consideration in the development of the sustainable organization is the examination of the processes the organization uses to act on and transform this flow into products. These products can be the end products of the organization, but the effect on the various forms of capital, equipment, and relationships with the environment must also be considered. When one undertakes to define the strategies an organization uses to learn from and adapt to the environment, it becomes necessary to have a model of the nature of an organization to make sense of the information.

In creating an organization that is capable of learning, the role of structure is to establish boundaries within the organization and between the organization and its environment. These boundaries are operationalized in terms of roles, regulations, responsibilities, and relationships. They are applied in areas such as system governance, maintenance of strategic resources, and the transformation of operating resources into products or services that are perceived to add value to the community (a sustainable organization's ecosystem). The relevant issue here is for structure to remain a process with an optimal balance between defining characteristics and flexibility, and not to allow rigidity to cause the organization to lose its adaptive qualities.

The Language of Organization

The process of strategic learning assumes that two types of interactions can be combined to create an organization: those interactions that are structuring and support repeated patterns of interaction, and those interactions that occur within a structural or prescribed framework. There is a significant difference between structural elements and structuring processes. Structural elements (such as an organizational chart or a cultural ritual) were structuring processes (such as functional assignments) at one time in the organization's history, but they were transformed from an active process involving people into a depersonalized, nonliving thing via the actions of a semantic operation called "nominalization."[11] In this linguistic process, a process word or verb in the deep semantic structure (which occurs in a person's unconscious mind) appears in his or her everyday speech (the surface structure of grammar) as a thing or a noun. Nominalizations distract attention away from ongoing or developing processes by confusing them with unchangeable objects. In psychotherapy, a client is assisted in recognizing nominalizations in order to show him or her that what had been considered an event that was over or beyond control is in fact an ongoing process that can be changed. In the case of strategic learning, the essence of creating an organization that is capable of learning and adapting to new situations is the reduction of structural (nominalized) elements into structuring or defining processes.

From the strategic learning perspective, an organization is an artifact of language. In effect, the organization becomes a function of the language used to describe it through the daily interactions and behavior of its constituents. The process of description creates the organization in the minds of the originators. It is the commonly held paradigm or mental model that can be understood by an outside observer when it is externalized through the behavior of its members. The success of the management of an organization in communicating this set of concepts to others mediates the clarity of the organization's purpose as it grows beyond the influence of its originators.

There is a reciprocal relationship between structure and flexibility. Organizations must decide to trade structure (certainty in handling information) for flexibility (the capacity to tolerate variance). When an organization opts to overbalance in favor of structural responses to the environment, it risks (1) inflexibility, resulting in the inability to adapt to changing situations, and (2) the danger inherent in a complex system moving toward maximum organization, also known as self-organized criticality. Inflexibility tends to be obvious; self-organized criticality is more subtle, but on examination can be readily discerned in circumstances such as those that resulted in the disintegration of Soviet hegemony. Bennis and Slater anticipated these events in their observations of the dynamics of information flow in large systems. They noted that as institutions increase in size (and attendant complexity), they become unmanageable. This is due to the unwieldy, traditional, bureaucratic top–down chains of command and their tendency to suppress and distort the flow of vital feedback on operations. The net effect of this is that these organizations move further and further out of touch with the real world through their structural inability to incorporate responses to variance in their operations.[12]

Balance and Renewal

Models of self-organized criticality demonstrate that complex systems can organize themselves to a critical state in which a minor event starts a chain reaction that can lead to a radical reordering or even destruction of the integrity of the system.[13] Although complex systems tend to produce a greater number of minor events, rather than catastrophes, chain reactions of all sizes are a part of the dynamics. The same mechanism that generates minor events leads to major events. Bak and Chen describe a remarkably simple illustration of self-organized criticality: the sandpile. An experimental apparatus was designed to drop sand, one grain at a time, onto a point on a smooth, circular surface. Initially, the grains stay close to the point where they fall onto the surface. Gradually, a gently sloping pile takes shape. From time to time, the slope becomes too steep and grains slide down the face of the pile. This triggers a small avalanche. With the gradual addition of more sand, the pile increases in size and the slope becomes more steep. The size of the typical avalanche increases and grains are carried off the slope; they even fall off the disc upon which the pile was built. The pile is balanced when it reaches a point where the amount of sand being added is equaled, on average, by the sand falling off the edge. When this point of balance is reached, the pile can be said to have reached a critical state. At criticality, any grain added to the pile can cause an avalanche, including a catastrophic (for the sandpile) event. It is also important to note that, in these models, complex systems never reach equilibrium but evolve from one metastable state to the next. In this state, the structural elements are like glass, very hard and inflexible, but they are also very brittle and vulnerable to specific forms of stress. When these elements are over-stressed, like glass they will shatter.

Another way of understanding the balance between an organization's capacity for renewal and self-organized criticality is Toffler's novelty ratio.[14] The novelty ratio reflects the degree of newness in a system; it is the ratio of new to old. Toffler points out that there are moments in the life cycle of the firm when it must cope with very high levels of novelty, and other times when the level of novelty is low. The governors of an organization must be able to identify the current level of novelty in its environment and operate the firm accordingly. For example, if a firm is in a low-novelty situation, incremental management could be indicated to adjust increments of market share, productivity, retention, and so on. In a context in which novelty is high, more radical forms of governance will be necessary to keep the organization viable. These are circumstances in which the behaviors associated with leadership need to be nurtured and supported. For an example, if an organization is unable to detect, identify, and relate significant shifts in the environment to its operations, it will quickly find that the items in its inventory are outmoded or that the composition of the work force has changed to a point where workers' goals are out of sync with those of the firm.

Organizational Governance: Where Leadership and Design Intersect

Leadership and management are complementary and interdependent roles. When one dominates the other, the organization suffers. Converting industries must strive to balance these two roles in the process of governance. An organization that is leader-intensive quickly becomes a caricature of itself. Its behavior appears to be hyperkinetic as it swings to face challenge after challenge. It can identify solutions, but it lacks the capability to keep the solution in place for a meaningful period so that a resolution can be reached. Management-intensive organizations focus on their predetermined, and infrequently revisited, polices, procedures, and plans. This focus for acting is maintained in the face of virtually any amount of environmental input to the contrary.

This component of the strategic learning process addresses the integration of the leadership dynamic and organizational design through the development of a hierarchy of directive behavior. This system is designed to link and coordinate all of the various components of directive behavior that must occur for an organization to be sustainable. It is composed of two channels, each consisting of five different levels. These levels define the relevant behavior for the various forms of energy that drive the organization. The levels are integrated through feedback loops that offer leaders the opportunity to examine the various processes and initiate necessary changes. The two channels are reciprocal. One channel focuses the energy contained in structuring processes, while the other channel consists of structural elements. In a renewable, adaptive, learning organization, each level must contain appropriate amounts of both channels. Organizations that lack balance between the channels at any level create specific forms of crises. The specific character of the crisis will relate to the nature of the transformation of energy and information as they pass between the levels that are out of balance. For example, assume an organization that has reached clarity about its core vision and mission. Using this knowledge, it has developed a set of strategic-level goals. It has not, however, taken into account information flowing up from the action and program levels that contradicts assumptions that underlie the strategic goals. With these strategies based on unrealistic assumptions, successful implementation will be virtually impossible.

As one progresses through the hierarchy, the levels express a reciprocal relationship between objectivity and change as a result of the changing balance between processes and structural elements. The first level, *vision*, is extremely subjective. It may include expressions of values and beliefs that guide the operation of the system. Statements of essential values cannot be readily changed without striking directly at the core of the organization's identity. These concepts, or their interpretations, define and frame the basic ground upon which the organization will operate. Paradoxically, therefore, while this level is built from the least concrete material, it must become structurally oriented so that it becomes the least flexible. The organization must have other levels that can be adjusted to meet the outcomes of its various leanings without altering the core values of the system. Therefore, each of the other four levels in the hierarchy is progressively easier to change through the management of structuring processes based on the learning of the organization.

The vision is transformed into directive action through the development of the organization's mission. It is the first step toward full objectification of the vision. Typically this is expressed through the *mission statement*. The mission statement must link the vision with succeeding levels by describing the processes or actions that will lead to the fulfillment of the vision.

The middle level of the hierarchy contains *strategic goals*. These are specific statements for each product of the organization. Strategic goals are the point of balance in the process of the vision's transformation into *action*. They lie midway between these two points. This is the level where specific and objective results can be assessed against the system's ability to fulfill its mission. Strategic goals should be (1) clear to all who are guided by them, (2) quantifiable, with yes/no indicators of success, (3) related to critical success factors for the system's environment, and (4) derived from competitive information and environmental scanning that is related to and then incorporated with benchmarking information.

The fourth level of the hierarchy holds *operational goals*. These goals are related to a system's specific functional components and relate the component's capacity to deliver essential services to the strategic actions of the larger system. Operational goals are derived from strategic goals and are informed by consumer requirements and benchmarking information. Each of the hierarchy's operational goals must be linked to a specific strategic goal.

The base of the hierarchy is made up of *outcome objectives*. Outcome objectives form the component parts of the operational goals. They communicate to performers what they are expected to do and how well they are expected to do it. These objectives should be direct, be written in behavioral terms, and address observable and quantifiable actions or sets of actions that are paired with measurable outcomes.

Most organizations have addressed each of these five levels. Typically, some levels are dealt with implicitly, leading to misunderstandings and misinterpretations. In this way, systems can quickly stray from their original intentions and designs and become dysfunctional. The other component of strategic learning that is frequently absent in other systems is feedback between levels. Usually, feedback systems exist between strategic and operational levels and between individual performers and operational units. The process breaks down in the use of feedback to revisit the organization's mission. As the mission becomes increasingly out of sync with the environment, the system's sustainability becomes jeopardized. Without leaders to use double-loop learning to review the mission, drift is inevitable.

The Journey into Strategy

The strategy of an organization is the articulation of a vision; it describes how the resources of the organization can be allocated to realize the vision. The strategy is also the point of balance in the system that integrates the internal, personal reality of each member of an organization with the pragmatic realities that the organization must address every day. On the level of the experience of the organization's governors, the vision is most closely linked to the outcomes of action plans that must be executed for the strategy and mission to be fulfilled. The reality of the organization becomes relevant at the level where mission, strategy, and program goals are addressed.

The journey into strategy for an organization is the same as the transformative journey of a leader. This journey gives the organization the opportunity to incorporate the capacity for learning into its operations. It is a vital quest that has the potential to change the organization's world. This is the true nature of the task that faces converting industries. The industries must reorient themselves, but this is not possible until the organization's governance is first reoriented. New visions and missions must be sought.

When we talk about changing systems, we ultimately talk about changing ourselves. Systems are our creations. If we do not use the insights from our learning and growth to manage the processes of the system, the system will use its structures to manage us. If we allow this, we surrender the best of our selves, our power and our future, to mindless and empty creations. To take back control of these systems, we must act as fully human. We must open ourselves to experience and experiment and continue our learning and growth. Ultimately, it is our legacy to accept that we can become more than our biology.

Notes

1. Ian I. Mitroff and Thierry C. Pauchant, *"We're So Big and Powerful Nothing Bad Can Happen to Us"*: An Investigation of America's Crisis Prone Corporations (New York: Birch Lane Press/Carol Publishing Group, 1990).
2. Ibid.
3. Ibid.
4. Morgan W. McCall, Michael M. Lombardo, and Ann M. Morrison, *The Lessons of Experience* (Lexington, MA: Lexington Books, 1988).
5. Abraham Zaleznik, *The Managerial Mystique* (New York: Harper and Row, 1989).

6. Ibid.

7. Joseph Campbell, *The Hero with a Thousand Faces* (Princeton University Press, 1968).

8. Zaleznik, *The Managerial Mystique*.

9. Chris Argyris, *Overcoming Organizational Defenses* (Boston: Allyn and Bacon, 1990).

10. James M. Kouzes and Barry Z. Posner, *The Leadership Challenge* (San Francisco: Jossey-Bass, 1990).

11. Richard Bandler and John Grinder, *The Structure of Magic I* (Palo Alto, CA: Science and Behavior Books, 1975).

12. Warren G. Bennis and Philip E. Slater, "Democracy is inevitable," *Harvard Business Review* (April 1964).

13. Per Bak and Kan Chen, "Self-organized criticality," *Scientific American* (January 1991).

14. Alvin Toffler, *The Adaptive Corporation* (New York: Bantam, 1985).

Part II
Conversion and Adjustment Experience in the United States

4

DOMENICK BERTELLI

Military Contractor Conversion in the United States

For most of the period since the end of the Cold War, defense conversion has been regarded as the equivalent of alchemy—impossible without magic, any success surely illusionary. From *Newsweek* to the *Economist* to the *Harvard Business Review*, conversion has been mocked amid sober eulogies for those poor employees who would inevitably be dislocated. The implicit message was that the only way to save those jobs and communities was through sustained defense spending. Perhaps the most quoted authority on conversion was Norman Augustine, chairman of Martin Marietta, who said "the record of conversion is unblemished by success." Considering that oft-repeated warning, it is extremely ironic (if little noted) that his own company is now trying to convert.

Would be free-market champions and prophets have railed about the different cultures of defense contracting and commercial production, and recounted sternly the 1970s "disaster" stories of Rohr, Grumman, and Boeing Vertol. They draw fangs to mock Grumman canoes, Kaman's Ovation guitars, and EDO's golf clubs. Their standard conclusion: firms are helpless; dislocation will be severe in some regions,

This research was supported by grants from the Joyce Mertz-Gilmore Foundation, Dr. George Wallerstein, Rockefeller Family Associates, Malcolm Wiener, the Wallach Foundation, the Everett Public Service Internship Program, the CEP Board of Directors, and members of CEP. The author gratefully acknowledges guidance, assistance, and/or comments from Jurgen Brauer, John Connor, Lloyd Dumas, Lew Franklin, John Tepper Marlin, Erik Pages, James Raffel, Peter Rose, and Lee Thomas.

but will not affect the whole nation; the government might be wise to address some adjustment programs; the markets will take care of restructuring. Few have noted the amazing irony that conversion naysayers—many of whom built their careers through the military-industrial complex, the most monolithic centralized-planning bureaucracy left in the world—have now become advocates of free-market capitalism in the face of military spending cuts.

What administration officials, Congress, businesspeople, and labor unions have slowly realized, acknowledging the growing number of successful conversion stories, is that:

1.   Firms are not helpless—though they are hindered by some defense-culture legacies and the inaccessibility of finance.
2.   The impact of defense downsizing is larger than expected among dependent regions and industries.
3.   Because of the role of the Department of Defense (DoD) in funding research and development (R&D) and in procurement of cutting-edge technologies, the impact of downsizing is economywide.
4.   Conversion needs reflect broader policy needs in the areas of technology development and transfer, industrial policy, training, and economic development without which we will be unable to slow—let alone reverse—the deindustrialization of the United States.[1]

By peering through the dust clouds generated by consolidating defense industries one can find much evidence that real conversion and diversification are happening—however haphazardly—and that almost every contractor is trying it. For large firms, there is a clear difference between the posturing of CEOs and the projects they are willing to try. For small firms, the will is there, but the working capital, information on government programs, and some of the requisite commercial know-how are lacking. For everyone concerned, reinforcing myths have critically delayed progress and the lack of a common dialogue has muddled and retarded the overall economic conversion agenda.

Evidence of Conversion

According to a 1991 survey of high-level defense industry executives undertaken by the Winbridge Group, 48 percent of executives responding reported "strategic and financial success" in selling their products in commercial markets.[2] Seventy-eight percent reported that they would pursue diversification projects over the following five years. Even two-thirds of those *opposed* to conversion because of past failures said their firms had technology with commercial potential.

A recent survey of Southern California aerospace companies found that nearly every company contacted is moving toward increased commercialization of its businesses, with smaller firms pursuing conversion opportunities most vigorously.[3] The study also notes the inadequacy of many conversion business plans, an observation discussed in greater detail below.

A 1990 survey undertaken by the Aerospace Industries Association found that bringing work in-house and moving workers to commercial programs appeared to be favorite contractor responses to military spending cuts. The survey of nineteen "top Pentagon contractors or key system and subsystem suppliers" reported that 61 percent moved workers from defense to commercial programs. Forty-four percent also reported changing the focus of product lines within plants.[4] Analysis of a National Science Foundation data base on engineers accumulated between 1980 and 1986 revealed that nearly one-quarter of engineers employed in defense work in 1982 had shifted to nondefense work by 1986.[5]

Three compendiums of conversion and diversification examples published in the early 1990s together tell more than seventy stories of companies finding new applications for defense technology.[6] With additional research, the Council on Economic Priorities (CEP) in New York City now has a data base with over a hundred examples.

Among defense contractors whom one would not think of as conversion companies are:

Martin Marietta. One booth at the EXPO 2000 technology trade show held in Baltimore in December 1992 featured representatives from a 130-person group based in Florida. When some of the engineers in the group saw their defense markets shrinking, they started thinking about commercial projects. They discovered that technology they had developed for combat night vision and aerial mine detection could also be used to scan handwriting and to detect toxic waste sites, among other possibilities. They are seeking commercial markets. Referring to Norman Augustine, chairman of Martin Marietta and loud conversion critic, one of his associates remarked, "with Norm you have to watch what he does, not what he says."

Loral. One diversification project the company is trying, in partnership with Siemens, is to use technology developed to store, distribute, and analyze reconnaissance images for the military for the growing market in biomedical imaging. In September 1991, the venture won a contract with a potential value of $350 million to install new equipment in military hospitals.[7]

Lockheed Missiles and Space Co. Lockheed is using antisubmarine warfare technology to detect oil spills, track their movement, and dispose of them.[8] Lockheed has also gone after railcar contracts, participated in Calstart, the consortium developed to make electric cars in Southern California, and, recently, signed a $700 million contract to help build Motorola's Iridium satellites.

Northrop Corp. Northrop, one of the most defense-dependent contractors, is spending $32 million on a project to develop high-efficiency buses.[9] Northrop also announced plans to open a commercial aircraft division in early 1993. At the time, the company announced the goal of increasing commercial revenues to one-third of total revenues.[10]

These projects are not large-scale tank-to-tractor examples, but are representative of what is possible, and what is being replicated across defense industries—small divisions within companies assessing core technologies and finding new applications. The vast majority of successful conversion projects are undertaken by small divisions within companies, small companies, or companies "spun out" of large companies. Loral and Lockheed have benefited from teaming with commercial partners. All these companies have benefited from the deeper financial pockets that come with larger size.

More important, the companies are applying technologies developed with taxpayer money. One consultant contacted by the Conversion Information Center (CIC) of C&P estimated that top-25 contractor Grumman, headquartered on Long Island in New York, had already identified more than $10 million worth of new markets that could be tapped with existing corporate patents, but had taken little action in pursuing them because they are "small potatoes" relative to defense systems. That Westinghouse has generated over $500 million in nondefense business through its efforts to diversify defense-intensive divisions suggests that the $10 million estimate is at least plausible.

The Grumman and Westinghouse cases suggest the answer to a question frequently asked by critics of conversion: If there were money to be made in other sectors, why wouldn't the contractors be diving into those markets already? The answer, supported by numerous contractor testimonials, is threefold: (1) in many cases they are; (2) in the nonentrepreneurial culture of defense manufacturing, there have been few incentives and, in most companies, no process to investigate alternative markets; and (3) where companies are not trying it, it is because profit margins are not as high in nondefense markets. Business conditions are also less regular and less predictable outside defense.

Citing just this point, many contractors have stated that they would gladly enter mass-transportation markets if firm, long-term public commitments were made to those markets.[11] Two of the famous "horror stories," the "conversion failures" of Boeing-Vertol and Rohr, derived in part from the federal government backing away from commitments to establish standards and partially fund the development of urban mass-transit systems.

The reinforcing myth that every potential market niche is already filled with highly competitive companies is also fallacious. First, if all possible commercial markets were filled, no new businesses would ever start up or diversify. Second, many defense firms, after long years of preferential access to government R&D money, really do know how to make better mousetraps; that is, they could make products that by virtue of technological superiority would create new niches and/or be competitive in old ones. Third, if all useful government-created markets were already established and fulfilled, we would be living in a much different and happier world.

So why are defense firms not diversifying in the present, tough climate? Many are, and as the development cycles for thousands of new goods and services come to fruition, this will become clear. Big firms try to deny that they are diversifying—let alone converting. When cornered, they sometimes elliptically describe conversion ventures as (for example) "seeking alternate markets using an available capacity."[12] Many firms are afraid to reveal projects to potential competitors, or to the Department of Defense, which many fear will penalize companies that diversify by shifting contracts to more dependent (and thus vulnerable) firms. With better incentives (some as simple as a directive from the secretary of defense encouraging diversification planning), many more firms would be tackling and overcoming the technical and sociological barriers hindering the transition.

Subsidies, too, can create appropriate incentives for conversion, but it is essential that accountability—especially in terms of job creation—be built into relevant laws.[13] When the government tried to help the steel industry in the early 1980s, it gave away too much (with too few strings attached) to companies like USX, which simply funneled assets to other divisions. If the path to conversion has to be paved with gold, it's not worth it.

In testimony before Congress in May 1993, several corporate representatives said that conversion would become much easier for them if they could more easily acquire the patents that derive from government-sponsored R&D.[14] Mirroring moves last year to substantially reduce or eliminate recoupment charges,[15] industry-suggested changes might spur more commercialization of defense technologies, but it is not clear that the public sector would get a fair return on public funds invested in the technology development if they were adopted.

In May of 1994, the Call to Action, a labor-led conversion coalition in New England, helped pass two pieces of landmark legislation in the Connecticut General Assembly. The first, the Act Concerning Economic Development Program Accountability, ensures that job creation and retention will be a priority at all phases of the economic development process, requires companies receiving over $250,000 in assistance to submit a business accountability plan, and establishes mechanisms for community, labor, municipal, and legislative oversight to ensure that businesses receiving public funds are held accountable. The second, the Act Concerning Defense Diversification, establishes the first alternative use committee (AUC) legislation in the country.[16]

What this discussion suggests, and what becomes clear after digging deeper into conversion, is that there is a lot more at play than technical questions about retooling and identifying new markets. The conversion debate has become a forum for discussing—and influencing—a full gamut of policy issues ranging from military force structures to all nuances of U.S. industrial policy. Before sketching firm conversion experiences, it is worth examining in brief the political and economic context in which they take place.

Dueling Definitions

Conversion means different things to different people, which constitutes a very big problem in realizing the kind of progressive agenda outlined by such renowned advocates as Robert Reich, Ira Magaziner,

Lloyd Dumas, Ann Markusen, John Tepper Marlin, and Joel Yudken. A broad range of agendas is promoted under the conversion banner. There are labor groups worried about job loss and plant reuse; contractor managers seeking manufacturing-extension assistance and diversification opportunities; and community groups concerned with new development to replace shuttered defense plants or military bases being closed. Religious and peace groups band together seeking to demilitarize local economies, and environmentalists try to draw attention to defense-related toxic contamination and to spur cleanup. Student groups concerned about the inroads made by the military into academia in the 1980s promote their own style of conversion, as do displaced military personnel concerned about benefits, training, and outplacement.

At the federal level, some conversion themes have been coopted by a competitiveness lobby hoping to take advantage of broader post–Cold War sea changes to realize a more civil-oriented technology (or industrial) policy. Their interests often intersect with those of Hawks concerned about preserving the defense industrial base. Defense Secretary William Perry has made a personal crusade of contracting or mil-spec reform as a path to making defense firms viable in commercial markets. A broad high-tech lobby has adopted conversion terminology to advance its agenda (largely realized in early 1994) of removing COCOM restrictions on exports. Universities weigh in across the spectrum, some supporting decentralization, democratization, and demilitarization of U.S. R&D activities, others squawking loudly about prospective cuts. Contractors seeking funding to guarantee ever-larger volumes of arms exports and contractors in damage-control mode trying to sustain current defense programs and preferential access to government R&D funding have also adopted much of the conversion rhetoric (if little of the spirit) and have had a heavy presence in shaping conversion programs.

Labor unions have intensified their efforts on conversion behind the leadership of the Industrial Union Department (IUD) of the AFL-CIO, the International Association of Machinists and Aerospace Workers (IAM), and the United Automobile, Aerospace, and Agricultural Implement Workers of America (UAW), the last of which showed breakthrough leadership in putting together the Call to Action. Labor sees conversion as part of a broader campaign to save jobs, create new jobs, institutionalize worker participation in workplace transformation, and redirect the philosophy of technological innovation and automation to make it more human-centered. These concerns have been addressed through the interunion Technology Working Group and the broad-based Workplace Economic Conversion Action Network (WE*CAN), which also includes more than thirty community, environmental, policy, peace, and religious organizations. These groups, though more influential now than a few years ago, are still dramatically over-matched by the industrial lobbies in terms of resources and access to decision-making processes.

There are also formidable lobbies within the government: bureaucrats trying to expand their turf, defense research agencies scrambling to justify their continued existence with falling defense R&D, and nondefense research agencies trying to expand their budgets, mandates, and functions. So far, the relative winners have been the defense-dependent bureaucracies.

To the environmental, corporate social responsibility, and arms control communities, conversion is a strategy for paring the military, minimizing dislocation, and redirecting R&D and procurement priorities. To many defense employees with whom I have talked, conversion has vague connotations of disaster or utopianism. Mentioning "conversion" without context at an aerospace trade show in 1992 elicited a comparable reaction to what might be expected at the mention of "supply-side economics" in South-Central Los Angeles.

To the casual observer, conversion usually connotes notions of making new products with defense technology and production facilities. To the colonel in the Pentagon, it means sustaining defense plants through a dual-use industrial policy so as to reduce the cost of keeping critical suppliers afloat and retaining the capacity to build up again. That is, conversion in the Pentagon extends little beyond notions of keeping the military-industrial base "warm."

Conversion can be a confluence of many of the above agendas, and will have to be if we are really going to utilize existing assets efficiently in meeting current economic and environmental problems. To date, however, conversion *legislation* has been mostly a confluence of the interests of the "competitiveness" lobby, would-be defenders of the defense-industrial base, big contractors, and the armed services (who saw to it that numerous adjustment programs were provided for mustered-out troops and DoD civilian personnel).

With respect to technology policy and economic development policy (particularly on the state level), addressing the specific problems of defense conversion has spurred hard thinking and government action on a variety of technology and development fronts: training, small-business incubation, sustainable job creation, linking of research institutions and industry, and the integration of all of the above. Such thinking arguably should have been done a decade ago. The concept of conversion has already been a catalyst for enacting more progressive policies in many places from California to the Northeast.

The process has gone badly awry in some places, though—notably in Arizona, where a conversion bill was hijacked and amended to entice companies to bring in *more* defense jobs. One state development official explained the logic of the bill in Orwellian terms: "Sometimes conversion doesn't just mean swords to plowshares; sometimes it means more swords."

The Technology Reinvestment Project

On the federal level, conversion programs have been something of a hodgepodge. October 1993 saw the passage of $1.7 billion in technology, training, and adjustment programs hybridized through the political process. Explaining the legislation just after it passed, one Senate staffer remarked, "The [House-Senate] conference committee was asked to choose between two very different bills. Their answer was yes."

These programs constitute the core of President Clinton's new Defense Conversion Reinvestment Initiative (DCRI). Some of the dual-use programs are smart defense policy and the broader Clinton agenda of building up the National Institute for Standards and Technology in the Department of Commerce as a civilian technology agency is a step in the right direction. But much of the program fits with the Pentagon conception of maintaining the status quo, and this has engendered a great deal of disenchantment among other constituencies.

The jewel in the crown of the DCRI is the Technology Reinvestment Program (TRP). Billed in press releases as a way to save and create jobs, unlock defense technologies for civil markets, and spur environmental and transportation research, it has accomplished none of these things and the program's administrators have gone on record saying "defense conversion [is] not what we're about."[17] Broader criticisms of the DCRI stem from the fact that the initiatives are poorly coordinated. There are also cries of protest because large chunks of funding are going for such programs as Junior Reserve Officer Training (Junior ROTC), which garnered $73 million in "conversion" funding in fiscal year (FY) 1994.

The initial announcement of the DCRI led to a fair amount of confusion and lost momentum in the progressive community. Those not following the issue closely read about conversion funding and, assuming their definition, thought "victory" and moved on. Those following it closely were wrenched between seeing improvement over past programs, and realizing that the new approach was not the comprehensive program it appeared to be.

It is hard to be positive from the progressive perspective under any circumstances. Even after cuts, U.S. defense spending is enormous in comparison with that of other countries. Taking into account the deep defense cuts ordered by Boris Yeltsin after the dissolution of the Soviet Union, we now outspend Russia about five to one. According to figures in a 1992 House Armed Services Committee report, the United States outspent the next ten countries (after Russia) *combined* by a margin of about 2 : 1 in 1990. The Council on Economic Priorities estimates that by 1993, U.S. military spending has risen to between 40 and 50 percent of the *world* total.[18]

Other Conversion Angles

The main priorities in conversion should be: (1) arguing for conversion rather than increasing arms exports as a means of addressing economic decline and preserving jobs; and (2) redirecting as much of the defense technology and establishment created during the 1980s as possible toward productive civilian ends. In conversion it is particularly important to address the human dimension of community dislocation and economic revitalization—in the long term, conversion blends with broader issues of sustainable development, humanizing technology, and improving workplace conditions. Unless we bring about real disarmament and a significant reduction in the arms trade, we will eventually be back where we are now in terms of spending—and likely in a worse place in terms of global security and stability. Despite conversion legislation, the United States in 1992 licensed $63 billion in arms sales, a tripling over the previous year. Clearly, then, notions of conversion have still not been significantly integrated into broader notions of cooperative security and Third World development.

Because of the difficulty involved in reutilizing some facilities—sometimes the machinery is just too arcane and the organizational structure just too unadaptable—it may be worthwhile to dedicate more effort to reutilizing defense technology and research institutions. Plant conversion is preferable, but harder to attain politically and financially, considering the hostility to conversion in corporate board rooms and on Wall Street. It is much easier to encourage diversification through tax incentives and well-structured technology policies than it is to encourage true conversion. Successful contractors repeatedly say that the sociological barriers to conversion are harder to overcome than the technological ones (see chapters 2 and 3). That is not to say that the technological barriers cannot sometimes be intractable.

Conversion advocates often raise issues of "workplace democracy" in developing the argument, advocating such provisions as mandatory alternative use committees (AUCs) set up at each military-oriented facility to plan for its conversion. This introduces heavy baggage into conversion efforts, as large parts of the possible conversion coalition—especially business—pack their bags at the mere mention of alternative use committees. Even if such provisions had any prospect of passage in Congress,[19] it is doubtful that they would ever be generally acceptable to military contractors.

A slew of recent business and academic literature,[20] as well as many conversion examples,[21] argue that companies tune out employee input at their own peril (see chapter 2). As research spreads about the value of employee participation in remaking companies, the climate for conversion and prospects for success improve. Efforts directed at convincing managers of the value of labor–management alternative use committees (such as those involved in the landmark 1994 Connecticut state legislation mentioned earlier) seem to hold more promise.

Why Are Contractors Hostile to Conversion?

A recent NATO research paper on conversion noted:

> A Vietnam era study of the diversification of twelve defense firms noted that the subculture of the executives contains numerous accounts of failures to diversify, a belief that the defense customer does not favor

commercial diversification and a recognition that there is little indication that the owners of defense firms or the financial community wish defense manufacturers to diversify.[22]

This more or less describes the modern climate as well.

Larger contractors are outwardly hostile to conversion notions and federal conversion programs for a number of reasons. For one thing, defense contractors receive much greater access to federal R&D funding under current spending patterns than they can expect if a broad conversion program is put in place. For big contractors, the status quo of progress payments and fairly reliable follow-ons is better than any prospective alternative. While many contractors appear outwardly hostile, they are in fact attempting conversion. They prefer a low profile to keep ahead of competitors with similar capabilities that might pursue the same nondefense niches. The overblown attacks on conversion emanating from large companies may therefore partly reflect corporate bluffing to throw potential competitors off the track.

Managing ability is not a comparative asset at defense contractors when they enter commercial markets. Recurring scandals suggest these contractors are poorly managed in any case, but they are also geared to monopsony and weighed down by compliance-related overheads. Most defense contractors can be better thought of as extensions of government bureaucracy than as private companies struggling in the marketplace. As a result, managers are conditioned to overcomply with government regulations and "sell" (read "bill to the government") rather than trim resulting overhead costs. The oft-mentioned "wall" between defense and commercial production at large contractors has much more to do with management hurdles and government accounting rules than with technical barriers. The whole atmosphere is geared to high profits, highly predictable cash flows, and risk aversion. Culturally and organizationally, the structures of contracting companies discourage entrepreneurialism.

Furthermore, to embrace conversion offends the Pentagon, which would prefer to hold the line against defense cuts by any means possible. A company that is diversifying is less vulnerable to cuts, the thinking goes, which will diminish the wailing to preserve jobs that the Pentagon relies upon to save systems. Many contractors report threats of retribution. (Some contractors have also reported threats from the Pentagon that contracts would be cut off if the companies were to enter joint ventures of any nature with Russian firms.) It should be noted that this charge is very difficult to document and can be self-serving to contractors. At least half the problem probably lies with nervous contractors who, not having received explicit threats, are wary of retaliation or of singling themselves out for cuts because of apparently enhanced capacity to cope.

To embrace conversion worries market analysts who seem convinced that conversion is impossible. Dismantling companies and laying off employees, conversely, gets Wall Street excited. There is no safer bet than that a company's stock will rise immediately after it announces layoffs. Conversely, conversion makes Wall Street panic; it implies unaccustomed risk for the companies involved, and implies investments that likely will not pay off for several years. One brokerage house that thought of creating a social investment fund to spur conversion admitted that the firm could not recommend investment in one of the most successful conversion companies because of the probability that significant returns would not be realized for three to five years. In sum, companies would prefer to avoid high-profile conversion programs for fear of stock market consequences. Beyond this, some of the pressure for conversion has been taken off by the boom in arms exports.

Even when contractors try to convert, they are often set back by concerns unrelated to product and market. First of all, financing for conversion is hard to come by. Bankers often do not understand the high-tech ventures proposed, contractors often do not have proper business plans, and banks are wary of financing any manufacturing companies right now because of uncertainties related to both the costs of health care reform and the North American Free Trade Agreement (NAFTA). Consequently, many companies have had the experience of winning commercial contracts and having to back out for inability to find financing.[23] Without financing, they cannot sustain cash flow while carrying out the work. (For most of these companies cash flow was formerly sustained by DoD progress payments.)

In addition, many companies are unfamiliar with and wary of government assistance programs. As a result, many contractors do not take advantage of manufacturing extension, management and employee training, technology transfer, business-plan-development assistance, and financing help available from state and federal governments. To a certain extent this reflects the fact that companies often do not appreciate their vulnerability until late in the game and associate government involvement with auditing and penalties.

Defense-dependent firms can be found in very diverse industries (from textiles to microchips), comprise a wide variety of sizes and capabilities, and operate under a wide array of regulatory and economic conditions. The details of conversion can vary significantly based on these and many other factors. One study found that large firms are twice as likely as small firms to place a high priority on reducing the size of their work force in response to cuts.[24] At the smallest end of the scale, layoffs are also more common as managers are forced to respond immediately due to tight overheads. Small to medium-sized firms are more likely to place a higher priority on employee welfare and sustaining the scale of operations. They are also more flexible and can more easily change course.

The more nonmilitary work there is in an industry, the better the prospects for firms and employees to find nonmilitary niches. Clearly, the more comparable the civil and defense work, the easier the transition.

The existence of a civilian-oriented marketing organization within the company is a great advantage. Most defense respondents attempting conversion report that marketing is the area in which they most want assistance. Availability of cash is also very important. This factor is often underappreciated; the big contractors, many of whom have large cash reserves at present, are less interested. Small firms, as discussed above, are usually trapped in a credit crunch. As one contractor put it, "Cash flow is the first casualty of conversion."

Strategies for Conversion

In looking at conversion one might think in terms of a "green wheels" model. Green Wheels are political, economic, and technological arrangements that create jobs and address civilian and regional needs with preexisting resources, technologies, and workers. "Green" reflects the environmental and sustainable-development goals of new initiatives, as well as the entrepreneurial spirit needed for success; "wheels" refers to the ability to turn companies and initiatives in new directions. It also implies the decentralized organization, with spokes of responsibility and activity revolving around a hub. The metaphor can be applied on both community and company levels.

The "hub" for companies attempting independent diversification (usually medium-sized or small companies, divisions of large companies, or companies that "spin out" of larger contractors) will be top and middle managers committed to conversion. The spokes of the wheel are employees and engineers working with managers to repackage, redesign, or create new products. The axle will most often be special revolving loan funds and lending programs that will help contractors make the difficult shift from military progress payments to market financing. Government programs designed in association with industry and trade associations can help grease the bearings by training managers in market research and marketing products.

There are three general types of contractors that seem to be able to carry out conversion successfully. The first includes companies that use technological superiority to enter commercial markets with more or less the same products they formerly sold (and in many cases continue to sell) in defense markets. Sometimes the product is put to the same uses (e.g., airplane hydraulics); sometimes to very different uses (e.g., complex algorithms). Prominent examples are Kavlico (Moorpark, California), which entered the burgeoning commercial passive sensor market; Martin Marietta (St. Petersburg, Florida), which applied remote sensor technology to civilian use; Data Products (Woodland Hills, California), which began marketing its durable hard boxes containing communications equipment to utility companies instead of to the Pentagon; Fail-Safe Technology Corporation (Los Angeles), which formerly sold its microcomputers only for use in missiles and satellites (where they helped prevent malfunction), and has expanded the product into mass-transit systems and banking markets; and Ball Systems Engineering Division (San Diego), which is utilizing its military testing range design experience to enable use of Los Angeles dispatch and track tow trucks on the highways.

Companies (often in such high-tech businesses as electronics, optics, and systems integration) that develop basic technologies for substantially new markets have also tended to succeed. This type of conversion often takes from three to ten years. Prominent examples are: AAI Corporation (Hunt Valley, Maryland), which moved into weather information, medical, and fire simulation equipment; Correll Manufacturing (Van Nuys, California), which entered the medical, computer, and lottery machinery industries; Cletronics (Medina, Ohio), which now produces magnetic-detection equipment for pacemakers; Perceptions, Inc. (Woodland Hills, California), which has adapted tank simulation programs into programs for training truck drivers and for entertainment; and Galileo Electro-Optics (Sturbridge, Massachusetts), which is now a producer of office and medical equipment. Westinghouse has taken this route, entering transportation markets, and producing special radars for law enforcement, as well as civil information systems. AGM (Tucson, Arizona) has applied hydraulics, valve, and packaging technologies to make wheelchair lifts; Reflectone Inc. (Tampa, Florida) now makes simulators for rides in amusement parks; Litton Ingalls has diversified from shipbuilding to manufacture of offshore oil drilling rigs and railcars; Loral (Hudson Valley, New York) now makes imagery equipment for hospitals; and EDO Corp. (College Point, New York) has moved from missile launch tubes and fighter plane fuel tanks into golf clubs and bicycle parts. Lockheed is now involved in environmental cleanup technologies, and Essex Industries (St. Louis) has diversified from making breathing devices for pilots into such areas as medical valves, fuel system components for vehicles, as well as other creative products.

Some companies have also succeeded with quirky projects, often driven by personal connections and interests, which have little relation to prior markets. These cases, in particular, deflate the myth that any commercial opportunity will already have someone exploiting it. Examples include Component Concepts, Inc. (Everett, Washington), which moved from testing defense components to environmental testing and cleanup; Instrument Systems Corporation (Jericho, New York), which moved from a defense-dependent communications base into garage doors, diapers, and T-shirts. Frisby Airborne Hydraulics (Freeport, New York) diversified into thermal disbursement technology, a project that began from a personal connection with an inventor and is leading to new products ranging from environmentally preferable machine coolants to isothermic ski boots that will keep feet warmer longer. There is also the case of Kaman Corp. (Bloomfield, Connecticut), which has put helicopter engineers and production workers into the production of Ovation guitars. Quadrax Corporation (Portsmouth, Rhode Island) has moved from sound-deadening submarine tiles to tennis rackets; and Tenneco has diversified its shipbuilding operations (in Newport News, Virginia) into design, construction, and repair of commercial power-generation equipment.

Finally, there are companies that have expanded preexisting commercial production when defense orders diminished. Some examples are: Hexel Inc., which enhanced its commercial chemical, resin, and fabrics production in response to defense cuts; Electromagnetic Sciences, which established a civilian products unit in 1982 and has expanded the division's production of inventory-tracking systems; California Amplifier, which shifted attention to its small commercial division serving the satellite dish and television industries while it deemphasized and eventually sold its military division; Giga-Tronics, which increased its focus on commercial radar and telecommunications satellite testing systems; and Varian Associates, which expanded its commercial electronics production while abandoning most of its lines of defense merchandise.

The second type of conversion is preferable from the larger perspective, as it leads to new markets and applies defense-derived, cutting-edge technologies to civilian and commercial problems that are not being sufficiently addressed by anyone else. The lack of direct connection to old markets, however, can lead to disruption. Companies often build new facilities in different places to exploit cheaper labor markets and various state-sponsored tax-sweeteners through which states sometimes cut each other's throats to lure jobs. In the broadest view, all types of conversion are good if they help dismantle the military-industrial complex and reduce pressure to export arms.

The first type of conversion, selling the same products in new markets, minimizes disruption, but many argue it robs Peter to pay Paul: the new sales acquired usually mean diminished sales at other more domestically oriented firms. Such competition is good under neoclassical models, but the more defense-dependent firms are sometimes the beneficiaries of government technical and financial assistance for which commercial firms are not eligible.

The third type of conversion is more removed from the hardest cultural and technical (though not necessarily financing) problems. It could be said that this type reduces to basic business strategy—which some argue is the case for much of conversion. One of the biggest differences between the demise of defense firms and, say, steel firms in the 1970s and 1980s is the difference in the relative power, bureaucratic backing, and standing of the respective industries; defense firms can command more attention.

Among firms participating in the Kearny study, 83 percent of respondents said they would rely on "existing technologies" to develop products, while 17 percent said they would commercialize new technologies. Many conversion examples (and virtually all large ones) involve the adaptation of military technologies to nonmilitary government markets. One company strategy might be to use nonmilitary government sales (or dual-use sales) to sustain the company through a more thoroughgoing transition to commercial markets.

Community-Based Conversion: Commonweals

For communities, to return to the green wheels metaphor, the hub for conversion is a coordinating company or nonprofit corporation that includes companies, labor unions, trade groups, community groups, research institutions, and training programs. These various actors form the spokes of the wheel. The engine that sets it in motion could be targeted federal funding invested in infrastructure renewal, environmental remediation, mass transit, low-emissions vehicles, energy-efficiency technology, medical technology, recycling, arms control verification, education, or construction of the data superhighway, among many other possible fields.

Government impetus can actually come in three main forms: (1) *"procurement pull"*—for new products, the first sale is often the toughest (the government has been the first customer in many of the industries that generate the most wealth in our economy); (2) *federal regulation*—regulations such as the California Clean Air Act improve living standards while creating new markets for products and services needed to achieve compliance; and (3) *technical assistance*—this can include manufacturing extension programs (designed to improve the productivity and capabilities of small shops), retraining and continuing education programs (to enhance the skills of the labor force), and R&D programs (to spur development of cutting-edge technologies and help transfer know-how into marketable products.

Of course, the ultimate test of these projects is in the marketplace where projects must eventually be self-sustaining, whether in domestic or world markets.

Through the consortia or community-based model, companies that might not otherwise be interested in conversion might be enticed to apply their resources in new directions. Two examples of the community-based approach are Calstart, the electric car consortium in southern California, and Career/Pro, a project to create jobs in environmental remediation.[25]

Conversion Policy

Government intervention in conversion is necessary to ensure the rationality of the drawdown, to make the best use of liberated resources in addressing new social priorities, and to minimize dislocation. And as I have argued, conversion policy becomes technology policy, economic development policy, and industrial policy over the long run.

In the past, conversion programs have been administered through the Pentagon and focused on large contractors. In the future, conversion programs should be administered through community-based consortia (or individual companies), with federal support, to convert medium-sized and smaller contractors (and divisions of larger contractors, or "spin-out" companies). They should be directed toward emerging markets, including government-created markets, that address social priorities in environmental remediation, mass transit, low-emissions vehicles, energy-efficiency technology, medical technology, infrastructure repair, recycling, education, and construction of the data superhighway, among many other fields.

It is possible to conceive of a variety of policies that would substantially improve the likelihood of successful conversion. There are currently twenty-six agencies that have a formal role in conversion programs. As a result, communities often do not know where to look for funding. Many conversion programs draw funding from non-defense-related budgets. Calstart, for example, received $2 million through a Department of Transportation program.

For these reasons, it would make sense to expand the clearinghouse for conversion created in the early 1990s.[26] The clearinghouse should provide not only information on federal programs specifically for conversion, but also (1) assessments of procurement funds in the budgets of other agencies that could be applied to conversion projects; (2) job-skills and employment-needs inventories; (3) resources to facilitate utilization of manufacturing extension and retraining services; (4) resources on the creation of flexible manufacturing networks and conversion consortia; and (5) a substantial data base of successful conversion examples and ongoing efforts.

Furthermore, the federal agency whose mandate is most clearly focused on conversion-related activities—the Office of Economic Adjustment—resides in the Department of Defense, while it should be located in a nondefense federal department, most logically the Department of Commerce. In fact, federal conversion programs in general should be coordinated through such a nondefense agency.

It would also be a good idea to better integrate job training and economic development programs so as to match people with jobs more effectively. Matching people with jobs deserves special emphasis because it is a problem that extends to all sectors of the economy. In addition, better coordination ties in with broader needs for reform in our education system.

The Defense Department still controls nearly 60 percent of government R&D funds (around $75 billion) and will control 50 percent even under proposed new technology policies. As recently as 1990, one-third of U.S. engineers worked on defense projects. From a policy point of view, it is particularly important to redirect these federal military R&D dollars to nonmilitary agencies and projects. Redirecting R&D is vital to creating new markets and building new world-class industries.

When there are contract cuts, often the first thing banks do is freeze lending to afflicted communities. Contractors consistently rate financing as their biggest obstacle in attempting conversion. It is important to improve financing conditions both for small to medium-sized military contractors trying to enter new civilian markets and for new civilian companies "spun out" of larger contractors. A revolving conversion loan fund capitalized at $3 billion would greatly assist hundreds of promising conversion projects that are currently stalled for lack of capital. The spin-out model would grant special capital provisions to startup companies. Tax breaks might be offered to large contractors that offer plant and equipment and/or license, sell, or otherwise transfer intellectual property rights for new technologies to the entrepreneurs. This model is gaining currency in some states. It fits quite well with the consortia model and very loosely describes Calstart's arrangement with Lockheed.

Manufacturing extension networks, which help upgrade small shops to the state of the art in equipment and techniques, have helped dramatically improve productivity of smaller shops in Japan and Europe. The sixfold increase in U.S. manufacturing extension funds over the last three years has largely been channeled through defense agencies and geared to defense manufacturing. At the same time, defense managers list market research as one of the areas where they are most eager for conversion-related assistance. It would therefore be wise for the federal government to create a funding pool for manufacturing extension, as well as small-business incubation, and administer it through state-based programs on a matching basis with state and private money. A model incubation program could be established to set guidelines for funding eligibility.

Laws dealing with government-funded R&D should promote use of technologies while generating maximum net social benefit. When the U.S. government finances research, either taxpayers should get a return or the technology should be disbursed to companies in the fastest time possible without discouraging cooperation on the part of individual corporate partners. Under current laws, patents for many new technologies go unutilized. There is a clear need for reform. One possible approach would be to shorten the patent's grant of exclusivity to three to eight years (depending on the time it takes to bring products to market) and then require that the technology be made available to other United States-based companies through licensing-on-demand. Small companies should be allowed to make greater use of patents that go unutilized by large corporate holders. All of this would promote faster commercialization and broader distribution of federally financed technological gains.

In 1992, the number of weapons export licenses tripled to $63 billion. The current export boom threatens U.S. and global security and is stalling the conversion process. It is important to begin taking steps toward a global international arms sales control regime. To start, the sheer volume of U.S. arms sales abroad should be significantly reduced. Laws prohibiting U.S. weapons sales to countries with poor human rights records are currently all but ignored. They should instead be rigorously enforced. A global arms registry should be established so that the volume of arms trade can be documented and regulated. The export of offensive weapons, such as fighter jets and attack helicopters, should be severely limited by international accord.

A sizable multilateral volunteer peacekeeping force should be developed under U.N. auspices with a mandate to demilitarize war zones through the confiscation of weapons. Incentives should be established through multilateral development lending agencies and the General Agreement on Tariffs and Trade (GATT) to reduce military spending and weapons purchases.

Barring significant change in the current security environment, the U.S. military budget should be reduced to no more than $180 billion (in 1993 dollars) by the year 2000. Up to $100 billion a year could be saved by closing more redundant bases and cutting at least 500,000 more troops than currently planned (lowering forces to 1.1 million).

Assessing Progress

Organizing and research efforts around the country over the last five years have generated many promising community-based conversion initiatives. Federal support through 1990 and 1992 laws, as well as state support, has served to catalyze many of these initiatives and to reorient local coordination and training programs. With a better federal information clearinghouse, these efforts will be even more productive.

But too much funding and decision-making authority is still vested in the Pentagon; we as a society have not transferred enough resources or made strong enough commitments to really drive large-scale efforts addressing the nation's pressing social and economic needs.

Such large-scale projects will be necessary to compensate for employment, manufacturing, and industrial policy gaps that have already grown and will continue to expand with a real drawdown. Moreover, our economic future and the future of our environment clearly depend on addressing these priorities.

With respect to resources, despite the declines from the oxygen-deprived heights of the 1980s, by the mid-1990s defense expenditures were still a few percentage points larger than the average during the Cold War. On the social level, we have already watched hundreds of thousands of workers shift to lower-paying, often menial jobs and dozens of communities enter long-term economic decline, while millions of manufacturing jobs have shifted overseas. Government programs have been predominantly reactive, slow, underutilized, largely underfunded—in general, too little and too late. For technology, the best we have managed is a questionable dual-use strategy that leaves the bulk of authority and funding in the Pentagon.

Conversion is happening. But in the broad sense, it is only just beginning. And, particularly, as conversion relates to broader issues such as addressing global environmental problems, the clock is ticking.

Appendix: Defense Conversion Case Study Summaries

Westinghouse (Pittsburgh, PA)

Westinghouse is organized into seven divisions, with electronic systems managing the bulk of DoD work and comprising about 25 percent of overall company revenues, $12.8 billion in 1991. In that year, the company received the eleventh largest total in prime defense contracts, doing work on the F-22 Advanced Tactical Fighter, submarine ballistic missile-launching systems, the MK-48 torpedo, the MK-50 torpedo, radar-jamming devices, Airborne Warning and Control System (AWACS), and avionics for the Comanche helicopter, among other projects.

In 1989, Westinghouse established the commercial systems division in an attempt to find new markets for defense-inspired technologies. The foundation of the division is the airspace management operation, makers of the ASR-9 and ARSR-4 radars. Westinghouse is now the top radar supplier to the Federal Aviation Administration and has contracted to install radar systems all over the world. In addition, the company has diversified into domestic drug interdiction through manufacture of surveillance radar, transportation (electric cars), transportation management (long-haul trucking and metro transit), security systems, law enforcement (specialized radars that can detect through walls and hand-held devices that can detect trace amounts of drugs or explosives), and civil systems (mail sorting, character recognition, image processing, and encryption devices).

Whereas nondefense sales accounted for only 16 percent of sales in 1986, they now account for 27 percent of sales. Some of this change is due to the decline of defense revenues. In March 1993, President Clinton went to the Westinghouse facility in Linthicum, Maryland, to announce his $20 billion five-year conversion program. The company has a declared goal of reducing defense dependence to 50 percent by 1995, but it is not clear it will meet this goal. According to a company spokesperson, the commercial systems division within the electronics division has developed over one-half billion dollars in new business since 1989, much of it deriving from defense technology.

An 11 percent shift to nondefense work over seven years, due partially to declining defense sales, might be criticized as small. Some of the shift is also attributable to purchase of other nondefense units (home security systems). The Linthicum plant has laid off 7,000 people since the late 1980s. The company's efforts would be hard for other companies to follow (though some, like Hughes, Martin Marietta, TRW, and Rockwell, are trying to penetrate the same markets).

Westinghouse is not a particularly good corporate citizen in other respects. Other divisions of Westinghouse manage parts of the nuclear weapons complex, including Savannah River. Westinghouse was well above industry averages in toxic inventory release and finished second behind only General Electric in the number of Occupational Safety and Health Administration (OSHA) violations accumulated between 1977 and 1990.

The company has lost more than $1 billion since 1991. Its stock market prices have plummeted. It is important to note, however, that these poor balance sheets reflect not the hazards of conversion, but ill-advised ventures into financial service markets that resulted in record-setting losses.

Galileo Electro-Optics (Sturbridge, MA)

Galileo was founded in 1959 with military funding and depended almost entirely on defense contracts until the mid-1980s. In 1982 the top managers began to worry that, having made more or less the same products for almost twenty-five years, they were too dependent on the survival of a few defense systems. With soaring deficits, they were concerned about coming cuts in defense. So they initiated an attempt at diversification (after two earlier failures) with the goal of expanding commercial business so as to reduce defense dependence to 25 percent of sales by the mid-1990s.

The strategy was to explore five market segments—office automation, remote sensors, medical technology, analytical instruments, and "unique little components that do special little jobs"—while continuing to develop their technology base in night-vision devices and specialized lasers. The crucial breakthrough was the development of a supplier relationship with Xerox.

Xerox machines were regarded as making the best copies in the industry at the time, but were notorious for breaking down. Galileo beat out Corning and Bausch and Lomb (much bigger companies) to become the new supplier of ion-generation devices for Xerox copiers. To win the contract, Galileo engineered a part that could perform at better than four times the speed of its predecessor, and could be delivered at less than one-third the cost. The technological breakthrough was significant enough that the same component first manufactured in 1985 has been designed into Xerox products through 2000. The company has delivered six million devices in eleven years, of which, the company claims, fewer than a hundred have been defective. Xerox is now Galileo's largest customer.

Galileo's president and CEO, Bill Hanley, states that the diversification process was conceptualized more in terms of end-state than from existing capacities. Working in tandem with a consultant, Hanley and top management worked out a plan to decide what markets they wanted and what skills they needed to get there. New products generally have a seven- to ten-year development cycle, underscoring the importance of getting an early start—a luxury many firms no longer have.

The consultant who worked on the project was a recent defector from a well-known consulting firm. When Galileo first approached some prestigious consulting firms, they came back to Galileo with proposals to help plan a new future for $1 million. This was far more than the company could afford—especially with the implicitly shaky prospects for success.

When the company did start, all of its machinery was government-owned and almost all sales were government-generated. Galileo started with a negative net worth. Business conditions for the company in the early part of the process were pretty good, though. Both defense and nondefense lines grew tremendously in the 1980s; between 1982 and 1988, employment at the firm nearly doubled from 330 to 631. By 1993, Galileo has about 1,000 customers (it gets about 80 percent of revenue from the largest twenty). Company sales are now about 95 percent commercial.

Unfortunately, the company suffered along with the rest of the Northeast economy with the end of the defense boom and the subsequent recession. With defense sales falling from $28 million in 1989 to $4.8 million in 1992, the company reduced its work force back to 316. In 1993, Galileo lost $1.04 million on sales of $32.9 million. One large investment house investigating the creation of a "conversion fund" decided that it could not recommend Galileo as a safe enough buy for the fund. (In one of the diversification efforts yet to see a substantial return, Galileo invested $5 million to adapt its military night-vision technology to build a component for a group developing a high-definition television prototype. So far, the investment has yielded only about $300,000 a year in revenue.)

But there was more to the work-force reduction than economic necessity. In the course of the transition, the ratio of salaried (roughly, management) to hourly workers went from about 1 : 1 to about 1 : 3. During this time, Galileo had 100 percent turnover in management ranks (about 85 percent through attrition; 15 percent continue to work at the company in nonmanagement roles). Hanley, who describes the process in terms of broad "reculturalization," claimed that the managers could not be retrained. He maintains that most went to other defense firms, "where they were happier," though no formal research was done on what became of them. Hanley brags that current employees are a "step or two" behind contemporaries in the industry, but that they don't mind because "[working for Galileo] is like playing for the Celtics"—a reference to his claim that Galileo engineers always succeed when addressing technical challenges.

Hanley sees a specific government conversion role only in financing assistance and reeducation, not in technology transfer and manufacturing extension. The call for finance and training is very common among conversion companies. It is important to remember, though, with respect to technology programs that Galileo is a company on the cutting edge in a highly specialized technological niche—and a company that recently received a $2 million matching grant from the National Institute for Standards and Technology (Department of Commerce) to develop microchannel plate technology.

To meet R&D needs, Galileo has a finely honed practice of contracting out what managers consider research work to universities (which under the normal agreements can publish findings two to three years after they are transferred to Galileo). The company does do a considerable amount of development work in-house, which occupies fully one-third of hourly employees. Many firms lack the size and experience to duplicate such a system without government guidance and financial help.

Hanley is more adamant about state and regional governments providing better services and expediting bureaucratic processes in general. When the company expanded in 1988, they decided to build the new plant in Virginia instead of in Massachusetts, largely because Virginia was more aggressive in seeking the business and jobs. The state government scouted property for the company and sent chartered planes on several occasions so that Galileo executives could come down and review possible plant sites. Hanley claims that they got the plant in Virginia running "in less time than it would have taken to get the sewage permit in Sturbridge."

When it came time to choose, the governor of Virginia escorted Hanley to the facility they finally bought (which Galileo claims cost one-fifth what an equivalent site would have cost in Massachusetts). When approaching the plant, Hanley remarked that the turnoff was a little hairy. Says Hanley, "Ten days later, the paint was dry on a new turnoff lane."

Galileo is full of praise for Virginia's Department of Economic Development, which helped expedite permits and provided some training. The department's director visits every six months to make sure Galileo's management is satisfied.

Kavlico (Ventura, CA)

Kavlico is a medium-sized second-tier contractor with revenues last year of $67 million. In the late 1980s, 95 percent of Kavlico's business was making sensors to measure pressure and position for missiles and every U.S.-built aircraft (both military and civilian). Overall defense dependence was about 85 percent.

Anticipating defense cuts, in 1988 the company started investigating other potential markets that would utilize its "core competencies." The new lines of sensors—for auto-emissions systems and brake and power-steering systems; for diesel engines used in trucks, trains, and earth-moving equipment; and, most recently, for power plants—now account for 70 percent of the company's business. Kavlico has grown from 250 to 725 people and expects to expand production facilities and add 300 more jobs over the next few years.

The company president also reports that the reorganization and thinking that went into commercial expansion have improved the quality and lowered the costs of the defense components he continues to manufacture. For Kavlico, conversion led to dramatic corporate growth. Kavilco is unlike some other companies that have converted in that the majority of the company's sales are to the private sector.

Kaman Aircraft (Bloomfield, CT)

Kaman was the seventieth largest contractor in FY 1991, receiving $212 million to make a variety of aerospace products, including military helicopters. Kaman Corp. had profits of $17 million in 1991 on revenues of $780 million. The Kaman Aerospace subsidiary employs about 1,500 people, mostly in Connecticut.

Since the early 1970s, Kaman has converted away from defense, reconverted during the Reagan military buildup in the 1980s, and more recently tried conversion again. In the 1970s diversification projects ranged from guitars to bearing manufacturing. By the late 1970s, defense dependence was less than 50 percent.

By the mid-1980s, defense dependence was back up to 95 percent. Since then, Kaman has reduced defense dependence to around 40 percent, with new ventures to produce parts for GE engines and Boeing passenger jets. The company recently received a $3 million grant from the Connecticut state government to help market the new K-Max helicopter, an "aerial truck" designed for logging, firefighting, and power-line construction. State and company officials involved in the project expect it to generate 500 new jobs at Kaman and 300 at regional subcontractors. As part of the deal, Kaman agreed to pay the state royalties up to $6 million (based on the number of helicopters sold and the time period in which they are sold) that will go back into a revolving conversion fund.

Science Applications International Corporation (La Jolla, CA)

The Science Applications International Corporation (SAIC), with $1.28 billion in annual revenues, provides high-technology services and products in the areas of national defense, health care, systems integration, environment, and energy. Based in southern California, the employee-owned company has more than 13,500 employees in more than 200 locations worldwide. SAIC was the thirty-seventh largest recipient of defense dollars in 1991.

The company has conversion projects running in both the United States and Russia. In the United States, SAIC has successfully pursued nondefense and commercial work, mostly in systems integration for such customers as the Departments of Energy and Veterans' Affairs. One conversion project took directed energy weapon technology developed for SDI and applied it to positron emission tomography, a diagnostic medical-imaging technique. Another project underway is the development of an electron-beam dry-scrubbing system that uses technology developed for nuclear-weapons-effects simulations. SAIC has reduced defense dependence from over 70 percent in the late 1980s to around 50 percent at present.

A third project is using a scanning tunneling microscope to develop a new method for sequencing DNA. The technology was developed and used mainly in classified government programs, most likely on the stealth fighter and bomber. This project is being undertaken in collaboration with the University of California at San Diego, several other companies, and potentially with the Department of Energy and the National Institutes of Health, representing an example of a government–university–industry consortium.

In June 1992, SAIC signed an agreement with Russian American Sciences Inc. to work on projects including conversion of defense technology to environmental programs and joint exploration of oceanographic and atmospheric data bases. In January 1993, Russia's Nuclear Energy Ministry (Minatom) reached an agreement with a group of U.S. companies led by SAIC to joint-produce and import to the United States molybdenum-99, a radioisotope with medical applications.

SAIC has also played an integral role in efforts to convert the Saratov Aviation Plant, about 500 miles south of Moscow. Working with the Center for International Security and Arms Control at Stanford University, the Federation for Enterprise Development, the Carnegie Corporation of New York, and the Institute of U.S.A. and Canada Studies of the Russian Academy of Sciences, SAIC has helped Saratov privatize into an employee-owned company while converting away from defense production. With plummeting orders from the Russian Defense Ministry, Saratov has gone from 50 percent defense production to less than 6 percent since the late 1980s. Increasing production of YAK 42 civilian aircraft has also been profitable.

Notes

1. Two million U.S. manufacturing jobs disappeared during the 1980s. Between 1989 and early 1993, employment in six major defense-related industries fell by 334,700, reflecting the loss of 23 percent of the jobs in those sectors, according to the Bureau of Labor Statistics.

2. Anthony J. Marolda, George F. Brown Jr., and Robert C. Fraser, *The Commercialization of Defense Technology: A Survey of Industry Experience* (Boston, MA: Fraser Group, DRI/McGraw-Hill Inc., and the Winbridge Group, Inc., No-

vember 1991). Because of ambiguity in some of the questionnaire responses, the authors note that the percentage might actually be as high as 76 percent.

3. A.T. Kearny Inc. and the Economic Development Corporation of Los Angeles County, "An industry in transition," cited in Anthony L. Velocci Jr., "Conversion approach appears flawed," *Aviation Week and Space Technology* (July 26, 1993). (Note the title given to a conversion article in a magazine largely dependent on advertising revenues from large aerospace customers.)

4. "AIA survey finds aerospace employment in decline since 1987 peak," *Aerospace Daily, 155* (August 28, 1990): 41.

5. Joshua Lerner, "The mobility of corporate scientists and engineers between civil and defense activities: Implications for economic competitiveness in the post–Cold War era," *Defense Economics, 3* (1992): 229–42.

6. Erik Pages, "Weathering the defense transition: A business-based approach to conversion," *Business Executives for National Security* (1992); Marie Jones, "Converting the Cold War economy: 63 companies change for the future," *Center for Economic Conversion* (1993); Greg Bischak and James Raffel, "Successful conversion experiences," *National Commission for Economic Conversion and Disarmament* (1993).

7. Debra Polsky, "Diversity, profits guide firms' guns-to-butter conversion: Renewed effort for non-defense sales inspires research at U.S. companies," *Defense News* (February 3, 1992).

8. Ibid.

9. Jeff Cole, "Arms makers are serving up a crush of requests for peace-conversion aid," *Wall Street Journal* (August 12, 1993).

10. Bruce A. Smith, "Northrop acts to boost commercial aircraft base," *Aviation Week & Space Technology* (November 2, 1992): 67.

11. See U.S. Senate Committee on Government Operations, Subcommittee on Executive Reorganization and Government Research, *National Economic Conversion Commission: Responses to Subcommittee Questionnaire*, September 1970.

12. CEP communication with a New York State industrial extension program representative, July 29, 1993; comparable explanations were made by defense-contractor employees at EXPO 2000, a technology trade show in Baltimore, December 1–3, 1992.

13. For a critical description of public subsidies and a catalog of existing state laws, see Greg LeRoy, *No More Candy Store: States and Cities Making Job Subsidies Accountable* (Chicago: Federation for Industrial Retention and Renewal and Washington, DC: Grassroots Policy Project, 1994).

14. Currently, the government keeps the patent rights for most inventions and negotiates exclusive licenses; Cooperative Research and Development Agreements (CRADAs) have different and variable rules. See Domenick Bertelli and Vatche Gabrielian, "Technology Transfer and Conversion" (CIC working paper, August 1993).

15. Recoupment charges were fees paid by contractors to the government when selling U.S. weapon systems abroad or any commercial systems that were judged to have derived from DoD-backed R&D. The fees were designed to compensate the government for R&D investments that led to corporate profits. They were largely abolished by executive order in 1992.

16. Alternative use committees are labor–management committees with the mission of seeking profitable civilian alternatives to current military-oriented products. For more on these bills or the Call to Action, see "A Call to Action: A Primer on Defense Conversion and Economic Rejuvenation," available through the Progressive Policy Institute, (617) 547–4474, or UAW Region 9A, (203) 674–0143.

17. McGraw-Hill's *Federal Technology Report* (June 12, 1994).

18. See Domenick Bertelli and John Tepper Marlin, "Defense Conversion: The Tasks Ahead," *CEP Research Report* (November 1992): 2.

19. The most that might be achieved is what was included in the FY 1994 House bill, which encourages AUCs—as opposed to mandating them—and offers some tax incentives.

20. For examples across the spectrum of available literature, see Barry Bluestone and Irving Bluestone, "Workers (and managers) of the world unite," *Technology Review* (November/December 1992); Aaron Bernstein, "Now labor can be part of the solution," *Business Week* (March 1, 1993); William N. Cooke, "Product quality improvement through employee participation: The effects of unionization and joint union-management administration," *Industrial and Labor Relations Review, 46*, 1 (October 1992); and Edward Cohen-Rosenthal and Cynthia E. Burton, *Mutual Gains: A Guide to Union-Management Cooperation* (New York: Praeger, 1987).

21. Two good examples are the conversion efforts of Frisby Airborne Hydraulics (nonunion) and A.M. General (unionized).

22. Clair Blong, Cordell C. Lukey, Edward T. Pasterick, and Bruce E. Sullivan, "Defense industrial conversion: Problems and prospects," paper prepared for the NATO Defense College Annual Symposium on Armed Forces in a Community of Shared Values, Rome, April 6–7, 1992, p. 6; citing John S. Gilmore and Dean C. Coddington, *Defense Industry Diversification: An Analysis with 12 Case Studies* (Washington, DC: U.S. Arms Control and Disarmament Agency, 1966), p. 7.

23. As a caveat, it should be noted that some conversion contractors (perhaps a quarter in the estimate of one industry expert) submit ridiculously low bids in attempts to get toeholds in new markets; banks are for the most part making wise decisions in avoiding loaning to such companies.

24. Economic Roundtable, *Los Angeles County Economic Adjustment Strategy for Defense Reductions* (Economic Roundtable, 1992), p. 131.

25. Domenick Bertelli, "Converting from defense: From iron triangles to green wheels," *CEP Research Report* (New York: CEP, August 1993).

26. The clearinghouse was set up with a toll-free telephone number: 1–800–345–1222.

5

ELIZABETH MUELLER

Retraining for What? Displaced Defense Workers and Federal Programs in Two Regions

Recent mass layoffs by defense contractors have concentrated the fallout from the end of the Cold War on particular groups of workers, firms, and communities. Because of lower levels of defense spending, defense-dependent plants are laying off workers or closing their doors, leaving workers and communities to fend for themselves in a leaner, less manufacturing-oriented labor market.

Notwithstanding the severity of the problem and its high visibility in defense-dependent communities, the programmatic response to defense layoffs has been meager in scale and seriously flawed in design. Despite the rhetoric around worker training, only $135 million of the total $1.7 billion Defense Authorization Act of 1993 was targeted toward the relocation and retraining of displaced civilian defense workers.[1] The Economic Dislocation and Worker Adjustment Act (EDWAA) established a program meant to aid workers displaced by causes ranging from the Clean Air Act to defense cuts. EDWAA more than doubled its funding level in 1992, reaching $577 million. Despite recent increases in funding, evaluations of programs for displaced defense industry workers suggest that only 9 percent of those eligible are being served.[2]

Yet, more troubling than the low level of funding for worker training programs is their design. There is a dearth of published information concerning the effectiveness of training programs in place for displaced *defense* workers. Information available on training programs for displaced workers in general shows serious problems in the accepted retraining model.[3] As currently conceived, retraining programs provide workers with brief periods of training in a limited range of skills. They are still beholden to their origins in programs for "disadvantaged" workers, emphasizing a length and type of training and types of services more appropriate to young workers entering the work force than to those with years of work experience and training.

Finally, these programs stand alone; that is, they are not linked to the well-funded technology initiatives included in conversion legislation or to other preexisting job creation programs. The stand-alone design of training services presumes the existence of appropriate jobs for retrained workers. It is a model more appropriate to frictional or even cyclical unemployment. Given structural shifts in the composition of growing sectors and occupations, favoring lower-paying service jobs over higher-wage manufacturing jobs, the assumption of adequate demand for laid-off workers is especially problematic. More attention must be given to linking training or adjustment services to job creation initiatives both conceptually and practically.

Through case studies of the experiences of workers in two different regions, it is possible to highlight the weaknesses of the current approach to adjustment and retraining services for displaced defense workers. While the two cases contrast sharply in everything from the structure of the local economy to the extent and quality of services offered, they do not contrast as neatly in the outcomes for workers. The problems workers faced in both cases in their search for non-defense industry jobs at comparable wages point out the inadequacy of the current, supply-side approach to worker displacement associated with defense cuts.

Method

To assess the effectiveness of current programs for displaced defense workers, information was collected on the experiences of displaced defense workers in two locations. The locations contrast in a number of characteristics, allowing consideration of contextual (demand-side) as well as individual (supply-side) characteristics in explaining the outcomes in each case. The factors highlighted through the use of these cases include regional characteristics such as the degree of defense dependency of the region, the size and diversity of the regional economy, the role of local community and political actors and institutions (including the company in question) in formulating and implementing a response to the layoffs or closure, and whether the layoffs were due to a plant closure or just a cutback at a facility still in operation. Research on the experiences of laid-off defense workers in earlier periods found that such contextual factors were more important than the individual characteristics of workers in explaining their prospects for reemployment.[4] In addition, these factors may help explain the different effects of the same federal programs across sites.

In both cases, survey data on the former employees were available. In St. Louis, two surveys were performed—one after the workers had been unemployed for one year, the second after two years without work. In New Jersey, a survey was conducted approximately one year after layoff. In addition to the survey data, interviews were conducted with laid-off workers in training programs, and with service providers and representatives of state agencies charged with funding or implementing worker adjustment and retraining programs under the provisions of either EDWAA or the Trade Adjustment Assistance (TAA) act (see Table 5.1).[5]

A case study approach is most appropriate to the analysis of the effectiveness of these programs for several reasons. First, the complexity of the problem and the wide array of possible factors that might influence the outcome for workers argue against the use of a simple comparison of survey data. Second, survey data alone would again emphasize factors related to the characteristics of workers and, as previous work has argued, contextual factors may be more important to our understanding of the success or failure of such programs for workers. Finally, to understand the importance of local factors, especially political factors, there is no substitute for interviews with key actors.[6]

Case 1: The Unisys Corporate Closure at Flemington, New Jersey

Located in a rural area whose largest town advertises itself as the site of the Lindbergh kidnapping trial, most Unisys workers do not think of themselves as part of a defense economy. While the region is the most rural in the state, with 45 percent of the county's land area in farms, job growth and residential development over the past thirteen years have contributed to the increasingly suburban character of the county.

Table 5.1

**The Economic Dislocation and Worker Adjustment Act
System: From Notification to Reemployment**

Layoffs announced:
    Firm notifies state's Dislocated Worker Unit (DWU), local elected officials and
    representatives of the work force, or, in the case of an unrepresented work
    force, each individual worker, 60 days in advance of an impending layoff of
    more than 100 workers or one-third of work force or of plant closure under
    the Worker Adjustment and Retraining Notification (WARN) act.[a]

First rapid response meeting:
    Within 48 hours, the Dislocated Worker Unit's Rapid Response Team should
    meet with plant management and representatives of the work force to discuss
    rapid response services.[b]

Mass informational meetings for work force:
    Between announcement of layoffs/closure and the event itself, the Rapid
    Response Team arranges a series of meetings with plant workers at which
    services available are described and, in some cases, workers are directly
    linked to services. Examples of direct linkage generally include registering
    workers for unemployment insurance on site.

Outplacement services:
    Outplacement services usually consist of résumé writing and interviewing
    workshops and are conducted by either state workers or employer-
    contracted private outplacement firms. Services may include financial
    counseling, assessment of workers' skills, and counseling on opportunities in
    the local labor market. Information and referrals to training programs may
    also be provided. Representatives of training programs may be brought in to
    discuss their programs and counsel workers on their options.

Retraining choice made:
    Workers decide whether or not to enter retraining programs.[c] Workers funded
    under EDWAA typically receive the standard six months of income support
    offered by unemployment insurance and enter training courses that average
    nine to twelve weeks. Career counseling and information provided on oppor-
    tunities in the local labor market vary.

Workers enter retraining:
    Workers approach public or proprietary schools. Private training institutes
    typically give their own placement tests and suggest appropriate courses.
    Schools are not required to provide students with information on their place-
    ment rates or on wages received by training graduates.

Workers reenter labor market:
    Workers leave retraining and reenter the labor market. Most schools do not
    guarantee placement and many do not provide even minimal placement
    services.

Notes:
[a]A recent GAO report found that half of all plant closures subject to WARN procedures did not provide notice and 29 percent of notices that were filed did not provide the full 60-day notice required (U.S. General Accounting Office, *Dislocated Workers: Worker Adjustment and Retraining Notification Act Not Meeting Its Goals*, GAO/HRD-93-18 [February 1993]).
[b]In practice, meetings often do not include labor representatives.
[c]Income support and therefore length and type of training course will vary depending on source of funding. Workers funded under the trade act are eligible to receive funding for income support and training course expenses for up to 52 weeks.

While regional job growth in the 1980s was spread across several sectors, the region retained a higher share of regional employment in manufacturing (25.2 percent) than the state as a whole (19.9 percent). The Unisys plant, which opened in 1980, and the neighboring Lipton Tea plant together provided a significant share of the region's manufacturing employment and contributed to the region's 29 percent growth rate in manufacturing over the decade. Other rapidly growing sectors included finance, insurance, real estate, and services. In absolute terms, the largest employment sectors in 1990 were wholesale and retail trade (9,000), services (7,900), and manufacturing (7,700).[7]

While the region has enjoyed a very tight labor market for the last decade, with unemployment falling to a low of 1.8 percent in 1988, the rate crept up to 4.0 percent in 1992 with recent plant closures.[8] The Unisys closure preceded the closure of several other large manufacturing employers in the region. Johanna Farms, Inc., closed its fluid-milk operations late in 1992, laying off 200 people.[9] Frenchtown Ceramics, another regional manufacturing employer, recently announced impending mass layoffs in compliance with the Worker Adjustment and Retraining Notification (WARN) act. In many ways, the case closely follows national trends. Regional manufacturing is declining, and future job growth is projected to lie in both high- and low-wage service occupations.[10]

The Raritan Township Unisys Plant employed 1,260 people in a state-of-the-art computer production facility at its peak in 1990.[11] Approximately 40 percent of the employees were directly involved in production, with the rest working in research, engineering, support functions, and administration. Opened in 1980 by Unisys's forerunner,

Burroughs, the plant was completely retooled between 1983 and 1988. By 1989, the facility had switched from a completely manual materials-handling system to an automated one, realizing dramatic increases in productivity and quality while delivering desktop computers to the Air Force. The plant received International Standards Organization 9001 quality control certification and won two of the first World Class Manufacturing Awards sponsored by the Advanced Manufacturing Systems Exposition.[12]

In spite of the plant's phenomenal improvement in productivity, it was slated for closure at the end of 1991 for strategic reasons. Given recent layoffs and plant closure announcements in local manufacturing plants, prospects for reemployment of plant workers in jobs of comparable skill and pay locally are grim. The most rapidly growing occupations in the region are poorly suited to the skills of production workers laid off from the plant. Not surprisingly, only 26 percent of surveyed former Unisys workers were employed eighteen months after the closure was announced and one year after the actual closure. Of those employed, 26.7 percent had taken a cut in pay.[13]

The lack of identification of the closure as defense-linked also worked against the workers. While the role of defense spending in the region is small compared with other regions, defense-related closures should trigger public sector efforts to help displaced workers. Workers are less likely to be aware of such programs in regions not recognized as defense-dependent. The two most commonly used programs for displaced workers are the Economic Dislocation and Worker Adjustment Act, funded under Title III of the Job Training and Partnership Act (JTPA), and the Trade Adjustment Assistance program, funded under the Trade Act. The main features of EDWAA include early notification of the impending closure and available services under a state-run "rapid response" system; job search, counseling, and career assessment services commonly labeled "adjustment services"; and retraining services. TAA places less emphasis on rapid response and adjustment services and more on income support and training services than does EDWAA.

These programs are most likely to work well in regions where a diversity of local actors put pressure on the system to respond quickly and appropriately to the needs of displaced workers and others affected by changes in national defense priorities. Such actors might include labor unions, local elected officials, local business leaders, and local community leaders. This is true since, in both programs, the onus is on workers or sympathetic officials to argue their case to federal agencies to receive adequate funding for services.[14] In the case of the Unisys closure, the work force was not unionized and therefore lacked access to the resources and information available through international unions.

Even local political leaders did not see the closure as defense-related. Local representatives and business leaders did not actively involve themselves in the issue of the plant closure or the services provided to workers, even when pushed by the "Raritan Valley Project" (RVP), a group of former Unisys employees working to find jobs for themselves. The workers were isolated from information on available services and not tied to any larger organization or political leadership able to help them push for more or better services. They were forced to start at the very beginning in identifying available programs and, ultimately, in designing their own response to their situation.

The isolated political context in which the workers found themselves made it extremely difficult for them to evaluate and then respond to the services they received from the state and federal agencies. At every point, the workers, through the RVP, found themselves forging their own approach with no local political support and against the opposition of the state bureaucracy. This is in marked contrast to the experience of the workers laid off in St. Louis.

Without any political leadership or support to give them access to information and clout, the Unisys workers/RVP were largely at the mercy of the company in terms of the level and quality of adjustment services they received. Arguably, a company planning to stay in the area would have more interest in obtaining high-quality services for its workers. A powerful company, employing a sizable work force, might even pressure the state to set up services quickly and provide financial support toward this end. In this case, Unisys was planning to close the plant and leave the region for good. In this context, community relations were not a top priority. Perhaps for this reason, their actions served to ensure that workers remained without access to information on services to which they were entitled and to reduce their chances of receiving other services.

Unisys prevented workers from attending early rapid response team meetings, where they might have learned all they were entitled to under EDWAA. Although EDWAA recommends the formation of a labor–management committee, complete with a paid, neutral chairperson as part of the rapid response process, the formation of the committee is optional and is often left up to the company. For companies that are not interested in promoting early response to a closure, there is a strong incentive not to form such a committee. This effectively prevents the work force from gaining valuable information about available programs. No such committee was formed at the Unisys plant. This contributed to the workers' lack of knowledge about relevant programs. For example, workers were unaware for several months after the announcement of the closure that they even qualified for EDWAA services and funds.

Likewise, the workers' lack of knowledge about the EDWAA system enabled Unisys to substitute an inferior outplacement program for services fundable as part of EDWAA rapid response services. The poor quality of counseling and assessment services as well as résumé writing assistance provided by this company meant that workers often made poor choices regarding participation in training courses. Workers were not apprised of the state of the regional labor market, given adequate information on growing occupations and corresponding skill requirements, or seriously counseled on their best options.[15]

Not realizing that they were entitled to services under EDWAA, the Unisys workers (organized as the Raritan Valley Project) took it upon themselves to certify the plant's work force for Trade Adjustment Assistance. To qualify for TAA act certification, it is necessary to prove that jobs were lost in part because of increased foreign imports. Either the company or the work force can try to certify the plant. It is clear, however, that a company closing its doors will have less incentive than its workers to ensure certification. The Unisys workers, knowing that in the previous year the plant's application for trade certification to cover an earlier layoff had been rejected, decided not to leave this in the hands of the company. They applied and had the plant certified themselves, claiming that imports of whole systems or components resulted in declining sales and production at the plant.

At the same time, the state applied for and received an EDWAA discretionary grant from the federal Department of Labor's national reserve fund to respond to the Unisys layoffs. Yet, because of the constant shortfalls caused by the formula used to allocate EDWAA monies at the start of the fiscal year, state officials decided not to use this money on programs for these workers, deciding instead to spend it in other areas on people who did not have access to TAA money. Again, the workers learned of this through their own contacts and were consistently denied information on how these funds would be used.

This conflict between the interests of state officials and the workers meant to be served by the program is a direct result of the consistent shortfalls and problems with the funding mechanism upon which EDWAA is based (see Table 5.2). Because initial allocations to the state are based on the state's unemployment rate, virtually any large layoff will require that the state apply for a discretionary grant—a process that can take a year or longer to result in cash in hand. In the meantime, the state's ability to respond to workers' immediate needs is dictated by its own budgetary constraints. Discretionary grant money cannot be used to reimburse states for money spent while waiting for the grant. This forces the state to divert money from other programs to cope with the layoffs. This problem is common to every state. Some states have developed alternative funding mechanisms (generally based on payroll taxes) to allow them to fund alternative programs early in the process.[16] In addition, workers laid off late in the fiscal year are less likely to receive state-level EDWAA funding, as funds are never adequate to cover all workers.

The Unisys workers were lucky to be eligible for both EDWAA and TAA. Since few defense plants produce for both defense and commercial markets in competition with foreign producers, this is not an option for most displaced defense workers. The shift to TAA funding in this case meant that the workers received more money for training and received income support for a longer period of time than they would have under EDWAA. As a result, they should have been able to take longer training courses than typical EDWAA recipients. In fact, the average length of the training courses that Unisys workers participated in was only 3.8 weeks.[17]

Workers also received assessment and counseling services from the TAA staff. TAA staff performed aptitude tests, including outmoded assessments of manual dexterity, that were purportedly meant to help place workers in appropriate training programs. In lieu of providing guidance on the state of the local labor market, TAA staff sent workers out to get nonbinding letters from potential employers expressing a willingness to interview trainees. This was not an adequate substitute for good labor market information.

When workers approached training schools, the importance of

Table 5.2

Economic Dislocation and Worker Adjustment Act Funding Hierarchy

1992 National Budget: $577 million

National level:
 80 percent allocated to states by formula each year.
 20 percent retained by secretary in national reserve fund, obtainable through discretionary grant process.

State level:
 Average state grant determined by state's unemployment rate in previous year.
 50 percent of state grants must be allocated to substrate areas at the start of the fiscal year.
 40 percent of state grant may be retained for administrative purposes.
 10 percent may be retained for emergency allocations.

Allowable expenses:
 Job search assistance; job development; training in job skills for which supply exceeds demand; supportive services; pre-layoff assistance; relocation assistance; early intervention services in cases of plant closures.

worker assessment and labor market information became clear. Workers reported in interviews that training schools often sold them on training in occupations that would not yield the wages claimed and that were not even likely to be available to graduates of these training programs. Workers' abilities to discern the veracity of trainers' claims were seriously undermined by the lack of guidance offered by both the private outplacement company and TAA staff.

While structural factors have been emphasized thus far, the match between training programs and workers' skills and characteristics is also important to successful retraining and placement. Within many of the training programs chosen by former Unisys workers, the clash between the characteristics of workers and the training offered was apparent. Nearly half of Unisys workers took advantage of training funds to enter a variety of programs. Yet their older age profile (common to defense workers in general), as well as their experience as manufacturing workers, made them a poor fit with most training programs. Many reported that, as they approached the end of their training, they were surprised to learn they were being trained for entry-level positions in their new field, at considerably lower wages than they had earned at Unisys. Since training schools collect their fees whether participants pass or fail their courses, they have no incentive to place them in courses that match their skill levels. Indeed, there is evidence that some schools coached workers through entrance exams in order to collect their TAA funds. Finally, there is also evidence that schools entice workers to enter programs based on promises of eventual high wages in management positions rather than on wages in the occupations for which they will be trained. Since most workers making use of retraining programs were production workers, this was particularly inappropriate.

Given the high rate of participation in training, why had so few Unisys workers found jobs after one year out of work?[18] In addition to the factors mentioned above—poor assessment and counseling, the short length of training courses—workers faced a bleak local labor market at the end of their training or outplacement program. To address this problem, the workers themselves developed a strategy meant to market themselves to potential employers, highlighting the training funds and other economic development money available through various state programs. They developed a marketing package that included a skills assessment of the group and a description of all the training monies and economic development loans that potential employers could make use of in hiring them. Ironically, such a strategy could have been employed by state officials through the use of on-the-job training (OJT) funds under EDWAA or TAA. Yet, perhaps because the development of on-the-job funding opportunities is very time-intensive and such funding has been criticized in the past for unfairly subsidizing employers to hire workers they would have hired anyway, such an approach has been largely overlooked. They received little encouragement from the state in their efforts. To date, they have not been able to place any portion of their group using this strategy.

In summary, the Unisys workers faced a difficult task for several reasons. First, their location in a rural, increasingly service-oriented economy meant that defense dependency was not a concern for local elected officials. Their plight was not met with a coordinated response from local officials, partly for this reason. Unisys, as a departing employer, had no incentive to push the state for better services. Second, the local labor market is moving away from the types of occupations most typical of those laid off. In this context, reemployment for most workers will be difficult without extensive retraining. This is especially true of workers in production-related occupations. Third, outplacement and counseling provided by representatives of TAA and training schools on workers' best options did not result in appropriate retraining placements. Most workers were retrained in service occupations offering considerably lower wages than they received at Unisys. While it may be too early to assess the long-range impacts of training on workers' job prospects and incomes, recent studies indicate that their prospects cannot be expected to change dramatically in the future.[19] In this context, the workers' own efforts took on added importance. Yet, without the support—both administrative and financial—of state agencies, they are unlikely to succeed. In regions where political and institutional support for services are weak, a very heavy burden would appear to fall on workers. Unfortunately, hard work on their part is no guarantee of success.

Case 2: The McDonnell-Douglas Layoffs in St. Louis, Missouri

The St. Louis case contrasts sharply with that of Unisys. The St. Louis regional economy is much larger, more diverse, and more heavily dependent on defense contracts for regional employment than is Raritan Township, New Jersey. In absolute terms, nonagricultural employment was 1.152 million in 1993.[20] The economy revolves around production of aircraft, missiles, space equipment, and automobiles, as well as educational, health, and business services. Traditional industries including primary metals, trucking and warehousing, and beverages (beer) are also large employers.[21] As in other regions, employment in traditional manufacturing sectors has been declining while service industries have grown, although at below the national rate.

The region's defense dependence is largely due to the predominance of one regional employer: McDonnell-Douglas. Although 720 firms receive prime contracts from the Department of Defense (DoD), McDonnell-Douglas received sixty-five times more defense dollars than the next biggest contractor in the region.[22] At their peak, in 1989, the company employed 42,300. With recent layoffs, they are now down to approximately 27,000.[23] Prior to defense downsizing, the region employed approximately 73,500 people in defense jobs, or 6.4 percent of the regional labor force. Another 85,000 people in the region are estimated to benefit indirectly from defense spending.[24]

Not surprisingly, given the importance of defense spending to the regional economy, regional economic and political elites came together when the first round of defense cuts were announced to design a coordinated effort meant primarily to diversify the regional economy. In July of 1990, the St. Louis county executive and the city's mayor, Vincent Schoemehl, announced the formation of a regional committee to plan and coordinate strategies that would lead to the diversification and growth of the region's economy.[25] The resultant committee, the St. Louis Economic Adjustment and Diversification Committee (SLEADC), includes representatives of the city of St. Louis, the five counties in the region, the Southwest Illinois Leadership Council as well as those of the states of Missouri and Illinois, and representatives of labor, industry and academia, reflecting the broad interest and concern over the impact of declining defense spending on the regional economy. The group received two federal planning grants to assist them in their efforts: a grant for $100,000 from the Pentagon's Office of Economic Adjustment, and another for $150,000 from the Commerce Department's Economic Development Administration.

In this context, efforts to develop programs for defense workers received a great deal of both public and state attention. The region dedicated state funds and a large federal discretionary grant to adjustment and training services for displaced McDonnell-Douglas workers. The region is also better equipped than most areas to deal with mass layoffs since it possesses strong employment and training institutions and has experience with mass layoffs and structural employment shifts due to earlier layoffs in the region's auto industry. The Metropolitan Re-Employment Project, with its strong ties to the regional network of community colleges, developed a comprehensive approach to rapid response, outplacement, and training referrals during these earlier layoffs.[26] They were able to build on this experience in developing the Worker Re-entry Program for laid-off McDonnell-Douglas workers.

Notably, regional efforts went beyond conventional state and federal programs for displaced workers. In response to a Department of Labor call for alternative approaches to displacement, representatives of the SLEADC and a local peace group, the St. Louis Economic Conversion Project, designed a program aimed at promoting the conversion of local, defense-dependent companies. This was intended to prevent the displacement of labor and eventually to promote growth of civilian industry. The resultant program, the Management Assistance and Technology Transfer Program (MATT), received initial funding of $500,000 for eighteen months, through June of 1994. The program's premise is that competitive manufacturing will require a transformation in management practices. Following Deming's principles of total quality and fifteen areas of excellence defined by the National Center for Manufacturing Sciences, companies are guided through an assessment of their current status and organizational needs. Companies are then assisted in finding and financing necessary consultant services.[27] According to one MATT board member, the program assumes that in many cases it is managers, rather than workers who need retraining. After little more than one year in operation, MATT had eighteen client firms.

This strategy, while currently limited in scale, represents an important conceptual advance over the conventional, supply-side approach to displacement. By emphasizing prevention over reaction, the program focuses on reorganization and retraining within an existing workplace rather than training that is loosely targeted to the needs of "growing occupations," regardless of the comparability of the jobs to workers' previous jobs. Obviously, in St. Louis, the ideal client for this program would be McDonnell-Douglas. Given the company's lack of interest in serious conversion efforts, the SLEADC has gone to the next tier down. At this early stage, it is impossible to predict how effective the program will be in converting its clients to civilian production.

As anticipated, McDonnell-Douglas began laying off workers in 1990, and layoffs continue to this date. In the first wave of layoffs, the state of Missouri was given advance warning and was able to implement rapid response procedures. In the second large layoff, coming shortly after a sudden contract cancellation, the company was exempted from WARN legislation, and the state and, therefore, the workers were given only two weeks notice of impending layoffs. Although the Missouri Division of Job Development and Training became aware of the potential layoffs at McDonnell-Douglas in May of 1990, company representatives did not agree to meet with them until late June. Initial rapid response meetings were attended by representatives from McDonnell-Douglas's human resources office, St. Louis Community College's Metropolitan Reemployment Project, the County Department of Human Resources, and Missouri Rapid Response.

Conspicuously absent were any representatives of organized labor. According to Cassell Williams, president of Local 837 of the International Association of Machinists and Aerospace Workers (IAM), union representatives were not invited to these meetings. Missouri Job Development and Training officials confirmed this, attributing it to the company's unwillingness to have union representatives present. While union employees represented a small portion of those laid off at this time (10 percent), they represented close to half those laid off in the sudden layoffs of early 1991. Yet, at this time no rapid response planning meeting was held with the company, since the team had already set up their procedures in the first wave meetings. Subsequent meetings, where workers were presented with information on available services, were held both on site and at the union hall, in an effort to include the unionized work force.

As a result of the state's planning meetings, forty-two rapid response sessions were held, covering 2,700 workers and beginning the week of July 15, 1990. In these meetings, an overview of the services available through the St. Louis Worker Re-Entry Program (developed by the Metropolitan Re-Employment Project) was presented to workers. The services included out-placement workshops covering résumé writing, interviewing skills, networking, job search strategies, and how to research employers; assessment and interest inventories; career exploration; job development and placement; funding available for training and retraining; and on-the-job training. Information was also presented on unemployment insurance and on job services programs available through the state's Division of Employment Security.

Representatives of McDonnell-Douglas management also attended rapid response meetings to inform workers of services offered by the company. The company established an outplacement center offering job fairs, professional seminars, and training classes. The classes offered included résumé writing, job search planning and networking, interviewing skills, and classes on coping with transition. This center was closed at the start of November of 1990 and the Worker Re-entry Program began to provide services to workers.

Initially, services to laid-off McDonnell-Douglas workers were provided both through an outplacement center funded by the company and through state-funded (JTPA-Title III) worker reentry centers. Once the A-12 contract was canceled and the layoffs announced, the state applied for a national reserve fund discretionary grant. Receipt of a

$3.375 million grant in February of 1991 allowed the state to set up a site in a facility donated by McDonnell-Douglas to serve only its own laid-off workers. The site included computers, office furnishings, and equipment. The state argued in its grant proposal that it was better to use formula funds to serve other firms and to dedicate a separate facility to McDonnell-Douglas employees. In June of 1993, the state received a grant from the Department of Labor's Defense Conversion Adjustment fund for $4 million to continue this program another two years. Due to the high level of funding dedicated to this center, the Worker Re-Entry Program was able to offer the McDonnell-Douglas workers a wider array of services than were available at its other sites.

Awareness of these services was high among laid-off McDonnell-Douglas workers. Criticisms came mainly from union and other non-technical workers who complained in focus groups that the services are oriented toward more highly educated and skilled employees. Worker Re-Entry Program staff noted that more educated workers were more likely to make use of the program's services. Both its director, Jerry Stockman, and Glenn Stinson, director of the state's Division of Job Development and Training, emphasized the efforts made to make blue-collar workers aware of the services available at the center.[28] Both speculated that many blue-collar workers expected to be called back to work at the company and were therefore not interested in participating.[29] Placement rates for those who did participate were high: over 74 percent in early summer of 1993.

The high level of funding of programs for displaced workers was *not* the result of active involvement on the part of local labor unions. While McDonnell-Douglas bears responsibility for cutting the unions out of early rapid response meetings, union leaders did not fight for a leadership role in subsequent program design or implementation, nor did they play a significant role in the regional diversification efforts. While local conversion activists have pushed labor leaders to be active participants in the process and to take a leadership role in developing an industrial policy for the region, most local labor leaders seem generally uninformed on conversion issues and not particularly interested. The McDonnell-Douglas local of the Machinists Union is understandably more interested in retaining employment at McDonnell-Douglas. Clearly, this strategy is tied to the company's strong anticonversion stance.

The prominence and political clout of McDonnell-Douglas was an important factor in determining the amount of attention and funding programs for displaced workers received in St. Louis. McDonnell-Douglas is able to exercise its clout to encourage the development of high-quality programs as part of its efforts to maintain good relations with the community. It is important to note that this is not a plant closure, but a contraction of a firm that plans to remain in the region.

Precisely because of the role played by defense spending in the regional economy and the importance of McDonnell-Douglas as a regional employer, the level and quality of services offered laid-off workers were high in St. Louis. In addition to structural factors, the local institutional setting was important to the service response to the layoffs. Services were provided by an established organization, with vast experience in providing services to displaced workers dating back to layoffs in the auto industry in previous decades. The state was highly motivated to raise the level of funds needed to attain this level of service. In contrast to the Unisys case, state officials had no interest in transferring these discretionary funds to other sites in the state. In addition, they spent state funds to provide services until the grant came in. This allowed a special center to be established just to deal with laid-off McDonnell-Douglas workers. Yet, beyond its fundraising activities and the program elements commonly invoked under EDWAA, the state was a passive participant. Due to past scandals, officials were reluctant to exercise the on-the-job training provisions of EDWAA, potentially able to link training to real opportunities. In a widely publicized case, the state had provided on-the-job training funds to McDonnell-Douglas to train defense workers transferred from Long Beach to produce C-17 aircraft in sheet metal assembly. They received over $700,000 of state funds for this purpose.

Yet, in spite of the higher quality and greater support on the part of company and state and local officials for programs for displaced workers, laid-off McDonnell-Douglas workers did not fare dramatically better than did Unisys workers. The 45 percent reemployment rate reported in the first survey of workers, conducted approximately one year after most were laid off, includes 14 percent who report that they have been rehired in defense companies, most likely by McDonnell-Douglas itself. Once this is taken into account, the reemployment rate looks closer to that experienced by Unisys at a similar point in time.[30]

In summary, the McDonnell-Douglas case contrasts sharply with the Unisys case (see Table 5.3). Workers were laid off from a plant that continued to operate in the region in the context of a high level of awareness of the problems of defense downsizing and economic conversion. In this context, programs for workers were well run and well funded. Yet, ultimately, the bulk of funds was spent on conventional retraining programs, unable to overcome the structural limitations of the local labor market. More innovative approaches, such as the MATT program, were not funded at a high enough level or were not able to reach the one company really able to make a difference—McDonnell-Douglas.

Comparison and Possible Explanations

Whether more weight is given to structurally or individually based explanations for workers' experiences, the St. Louis workers would be expected to receive better-quality, better-funded services than would the New Jersey workers. If these services were well designed, they would be expected to result in higher rates of reemployment for this group as well.[31] Yet, in spite of their apparently advantageous setting and individual characteristics, though the St. Louis workers did fare better, they did not fare dramatically better than the Unisys workers. It appears that both groups faced similar barriers to successful reemployment.

Traditionally, public programs meant to help unemployed workers find that jobs have been based on a supply-side approach, emphasizing the need to change workers' skills as the solution to their predicament. Less attention has been focused on defining the skill areas in which to train workers. The general presumption has been that it is not the quantity of jobs in the labor market that limits workers but rather their inadequate or inappropriate skills. The problem is a "mismatch" between workers' skills and those demanded in the labor market.

Defense workers differ from manufacturing workers in general in ways that are relevant to both their chances for reemployment and their compatibility with the design of current programs. Overall, defense workers are more often in professional and technical occupations than workers in nondefense manufacturing industries. They are more often male and white and are, on average, older than nondefense manufacturing workers.

Past studies of worker displacement have found that older, female, minority, and blue-collar workers had the most trouble adjusting to

Table 5.3

Survey Data for Unisys and McDonnell-Douglas Workers One Year after Layoff

	Unisys	McDonnell-Douglas
Demographics		
Modal age category	41–45	25–44
Percent male	45.8	75.0
Percent white	72.3	89.0
Percent engineer	12.3	22.0
Percent production	51.5	37.0
Percent administration	6.9	8.0
Percent other	29.3	33.0
Modal education category	High school graduate	Some college
Modal wage category	$10–$15/hour	$10–$20/hour
Mean years job tenure	11.9	Under 6
Percent union	0	37.0
Post-layoff experience		
Reemployment rate	26.7	45.0
Drop in wages	46.7	44.0
New occupational distribution		
Percent engineer	12.9	
Percent production	12.9	
Percent administration	29.0	
Percent other	45.2	
Percent retraining	49.6	16–40%[a]
Average length of course	38.0 weeks	
Average length of income support	12.0 months	6 months[a]

[a]Sixteen to twenty-seven percent of survey respondents participated in classroom training. This is from a survey conducted about two years after layoff (E. Terrence Jones and Development Strategies, Inc., "The layoffs at McDonnell-Douglas," December 1992). The rest of the McDonnell-Douglas figures are from E.T. Jones, "The layoffs at McDonnell-Douglas: A survey analysis," 1991). All Unisys data are from a survey of laid-off workers by the Project on Regional and Industrial Economics, Rutgers University, and the Raritan Valley Project, one year after layoff.

layoffs. Older workers were unemployed longer and suffered larger wage losses when reemployed. Female workers, suffering unemployment rates three times those of men after layoffs, remained unemployed longer and received lower wages when reemployed. Minorities also did poorly in reemployment and received lower wages than whites.[32] In occupational terms, unskilled and semiskilled manufacturing workers have had the most trouble adjusting.[33] Past studies have found that workers with higher levels of education have had better luck finding new jobs quickly and have suffered the least in terms of wage losses.[34] Because defense workers are paid more than their civilian counterparts, they can expect to suffer significant wage losses with reemployment in civilian industries.

Programs for displaced workers that focus on job search assistance are a poor match for older, blue-collar defense workers. For workers facing a large drop in wages without a long period of serious reorientation of their skills, the current system is inadequate.

Given the characteristics associated with successful reemployment and the design of current programs, the St. Louis workers would appear to have the best chance of success with the current model, based on their characteristics alone. St. Louis workers are more often young, white, male, and highly skilled than are the Unisys workers. On average, they have more years of education and earned higher wages and had fewer years on the job—all traits thought to favor workers in reemployment (see Table 5.3).

In contrast to arguments based primarily on the characteristics of workers, other analysts argue for the importance of a variety of factors that contribute to the political-economic context in which defense layoffs take place. Among the factors emphasized are economic structural factors such as the size and diversity of the local economy and the degree of defense dependency in the local economy. In addition, political or institutional factors are stressed, such as the role of local community political actors and institutions in shaping the public definition of the problem facing the region. This in turn shapes both the level of effort and the design of programs meant to respond to defense layoffs.

If the scale or structure of the local labor market were important, we would expect the St. Louis workers to be in a better position than the Unisys workers, primarily because of the size and composition of the regional labor market. While both labor markets are fairly tight, exhibiting low unemployment rates, the Hunterdon County market is very small, with most growth appearing in either high-wage service sectors for which workers would require extensive training or low-wage sectors inappropriate to their need to maintain themselves and their families at something approaching current income levels. However, in both cases, manufacturing occupations are not growing.[35]

In both cases, workers are facing a job market that will not provide jobs with similar wages even if jobs are the same. In many cases, workers will need to change fields. Early indicators suggest that there will not be enough well-paid positions for those wishing to switch. Those facing the most difficulty may be lower-level employees who received benefits and relatively high wages at defense firms but cannot hope to find similar jobs without substantially reorienting their skills.

St. Louis workers appear to be favored by the high level of awareness and public debate over the impact of defense cuts on the region. There is a high level of awareness of the problems of defense dependence and economic conversion issues among local policy makers, as well as the local business and economic development community. Consequently, the region has developed a coordinated regional strategy, albeit with inadequate representation of the financial sector and organized labor.

As a result of their efforts, they have received a large amount of federal funding for planning purposes, an innovative demonstration project, and the high-profile Worker Re-Entry Program. There is no comparable public sector or political effort in the New Jersey case. Although the state did write and receive funding for a discretionary grant, the process was secretive and did not include workers. At all stages the state was reluctant to work with the worker group or to go beyond the formal outlines of current EDWAA or TAA policy to link its efforts to compatible programs elsewhere in the state bureaucracy.

Because of the high level of interest on the part of local elected officials and the strong role of McDonnell-Douglas in the regional economy, St. Louis workers received well-funded and well-run services through the Worker Re-Entry Program. The program catered to the needs of skilled McDonnell-Douglas workers. In the Unisys case, the quality of services was clearly lower, with serious problems in the areas of outplacement and advising regarding training, leading to some inappropriate training placements. Not all factors favored the McDonnell-Douglas workers. The Unisys workers received income support for a longer period of time due to their participation in the TAA system rather than in EDWAA. Yet this difference again would lead us to expect a higher reemployment rate in St. Louis early on since workers would have been without unemployment insurance for several months in St. Louis at the time of the survey.

It is interesting to note that although the McDonnell-Douglas work force was unionized, this did not guarantee them access to early meetings in the rapid response process, nor did it ensure that labor had adequate input into the process. Ironically, though they were not successful, it was the Unisys work force that took the initiative to develop an agenda for policy. However, while organized labor was not an active participant in the regional planning process, a community organization centered on the issue of economic conversion did play an important and constructive role.

All of the indicators cited above would lead us to expect a higher reemployment rate for McDonnell-Douglas workers in St. Louis. And at first glance the figures appear to favor the St. Louis workers. But when adjusted to remove those reemployed at McDonnell-Douglas (14 percent), the reemployment rates are in fact quite close: 26.7 percent were reemployed a year after layoff in the Unisys case; 31 percent had found employment outside of McDonnell-Douglas in St. Louis after a comparable period of time.

Recommendations for Reform

Successful retraining and reemployment depend on an accurate assessment of the causes of displacement in the first place. Labor economists have identified and debated several sources of unemployment, which they label frictional, cyclical, and structural. Frictional unemployment can be defined as that due to normal job turnover—that is, temporary mismatches between those out of work and the jobs available. There is no lack of demand, nor is there a significant change in the types of jobs available or the skills they require. In defense layoffs, this might correspond to workers with generic skills in clerical work, for example. Cyclical unemployment is more problematic since it lasts longer, with workers dependent on the next upturn in the economy to find jobs. Again, the structure of demand for labor is assumed to be constant. This is the traditional justification for unemployment insurance. Finally, structural unemployment is defined as that due to changes in the mix of industries and occupations in the national economy, due to increased international competition, technological change, and institutional factors such as the downsizing of national defense production.

Defense workers involved in the production of items for which demand has severely decreased are structurally unemployed. They can neither wait out the downturn in demand nor count on outplacement services to match them with available jobs. They need to reorient themselves for available jobs, match themselves to federal or state-level efforts to create new jobs, or develop new alternatives for themselves.

While recognition is growing that displacement is generated by structural changes in the economy, policies have yet to catch up with this realization. The current administration has inherited a structure for addressing the problems of displaced workers that is aimed at lowering frictional unemployment or at helping marginal workers enter the labor force. The deeper issues raised by structural unemployment are beyond the scope of readjustment programs as currently conceived. The specific barriers to addressing structural unemployment in current programs revolve around three issues: (1) the lack of links to demand-side, job development initiatives; (2) the need to differentiate worker problems by skill level or demographic characteristics; and (3) the types of training currently emphasized by programs.

Linking Training to Jobs

As noted earlier, across the country manufacturing jobs are declining while service sector jobs continue to grow. The mismatch between the occupational makeup (and, therefore, skills and wages) of these two sectors makes reemployment difficult for laid-off manufacturing workers. This disjuncture makes it crucial to link training to proactive employment initiatives. Without such a link, workers will be expelled into a labor market that can offer them no more than underemployment.

Rather than wait for layoffs to occur, the first line of attack should be in preventing layoffs through job retention strategies when possible. While the WARN system is meant to provide advance warning of layoffs, it does not provide notice adequate to permit alternative use planning or employee buyouts of plants. In addition, evidence suggests that compliance is spotty at best, since no agency is charged with enforcement of the law. In order to promote alternatives to closures, early identification of companies at risk of closing is critical. Legislation aimed at requiring the Department of Defense to notify contractors of anticipated contract cutbacks and cancellations as part of the budget process would be a step toward this end. In addition to alternative use planning, elements of retention strategies should include adequate funding (and oversight) of on-the-job retraining, loans for feasibility studies and startup costs for employee stock ownership plans, including for new product development, and technical assistance to retrain management.

While both EDWAA and TAA have provisions for supporting on-the-job training for employers who hire displaced workers, these services appear to be underutilized. Most states have programs on line meant to develop jobs that could be linked to displaced workers.[36] Examples include funds for on-the-job training, feasibility studies for expansion, loan funds for expanding facilities, technical assistance programs, and so on. These programs contain elements of what is needed to promote the expansion of existing firms or the creation of new firms that could employ displaced workers. Yet current initiatives are only weakly linked to each other (if at all) and not linked at all to programs for displaced workers. Part of the blame for the lack of coordination across programs can be placed on recent budget cuts. According to state officials interviewed, many of these programs suffer from a lack of staff time and do not have the capacity to make these links themselves. In other cases, state officials appear unwilling to make the links. One Economic Development Authority official interviewed commented, "anything to do with laid off workers we don't get involved with . . . we finance business."[37] Officials viewed attempts to promote hiring of displaced workers through wage subsidies as interfering with the operation of private business. Apparently, they did not view other, primarily financial incentives to remain in the state the same way. This lack of concern for state employment in economic development agencies is inconsistent with their mission.

Matching Programs to Workers

The question upon which the retraining debate turns is, what type of training do workers need to find work at a comparable level of skill and pay? Also, how can workers with different types of skills or with different demographic characteristics be best served? Can one system serve all workers?

Workers laid off from occupations in decline will have a harder time finding new jobs than those with readily transferable skills. Adjustment and training services should recognize the different needs of workers with differing skill levels and educational backgrounds. In addition, older workers, typically at the peak of their career in earnings and skills, will have a harder time matching their skill and earnings levels in new occupations than will younger workers. Retraining for an entry-level position will not be adequate for them: they will need more intensive, long-term training than is currently funded to maintain their incomes. Similarly, skilled workers with advanced degrees should not be retrained for entry-level positions; they need training that will build on their skills while reorienting their application to new areas.

Current programs do not address these different needs. Instead, they emphasize short-term training and adjustment services better suited to the needs of workers with only modest training needs and good prospects for immediate reemployment. The EDWAA program, using the framework provided by the Job Training Partnership Act, was originally developed to help channel marginalized workers into the labor force. It focuses on outplacement and adjustment services. Ironically, this appears to favor better-skilled displaced defense workers. Although legally allowable, it only rarely provides for income support for workers during training. It is mid- or lower-skill-level workers who have the most serious retraining needs. The funds allocated for training are generally too little to provide for more than a few months of training, given the numbers of workers to be served. TAA is able to fund programs and provide income support for as long as one year.

Neither program, however, provides enough guidance to workers after layoff. As described earlier, this has led to poor training choices by workers who were often pressured into selecting courses by training school representatives. So that the needs of workers can be better served under the current system, their skills must be assessed early in the process. Rapid response services must be more comprehensive, performing skills assessment and directing workers to appropriate services before they are laid off. Likewise, workers and firms should be directed to OJT programs, business incubators, or business services such as those provided by the MATT program before layoffs occur.

The importance of regulatory oversight of training institutions cannot be overemphasized. Workers are particularly vulnerable to the promises and misinformation of training recruiters when they have not been adequately briefed on the condition of the local labor market and their options before entering retraining schools. Should the administration promote greater use of vouchers for training services, these issues will become increasingly important. Portable funding, while theoretically giving the worker more options, may be wasted if workers are not also offered guidance in selecting among available options. Making funding contingent on placement in permanent employment would help alleviate this problem.[38] Likewise, evidence suggests that greater use of community-based organizations, in place of state "service delivery areas," as the conduits for matching workers and programs will result in more effective programs.

Training for What?

Finally, the substance of training itself is of critical importance to the likelihood of finding adequate employment. Currently, under the EDWAA system, workers are to be trained in areas where jobs are growing. Given the high level of skill and experience of many displaced workers, and the low skill level of growing service industry occupations, this strategy is problematic. Again, this reflects the entry-level emphasis of other programs of the Job Training Partnership Act.

A second approach is to train people for the jobs of the future—an "if we train them, the jobs will come" approach. Such training, although hailed as the key to our future economic success by Secretary of Labor Robert Reich, is not encouraged by the current EDWAA system. And, without simultaneous and linked job development programs, high-level training will not result in reemployment in the short to medium term.

The real barrier to successful retraining is the lack of appropriate jobs for displaced, skilled workers. Is increasing the supply of highly trained workers the right approach when there are shifts in the structure of the labor market away from the occupations of those displaced? Existing state and federal programs can only marginally affect the level of demand in the labor market. To shape demand or increase it in a more significant way, the state or—more likely—the federal government will have to stimulate demand more directly. While not using the term "industrial policy," a significant share of defense conversion appropriations are going to technology-related initiatives meant to result in job development. Yet, to date, these programs have not integrated work-force development into their structure very well. The few work-force-related provisions focus on classroom training for engineers. The training provisions are not explicitly linked to funding for technology development.[39]

In the absence of links between training and job development programs, schools are offering training for entry-level positions where it is arguable that such training is not necessary. These courses are more appropriate for workers with only a high school degree and in need of language development—the traditional focus of the system. For middle-level workers, this type of training is inappropriate. In other cases, the necessary training could be purchased for significantly less at local community colleges. Without regulatory oversight of both the content and the cost of training courses, the government and workers may end up paying a lot of money for minimal return.

Unless serious attention is paid to the mismatch between the skills of displaced workers and the skills demanded in the labor market, reemployment will mean a severe drop in wages and skill. However, even if workers are placed in jobs at skill levels equal to those they hold in defense firms, they may face a drop in wages. In part, this is due to the decline in unionization in the economy and the general atmosphere of downsizing and benefit cutting. Government contracts (especially "cost-plus" type defense contracts) brought with them good wages and benefits and coverage by federal labor legislation.

A proactive conversion policy must include significant economic development initiatives, linked to retraining efforts and job retention strategies. Without these elements, workers in the most favorable circumstances can expect to have a very difficult readjustment, with a serious drop in wages at best. There is currently no high-wage alternative for displaced blue-collar workers.

Existing programs do not provide resources necessary to change occupations *and* maintain the wage level of previous employment. Adjustment services are aimed at rapid reemployment at whatever wage. Training is aimed at short-term skills upgrading for high-skill workers or job search and minor adjustments for low-skill workers. This approach is not appropriate when, in essence, an industry is being dissolved and growing sectors are inappropriate substitutes. In this context, the only possible chance for a positive transition to new work without massive declines in wages and living standards is through proactive job development policies. Although elements of these policies do exist in other programs funded by the states and the federal government, they remain the critical missing link in current programs for displaced workers.

Notes

1. Figures represent money actually appropriated for FY 1993 ("Defense reinvestment and economic growth initiatives, President Bill Clinton, budget authority," in Miriam Pemberton [ed.]) *Defense Industry Conversion: Strategies for Job Redevelopment* (Washington, DC: National Commission for Economic Conversion and Disarmament, March 1993), p. 54.

2. Office of Technology Assessment, *After the Cold War: Living with Lower Defense Spending.* OTA-ITE–457 (Washington, DC: U.S. Government Printing Office, February 1992), p. 77.

3. See SRI International, *Study of the Implementation of the Economic Dislocation and Worker Adjustment Assistance Act—Phase II* (Washington, DC: U.S. Department of Labor, Employment and Training Administration, November 1992); and Mathematica Policy Research, Inc., *International Trade and Worker Dislocation: Evaluation of the Trade Adjustment Assistance Program* (Washington, DC: U.S. Department of Labor, Employment and Training Administration, April 1993).

4. In a comparison of layoffs at Martin Marietta, Boeing, and Republic Aviation in the mid-1960s, Fishman et al. found that eight variables covering personal characteristics (age, sex, education, mobility, seniority, home ownership, dependents, and pre-layoff salary) explained between 7 and 29 percent of the variation in duration of unemployment and salary change for these workers (*Reemployment Experiences of Defense Workers: A Statistical Analysis of the Boeing, Martin, and Republic Layoffs,* prepared for the U.S. Arms Control and Disarmament Agency [Washington, DC: Government Printing Office, 1968]; cited in Sabina Deitrick, "Worker retraining and defense conversion: Lessons from prior defense cutbacks," presented at the Association of Collegiate Schools of Planning 35th Annual Meeting, Philadelphia, October 30, 1993, p. 15).

5. In St. Louis, all interviews were conducted by the author. In New Jersey, interviews were conducted by members of a team of student researchers, coordinated by the author. For more detail on the cases, see Elizabeth J. Mueller et al., "Retraining for what? Displaced workers come up against EDWAA," Rutgers University, Center for Urban Policy Research, Working Paper no. 57, September 1993; and Michael Oden et al., "Changing the future: Converting the St. Louis economy," Rutgers University, CUPR, Working Paper no. 59, November 1993.

6. For an excellent description of the appropriate use of case study methodology, see Robert K. Yin, *Case Study Research: Design and Methods.* Applied Social Research Methods Series, vol. 5. (Newbury Park, CA: Sage Publications, 1989).

7. New Jersey Department of Labor, Office of Research and Planning, Northern Region. *Regional Labor Market Review*, Bergen, Essex, Hudson, Hunterdon, Middlesex, Morris, Passaic, Somerset, Sussex, Union, and Warren Counties (Au-

gust 1992); "Jobs and beyond: Is New Jersey ready?" Annual Occupational Supply and Demand Report of the New Jersey Occupational Information Coordinating Committee (1989).

8. The low unemployment rate is an artifact of the relatively sparse prime age population in the region and the movement of already employed residents to the area due to new housing construction.

9. New Jersey Department of Labor, Office of Research and Planning, "Regional labor market review" (August 1992).

10. Ibid.

11. David P. Willis, "Partnership to stem flow of jobs from Hunterdon county," *The Courier-News*, January 27, 1993, p. B1.

12. "Unisys: Center of high technology in Raritan Township," *The News* (Frenchtown, NJ), March 7, 1991, p. 4.

13. A survey of 450 former Unisys employees was conducted by a team of graduate students in the Department of Urban Planning and Policy Development at Rutgers University in April of 1993. Results reported here are based on 132 responses.

14. They must either present their case for certification under the Trade Act to the federal Department of Labor in the case of TAA funding, or write a major grant application for discretionary funding of services from the secretary of labor's national reserve fund under EDWAA.

15. Mueller et al., "Retraining for what?"

16. California's Employment and Training Panel funds its programs this way. See Jim Raffel, *The New Economy.*

17. J. Lee and J. Merisotis. *Proprietary Schools: Programs, Policies and Prospects*, ASHE-ERIC Higher Education Report 5 (1990).

18. The timing of the survey—one year after layoff—may be seen as a weakness in the study since those still covered by unemployment insurance and COBRA might be expected to remain unemployed. However, at this point, all were approaching the end of such coverage and anecdotal evidence indicates that most people had stepped up their job searches in recent months in anticipation of the end of coverage.

19. Walter Corson et al., *International Trade and Worker Dislocation: Evaluation of the Trade Adjustment Assistance Act*, submitted to the U.S. Department of Labor, Employment and Training Administration, Office of Strategic Planning and Policy Development (Princeton: Mathematica Policy Research, Inc., 1993).

20. Missouri Department of Employment and Security, Total Non-Farm Employment by Industry Series. Total for 1993 for the month of August from "St. Louis MSA labor area summary" (September 1993).

21. See Oden et al., "Changing the future," table 1.

22. Defense Budget Project, *The Future of Defense Spending and Armaments Production in the St. Louis Area* (Washington, DC: Defense Budget Project, 1993).

23. Interview with Russ Signorino, senior labor market analyst, Division of Employment Security, Missouri Department of Labor and Industrial Relations.

24. St. Louis Economic Adjustment and Diversification Task Force. "St. Louis Economic Adjustment and Diversification Program" (1991), p. i.

25. Ibid., p. ii.

26. A study performed by Abt Associates on the effectiveness of the MRP found generally positive results, with those participating in JTPA training experiencing increased earnings following program participation (U.S. Department of Labor, Employment and Training Administration, "The St. Louis Metropolitan Reemployment Project: An impact evaluation," Research and Evaluation Report Series 93-B, 1993).

27. The Management Assistance and Technology Transfer Program provides 75 percent of the initial cost of the consultant's fee and 50 percent of the cost for second-stage, factory-level analysis. See Oden et al., "Changing the Future," pp. 51–2, for more information.

28. Awareness of programs seemed uneven, with the least skilled being least aware of available services. One focus group member—a former housekeeping employee—was attending a training course for paralegals financed by student loans while surviving on Aid to Families with Dependent Children (AFDC). She was completely unaware that her program could be at least partially paid for by training funds.

29. Given past contractions and subsequent "callbacks" of employees, many employees retain a wait-and-see attitude in the early stages of unemployment, which affects their willingness to make use of services. This appears to be more of an issue for semiskilled blue-collar workers in this case.

30. Figures on reemployment of those using services cannot be compared since only first-year figures are available for Unisys workers.

31. Whether or not the jobs they were placed in represented a positive outcome for the region is another issue.

32. Office of Technology Assessment, "Technology and structural unemployment: Reemploying displaced adults" (Washington, DC: Congress of the United States, 1986).

33. Marie Howland, *Plant Closings and Worker Displacement: The Regional Issues.* (Kalamazoo, MI: Upjohn Institute, 1988).

34. There is some evidence that in St. Louis, workers are being reemployed in manufacturing occupations at McDonnell-Douglas.

35. Gregory Bischak and James Raffel, "Defense Department drags feet on conversion law: Delayed notification of cuts and guidance to defense contractors," *The New Economy*, Vol. 4, no. 2, issue 18, Spring 1993.

36. For example, the state of New Jersey runs programs through both its Commerce and Economic Development Departments meant to encourage business startups by funding feasibility studies. It funds business incubators through the New Jersey Institute of Technology and Rutgers University. The Economic Development Authority runs at least fifteen programs to help businesses with their financial needs in plant expansion, purchase of machinery, new product development, and other needs. The Department of Commerce runs a technical assistance program for state businesses in which 400 field representatives inform businesses about available assistance programs.

37. Interview conducted by Jonathan Feldman with Caren Franzini, Deputy Director, Economic Development Authority, Trenton, April 19, 1993. See Mueller et al., *Retraining for What?*, p. 45.

38. California's Employment and Training Panel attempts to address some of the problems raised here. Using funds raised from a small premium on the unem-

ployment insurance taxes that employers pay, the state has created a program that emphasizes on-the-job training to upgrade skills of employed workers and—for displaced workers—training that builds on workers' existing skills rather than forcing retraining in a new area. In addition, the program ties the training funds to placement in a job held for at least ninety days. Preliminary studies indicate that the program has been more effective than have federal training programs in increasing workers' wages in their new jobs. The program better serves older, experienced workers than does the current EDWAA system (Peter T. Kilborn, "Innovative program in California aids those with outdated skills," the *New York Times*, November 27, 1992).

39. See "Program information packet for defense technology conversion, reinvestment, and transition assistance," Technology Reinvestment Project, ARPA, Department of Defense (March 10, 1993).

6

FRED ROSE

Organizing for Conversion: Peace and Labor Coalitions

In an era of both disarmament and poor economic performance, the concerns that have historically motivated the peace and labor movements have become the central issues of the day. How can we reorganize the economy to advance social goals rather than relying on military production to drive development? How do we shift from a military- to a civilian-oriented economy while maintaining stable employment at a living wage? National, state, and local policy makers are now grappling with these questions—questions that have long absorbed conversion activists.

A political struggle is under way to determine how our society will be restructured after the Cold War. Who will pay the costs or reap the benefits of this transformation? Conversion could serve the interests of the military-industrial complex through weapons exports and dual-use technologies that preserve the industrial capacity to produce weapons. These policies now being pursued by military-oriented firms and federal policy makers may save some jobs within the current organization of production, to the detriment of peace.[1] Other conversion strategies, such as community or corporate diversification, the downsizing of military corporations, and the transference of federal spending to social programs, advance the goal of peace, but frequently fail to replace good union jobs being lost in defense plants.[2]

The outcome of the conversion debate depends upon the coalitions that form around specific policies. If the peace movement cooperates with the business community or economic development agencies without labor, then conversion is likely to happen at the expense of jobs. If the labor movement and business cooperate alone, then peace will likely be the casualty. The goals of jobs and peace will only be achieved if the peace and labor movements are able to unite behind a common agenda.

At stake in this political struggle is the very meaning of conversion. The Pentagon defines conversion in terms of community adjustment, accepting that large numbers of workers from defense plants will be displaced. Many corporations similarly neglect job creation when they define conversion as downsizing or corporate diversification. Peace movement attention to cutting the military budget and shifting to social spending can fail to address immediate job dislocations. The struggle to build a peace and labor alliance is also a struggle to define conversion as a transfer of federal resources that preserves quality jobs.

The obvious need for a peace and labor coalition is to create a larger political constituency for change.[3] The peace and labor movements represent too small a proportion of the population to effect change in isolation. The membership of peace organizations peaked in the mid-1980s at about 10 million, or around 5.5 percent of the population over the age of sixteen.[4] Although the movement has become less active since that time, this serves as a reasonable estimate of the population of potential activists. Organized labor represented about 16 percent of the work force in 1991, with 16.6 million members. It is, of course, true that support for these movements exceeds the number of active members. Polls show that something on the order of one-third of the population tends to agree with fundamental positions of each movement, with considerable variation depending on the issue and the time. About one-third of the population consistently opposed the Gulf War, similar to the numbers who opposed military means to contain communism in the mid-1980s.[5] About one-third of the public also supported a ban on permanent replacement of strikers in 1992, and about one-third is predisposed to be sympathetic to labor over management in disputes.[6]

There is certainly overlap among the supporters of the peace and labor movements, which makes it difficult to estimate the potential size of a peace and labor coalition. The above figures demonstrate that neither movement alone represents a majority. Each needs to find allies if it is to achieve its goals. Because the peace and labor movements do draw their members largely from different socioeconomic communities, there is some reason to believe that these numbers may represent substantially different populations.

As important as the political calculus, but far less appreciated, is the role of coalitions for developing an inclusive political agenda. Single-issue movements pursue goals that appeal to a limited segment of society. Social movements in general tend to limit their attention to a few well-defined issues and are frequently unaware of the concerns of other movements or the negative consequences of their programs for other goals. In this, they reflect the organization of interest politics in society as a whole. Interest politics channels political participation into single-issue contests. But democracy also requires processes that integrate diverse groups into a community with a shared sense of values and purposes.[7] In our society such processes are generally lacking, both inside and outside social movements.

Coalitions require organizations to reframe their issues to encompass the goals of participating groups. If the peace movement is to work with labor, it must incorporate issues of jobs and economic justice into its understanding of peace. And if the labor movement is to cooperate with peace organizations, it must incorporate the social implications of economic development and government spending into its economic goals. In successful coalitions, participants learn to broaden their perspectives, develop a more inclusive understanding of issues, and perceive the value of working with other movements. Coalitions create the potential for building a majority politics through developing an agenda worthy of broad support.

The labor and peace movements, however, generally have not coalesced in this country, despite periodic cooperation. Media images of "hard hats" beating peace protesters during the Vietnam War dramatized this conflict. During the 1970s and 1980s, peace activists confronted defense workers at plant gates as they protested preparation for war. The AFL-CIO leadership supported U.S. Cold War policies throughout the period, acting as an agent of the Central Intelligence Agency and an ardent crusader against communism.[8]

Despite this history of conflict, union opposition to official AFL-CIO Cold War policies has increased throughout the past three decades. Labor opposition to the Vietnam War visibly challenged official policy and convinced national and local unions to establish independent foreign policy positions.[9] Some segments of the peace movement advanced conversion as a means of establishing closer ties with labor. A labor and peace coalition almost passed conversion legislation during the Carter administration, and this coalition has reemerged with the end of the Cold War to continue to promote conversion planning.[10] These cooperative attempts have always included a minority of both movements. Why has the conflict between the labor and peace movements continued? How are these movements learning to converge through building coalitions around conversion?

Case Studies

As a result of field work conducted between January 1991 and May 1992, three case studies of conversion coalitions have been developed. These labor/peace "joint ventures" include: (1) the International Brotherhood of Electrical Workers (IBEW) Local 2047 (at Unisys Corporation) and Minnesota Jobs with Peace; (2) the International Association of Machinists (IAM) Local 6 and the Peace Economy Project in Maine; and (3) the Washington State Labor Council and Washington State Sane Freeze (WSSF). Each coalition has continued to evolve since the time of this research. The descriptions given here therefore represent only the status of organizing in these communities at the time the studies were performed.

Organizing is entirely context-dependent. I therefore begin with a brief introduction highlighting the unique social conditions that existed in the communities and organizations under study.

The State of Washington

A study by the Council on Economic Priorities placed Washington State third among the states in vulnerability to cuts in defense spending.[11] People in Washington still speak of the "Boeing bust" that accompanied the end of the Vietnam War. Between 1969 and 1972, Boeing reduced employment by 60,000, and 140,000 people in the region lost jobs. Reagan's military buildup brought a new boom in contracts to Washington in the 1980s. By 1987, 8 percent of Washington's civilian work force, or 160,000 jobs, was tied to defense spending. An additional 49,000 active-duty personnel live in the state.[12]

Historically, the shipbuilding and aerospace sectors have been the largest recipients of Department of Defense prime contracts in Washington. Boeing receives the lion's share, about two-thirds of the state's total. Boeing announced layoffs of 5,000 people in 1990 and 2,500 in

1991. The decline in Pentagon contracts to shipbuilders meant that by the latter year, only 2.5 percent of the state's prime contracts supported this declining industry in the state. Washington has historically been among the strongest union states in the country due to organizing in the shipyards, Boeing, and the timber industry. In the 1950s, over half the work force was organized, the highest rate nationally. By 1982, this had fallen to a third of the work force, which was still 50 percent higher than the national average.[13]

In 1990, the Washington legislature passed the first state program for economic conversion. In the wake of the collapse of the Berlin Wall, and with national attention focused on the peace dividend, the bill passed by a large majority. It allocated $200,000 for collecting information about shifts in defense spending and their effects on companies and communities; educating the public about defense cuts; and assisting firms, communities, and labor with diversification efforts.

The legislation was the culmination of a three-year campaign by Washington State Sane Freeze, with some church and labor assistance. WSSF had built some influence in the state legislature through effective campaigning in key elections. Because of this, it was able to convince the legislature in 1988 to fund a study about the state's dependence on military spending. That study documented the need for conversion planning and became the basis for arguing for a state conversion program. The state program was defeated in 1989, but then passed the next year.

WSSF sought support from labor, religious, and community organizations for its conversion efforts. It worked with sympathetic union representatives to convince the Washington State Labor Council to establish a conversion committee. The committee's mandate was later broadened to address job diversification throughout the economy. WSSF worked with the labor committee to develop a conference about conversion for the labor community. However, because of pressure from unions from the nuclear industry who opposed working with WSSF, the state labor council would not allow the peace organization to cosponsor the conversion conference. Thereafter, WSSF continued to work with some supportive labor leaders, but never achieved official support from the state labor council. Thus, individual union representatives cooperated with WSSF's legislative effort outside of any official policy or endorsement.

The State of Minnesota

Four corporations receive over 80 percent of Minnesota's defense contracts: Honeywell, Unisys, FMC, and Control Data. These big contractors are concentrated in the Minneapolis–St. Paul area, and over 95 percent of the state's defense contracts come to the cities. The defense sector in the state is concentrated in a few industries as well, particularly computers, transportation equipment, communication equipment, and nonelectrical machinery. Between 1987 and 1989, military procurement dollars in Minnesota declined $639 million or 29 percent, costing the state 29,500 jobs. The sectors most impacted by these cuts were scientific instruments, communications equipment, and electric industrial appliances. Of the 85,000 remaining defense jobs, 27,000 are at risk over the next five years.[14] All the large corporations have laid off thousands of employees over the past five years, but Unisys has been the hardest hit, cutting about 5,000 workers between 1986 and 1991. Minnesota is a moderately unionized state, ranking about fifteenth in the country. About a quarter of the work force was organized in 1982. The public sector is over twice as organized as the private in the state.[15]

IBEW Local 2047 at Unisys has been working with Minnesota Jobs with Peace since 1985 to convince the company to shift production toward civilian products that would preserve jobs at the St. Paul plant. The state AFL-CIO brought the union and peace organizations together after a new round of layoffs was announced. Activists in the union worked with Jobs with Peace to develop a list of products with market potential that could be built in the plant, using existing resources and workers. The corporation resisted all efforts to include its work force and the community in conversion planning. The conversion campaign organized pickets which drew the mayor and governor, sponsored educational events, and introduced stockholder resolutions to pressure the company. Eventually the company agreed to meet with union members, but without community representatives. At this writing, these meetings had not yet produced any tangible results. Unisys even announced it would produce one of the alternative products suggested by the union—a satellite-based remote sensing system—but at a plant in Salt Lake City, Utah, rather than in Minnesota. Through this struggle, the peace and labor organizations have built a strong alliance.

The State of Maine

About 6 percent of Maine's civilian employment and 9 percent of its total (civilian and military) employment depend directly or indirectly on the military budget.[16] Three regions of the state receive the bulk of these benefits, and these currently face major job losses. In the Bath–Brunswick region of the coast, 46 percent of jobs derive from defense contracts at Bath Iron Works (BIW) and the Brunswick Naval Air Station. Loring Air Force Base in the far north of Maine supports 17 percent of the jobs in Aroostook County. The base is slated to be closed by 1994. And York County on the southern border with New Hampshire has depended on the Portsmouth Naval Shipyard, which is laying off workers, and on the now closed Pease Air Force Base. The Council on Economic Priorities ranks Maine eighteenth among states hardest hit by military cuts.[17]

Bath Iron Works (BIW), Maine's largest private employer, provided 11,800 jobs in 1991, almost 2 percent of the state's work force. In the past, BIW built commercial as well as military ships, but by 1991 it was about 95 percent dependent on the Navy. This one company received 78 percent of the state's defense contracts in 1989. But BIW laid off 2,500 people between 1991 and mid-1992. In the next few years, it anticipates significant cuts as it competes for contracts to build a declining number of Navy ships. The 106-year-old company is owned by an investment banking firm in New York City, but is operated by local managers with family ties to the company.

Maine has historically not been a union state, ranking twenty-seventh in the country in 1982. Only 15.2 percent of the work force was organized in 1986, below the national average. The largest unionized sectors are papermaking, shipbuilding, and the public sector. Almost half the public sector is organized, while only 11 percent of the private sector is.[18]

The Peace Economy Project, an affiliate of the statewide Maine Peace Campaign, has worked with the union and management at Bath Iron Works to promote conversion planning. The project seeks to involve all stakeholders in a cooperative process of planning for conversion and sustainable development. BIW has been willing to consider conversion options and joined in public discussion of the issue. This cooperation is the result of BIW's strong ties to the community as a locally managed company and the CEO's long-time interest in the issue of peace. The machinist union at BIW, IAM Local 56, joined the discussion as well, recognizing the need to find some alternative to shrinking defense contracts. The Peace Economy Project, with labor and management representation, has facilitated the development of local and state conversion planning processes, provided political support for conversion legislation, served as a conduit for information and networking, and sponsored educational programs about conversion. It has also prodded BIW to plan for conversion.

Cooperation and Conflict between the Peace and Labor Movements

In each of these cases, peace and labor organizations experience significant tensions even as they cooperate. Tensions follow familiar patterns around organizing styles, issues, and political interpretations. The following examples from these cases underline some of the differences between labor and peace organizations.

Unions generally perceive conversion as a strategy to save jobs. Farsighted labor leaders, such as former IAM International President William Winpisinger, have long recognized that greater and more stable employment would result from spending for social programs rather than for the military. However, conversion has only gained wide support within the labor movement with the end of the Cold War and the realization of long-term cuts in defense spending. One defense worker captured worker motivations, describing her experience in this way:

> I was working at the shop and saw people go out the door who I had worked with for fifteen years. We raised our kids together, we became grandmas together. So it was very personal, and you know you're going to fight for your family. At the time [I had no idea who the peace organization was] and I didn't care, when they're laying off hundreds and hundreds of my co-workers. We were willing to try anything to save our jobs.[19]

This contrasts with the peace movement's goals for conversion, which usually relate to disentangling people from dependence on the military economy. In the words of Lloyd Dumas,

Those who advocate conversion are perhaps driven by one or both of two differing, though certainly compatible visions: that of an economic system unburdened of the debilitating effects of excessive military spending . . . and that of a world turned away from an obsession with the means of self destruction and coercion. . . . Conversion is a practical political strategy. Advanced planning for conversion should reassure those whose livelihood currently depends on continued funding of military projects that the curtailment or elimination of these activities will not cost them their jobs. . . . This in turn should help to free legislators who must vote on military appropriations from being held hostage to the military budget.[20]

Thus, conversion for the peace movement is part of a larger strategy for shifting federal spending priorities and advancing peace.

Peace and labor organizations frequently differ in the magnitude of change they seek, which reflects their distinct goals. Peace activists are more likely to view conversion as a means to increase local control over economic development and corporate decision making, as captured in the following statement:

I'm talking about a basic shift of power. I think that at this point we cannot let go [of the fact] that we're not just talking about shifting product lines. To me it would not be a success for us to convert a plant away from making weapons to making electric tooth brushes. There's got to be an environmental component and a community component and a workers component. What we're talking about is challenging the way in which production decisions are made. That means that there [needs to be] an element in the decision making that involves the workers.[21]

By contrast, many union activists for conversion have far more modest and immediate goals. They seek to influence companies to preserve jobs, as this defense worker says:

We're not asking [the company] for us to tell them what to make. . . . All we're saying is "Look at us. We have intelligence; we have ideas. We're a highly skilled work force. Use it, use it to make more money for the company. Because if you make more money, we get a job." That's what it boils down to in a nutshell. [We don't even care to be] part of the process - just take the ideas. Accept them and let us help. We just want to cooperate. You would get so much more done if you had the president of the union, the head of labor relations and the head of defense standing in the cafeteria together. It would cut out all the adversarial words and thoughts and everything else. Sure, at contract time you can attend to your own business. You can't get out of that. But to me, this isn't a union/company thing. This is people trying to help the company.[22]

Unions and peace organizations part ways over organizing styles as well as goals. Unions bring their sense of urgency, highly structured organizations, and emphasis on immediate accomplishment. Peace organizations pay far greater attention to envisioning ultimate goals, group process, and broad education of the community and themselves. These differences are captured in the following contrast between a labor activist's experience working with the peace community and a peace activist's experience working with labor. The union member expressed his frustration working with the peace organization in these terms:

These peace people don't understand that it's a war out here. The union just went through a major fight over decertification; and people who were good friends before, now won't talk to each other. It split fathers and sons. The contrast between giving people hell at a bar over the union vote and then going to a peace organization meeting where people sit around and eat cheese and sip herb tea is really frustrating. Those people seem like they're from a different solar system. I'd love to get three or four of them down here to spend six months in this office and then see what they think. Peace people are too intellectual and always want to work on the structure of the organization. The company could be closed by the time they get the structure together. The union is used to getting down to work and getting things done. We wouldn't talk to the governor more than once. If he wasn't listening the first time, then he'd read about it in the paper next day. This is a war, and you can't be nice about it. We face 350 new people out of work and we need to tell them something. We have a sense of urgency about it that I don't get from the peace people.[23]

Peace activists have a very different experience of unions when they seek to work together. As one activist explained:

You've got to kiss the ring, that's my short hand for paying deference. If I thought it was something especially made up for me personally, I might take it differently. It comes out of a different generation, a different educational experience. They had to fight a kind of fight where those kinds of things mattered, and it's understandable. Labor for the most part belongs to a very formal structure [and] organization in which they do kiss each others' rings and it does matter who does what first and who calls whom first and that you go through the proper channels. We're kind of flying by the seat of our pants, a lot of us [peace activists]. We're not used to doing that. There's all these things that are very different, enough to make people edgy. So they go to the mechanisms that they're used to working with, for the formal structure.

Why Conflict?

Coalitions between labor and peace organizations must bridge these different goals, perceptions of issues, and styles of organizing. Social-class differences are at the heart of the labor and peace controversy, while historical experiences of conflict also perpetuate the sense that the other movement is not an ally. Members of each movement will remain skeptical about cooperation until they have contrary experiences. The history of conflict adds to the cultural and structural barriers discussed here.

The divisions between the peace and labor movements fundamentally derive from social class. The peace movement is an expression of middle-class society and culture, particularly the professional middle class that makes up its activist core.[24] The labor movement, by contrast, generally reflects working-class politics, although there is considerable variation in the class background of different unions. The unions included in this study are blue-collar, skilled craft unions whose members fall squarely within the working class.

Members of the working and middle classes perceive politics and social action differently as a result of their class-based cultures. Class cultures derive from the structural characteristics of each class as a result of its position in the production process. The working and middle classes differ in terms of the kinds of work they perform, the way work is regulated, and the nature of the skills required.

Working-class jobs generally involve manual labor, and these tasks are amenable to managerial and technical control. Processes that manipulate material objects are accessible to machines that substitute for human labor. These can further be subdivided into standard tasks along Taylorist lines, which replace the skill of the worker with managerial control. The experience of very circumscribed control over time, physical movement, the pace of work, and the work environment defines working-class life on the job. One observer describes this experience in these terms:

> Indeed, the very evidence of his daily work life brings home to the manual worker the degree to which he is directed in his behavior with only limited free choice available. From the moment of starting work by punching a time clock, through work routines that are established at fixed times, until the day ends at the same mechanical time recorder, there is impressed upon the industrial worker his narrow niche in a complex and ordered system of interdependency . . . a system over which he, as an individual, exercises little direct control.[25]

In other words, working-class work is highly regulated by external authority. Supervisors and employers enforce compliance through a well-established system of rewards and punishments. For the working class, outsiders define the goals and rules by which they work. When the work is unionized, workers contribute to defining the rules, but the form of regulation remains the same. When, what, and how work will be done are established, and the employee must conform or suffer well-defined consequences.

In an externally regulated society, individuals remain separate from authority and conform only when forced by the threat of punishment or the promise of rewards. Individuals often seek to escape the rules, to "get away" with whatever is possible, to locate those places and situations that authority has not yet controlled. In such a system, the individual stands outside of authority and is at war with it. Paul Willis describes this working-class reality in his seminal analysis of work culture as it develops among schoolboys:

> Opposition to school is principally manifested in the struggle to win symbolic and physical space from the institution and its rules and to defeat its main perceived purpose: to make you work.[26]

Middle-class jobs are generally distinguished from working-class jobs in that they involve some aspect of knowledge or mental work that is not so readily accessible to machines or subdivision of the work process. This is particularly true of the professional middle class. The definition of "profession" has long emphasized special training and control over knowledge and work.[27] Middle-class work requires some level of analysis and interpretation of individual situations that cannot be standardized into mechanical processes alone. Such knowledge and thinking cannot be regulated as mechanical tasks are, and are thus less accessible to managerial control. As a result, middle-class work processes inherently involve greater independence.

Whereas working-class work is regulated externally, middle-class work is regulated internally. Mental work cannot be accomplished on a set schedule or supervised from the outside. Instead, the worker must internalize the motivation and ambition to achieve. Individuals accomplish tasks and conform to rules based on personally accepted ideas about right and wrong as well as desires about how others will perceive them. Outsiders are rarely called upon to impose order explicitly, but individuals regulate themselves. Work hours are often flexible, and employers generally trust their employees to devote the prescribed time to their work. The emphasis at work is on completing tasks in the best way possible, and individuals have significant freedom in organizing their own time. Individuals are also usually trusted to use their own judgments about needing to leave work for personal or health reasons.

Lawyers, doctors, and university professors are examples of internal regulation. Individuals retain considerable autonomy over their daily routines and the organization of their work. Standards for accomplishment are set by peers based on commonly accepted norms. Employers cannot judge the expertise of their professionals except through the advice of other experts. Tasks cannot be supervised or rewarded or punished in isolation, but only results can be judged over a period of time. Therefore, regulation shifts from daily routines, which are the focus of working-class regulation, to results, with significant middle-class control over the process through which goals are accomplished.

Of course, neither working- nor middle-class society is a pure type. Both utilize internal and external forms of regulation to some degree, as with any society. In the United States there are forms of external authority that everyone confronts, such as the police, courts, or the Internal Revenue Service. While these impose rewards and punishments on all, they do tend to discriminate by class as well as by race, gender, and other social groupings. Less powerful groups are subject to greater levels of explicit force. Furthermore, society as a whole teaches all members to conform to values to some degree. However, comparatively speaking, middle-class life is far more regulated by internalized morals while working-class life is maintained through external rewards and punishments.

Class-Based Models of Organizing

Class-based experiences of social regulation produce characteristic beliefs about human motivations, politics, and social change. Working- and middle-class movements advance distinct forms of organizing as a direct outgrowth of different class positions and cultures. Working-class movements tend to approach organizing as a process of interest mobilization, as a consequence of their experience of external regulation. Middle-class movements generally perceive change as a process of education about values and raising consciousness, as a consequence of their experience of internalized norms, ambitions, and responsibilities. These differences, as well as their relationships to forms of social regulation, are examined below.

In a society regulated by external authority, individuals experience their wants and needs as interests that are opposed by the power of outside groups.[28] External authority produces a clear sense of individual and group interests vis-à-vis those in authority. In this power struggle, interests are met through winning against the interests of others. One union organizer likens this to nature where, "The stronger always defeats the weaker, like the U.S. outstretching the USSR and winning the Cold War."

For example, the goals of the International Brotherhood of Electrical Workers (IBEW) illustrate the focus on immediate gains to be won through conflict with management. Their goals include:

- To promote reasonable methods of work;
- To settle all disputes between employers and employees by arbitration (if possible);
- To secure employment;
- To reduce the hours of daily labor;
- To secure adequate pay for our work;
- To seek a higher and higher standard of living;
- To seek security for the individual.[29]

The community organizing tradition, which developed from organizing in working-class neighborhoods, also explicitly focuses on interests. The Midwest Academy, training institute for the Citizen Action network of community organizations, states that "The first principle of direct action organizing is that it aims to win real and immediate improvements in people's lives."[30] An organizer's first task is to identify local interests. One organizer explains, "The wider and deeper the appeal of the issue, the better. Listen for issues people feel strongly about, things that make them angry. . . . The organizer's job is to ensure that the issue has pragmatism as well as common self-interest."[31]

In working-class organizing, other groups are also assumed to be motivated by self-interest. The organization's goal is to unite sufficient numbers of people with common interests against these others. As a result, working-class organizations place considerable priority on discerning friends and foes as part of a calculation of relative power. As one organizer describes, "Now, we all know there are only two parties: there are the bosses and there are workers, and when workers unite they have a union and there are still two parties—there are bosses and there are workers who are now united."[32]

Working-class organizing is a strategic contest, in which movements strive to build the force of numbers acting collectively to outweigh the resources and institutional power controlled by corporations or government. As the Midwest Academy's organizing manual explains, "The second principle of direct action organizing is that it gives people a sense of their own real power. . . . The third principle . . . is that it attempts to alter the relations of power between people's organizations and their real enemies."[33] The overall goal is to build the organization in order to be able to challenge the power of management or other forces successfully.

Education plays an important role in working-class organizing by contributing to the success of interest organizing. Union organizers seek to educate potential members about the role of the union in advancing their interests. Another educational agenda is to raise members' awareness about their own interests, be they safety and health, bargaining issues, or union rights. Other organizers promote education as a way to build a sense of ownership of the union, to learn "that the union is not an outside third party but that they themselves are the union. . . . This education simply means that during the campaign most workers realize that their risks are worth it because they are meeting their own needs by developing their own vehicle to meet those needs."[34] In all these cases, education is dedicated to informing people about their interests and the role of the union in advancing these.

In contrast with interest organizing, the professional middle class, which is governed by internal forms of regulation, experiences the barriers to change as the values, norms, and sense of responsibility of others. Professionals are the primary locus of expertise in society, and their source of influence is through ideas. They are generally poorly organized to assert direct forms of political power, but seek to persuade others through education and communication. Organizing, then, becomes a process of education about values, raising awareness about issues, and developing new attitudes about life-styles and social relationships.[35] One peace activist summarized this approach: "Wherever the culture in society becomes prepared to handle change, then you have success. Real social change begins with education; you need to change how people think first before you can change how they act. Education is the key."[36] Or, as Maine's Peace Economy Project, renamed the Economic Conversion Project, explained in its 1991 report,

> We are reminded of the difficulties and importance of our task—of shifting from old, militaristic ways of thinking and acting to new ways founded on redefining security to encompass environmental health, social well-being, the development of an economy that is equitable and sustainable over the long-term and commitment to resolve political crises through diplomacy rather than violence.

John Lofland et al. have identified six approaches to social change within the peace movement that all have this same basic structure of value- or education-driven change. The first, "transcender theory," proposes that a rapid shift in consciousness will result from exposing people to the real nature of problems. "Educator theory" says that people exposed to new ideas and information gradually come to alter their own ways of thinking. The third group of "intellectuals" see themselves as reorganizing and developing the ideas that others will use to educate for change. Those who adhere to "politician theory" seek to build credibility for realistic policies through a rational dialogue with the public and Congress. "Protest theory" says that ideas are not sufficient to attract people's attention and move them to think, but through noncooperation and protest, it is possible to force others to confront one's ideas and shift their ways of thinking. The final approach is "prophet theory," which strives through morally right acts to provide an example to others in order to alter their thoughts and actions.[37]

Many activists in middle-class movements participate in traditional interest politics. Lofland and his colleagues estimate that the peace movement around 1980 was about evenly divided between the practically minded "politician" activists and the rest of the movement that lacked a focused political presence.[38] These two groups clashed over such questions as the priority of means versus ends, the limitations of legislative politics, and the appropriate role for the peace movement. The "politicians" promoted education to develop a vocal public that can convince legislators that if they do not vote properly, they will be defeated at the polls. The alternative approach promotes new types of awareness, from the spiritual side of visualizing world peace, to the more materialist goal of changing life-styles. Within this spectrum, greater attention is paid to pragmatic interest politics among legislatively and electorally oriented peace organizations. For these organizations, the educational agenda is not sufficient in itself, but is channeled into specific political actions to pass legislation. Yet, even the pragmatic wing of the movement continues to emphasize the central role of education.

As a result, middle-class movements explain their positions in the language of strong moral arguments, and never in terms of advancing the interests of a particular group. Indeed, one of the defining features of these movements is that they advance universal goals and not the explicit interests of their class.[39]

Lest educational organizing sound naive, it is worth noting that middle-class movements have effected enormous social change in the past thirty years based on this approach of consciousness raising. In an assessment of the accomplishments of the 1960s' movements, Maurice Isserman and Michael Kazin observe, "The movements and events of the 1960s generated an attitudinal penumbra that glimmered long after the Students for a Democratic Society (SDS) and the Student Nonviolent Coordinating Committee (SNCC) had been eclipsed."[40] They list the legacy of the New Left as changed perceptions of race and gender, a new critical attitude about foreign intervention, altered language of politics that is more antiestablishment and populist, and an ongoing influence on intellectual life and the media. The ending of the Vietnam War, the development of opposition to Reagan's military buildup, rising environmental consciousness, and increased acceptance of equality for women are primary examples of changes in values and consciousness based on the broad educational and cultural work of middle-class movements.

In analyzing working-class interest organizing and middle-class value and education organizing, I do not mean to suggest that working-class people are motivated solely by interests while middle-class people act only on values or beliefs. All social groups are motivated by interests, beliefs, and values. However, the labor movement and working class themselves tend to frame their organizing in the language and logic of interests. Middle-class organizations tend to conceive of their organizing in the language and framework of values and consciousness. These class-based self-perceptions and ideas are incomplete. Working-class movements tend to be unaware of the values and beliefs that underlie their stated interests, whereas middle-class movements tend to underplay the interests that shape their values. Nevertheless, the language of interests versus values distinguishes working- from middle-class culture.

Working- and middle-class social movements pursue conflicting goals as a result of their cultural biases expressed within the present organization of society. Working-class movements seek to fulfill immediate needs in an economic system that functions without reference to values. In a market economy, social goals such as efficiency and wealth are supposed to result from pursuit of individual self-interest. Thus, as labor pursues economic goals, it is systematically guided away from other social values by the economic system in which it functions.

Middle-class movements, by contrast, generally promote changes in social values without reference to economic interests. They function in political and social spheres that are supposed to serve the common good and not advance individual interests. Decisions about such matters as war and peace advance noneconomic goals, and their economic consequences are frequently not recognized. Therefore, movements devoted to such issues are systematically channeled away from addressing economics. In sum, the divisions between the labor and peace movements emerge from class-cultural ways of perceiving goals within a society that systematically divides economics from social values.

Cross-Class Coalitions

If single-class movements are limited by their class-based forms of organizing, then coalitions between working- and middle-class movements have the potential to transcend these divisions. Coalitions between labor and the peace movement must develop hybrid forms of organizing that build on the strengths of both the interest and the education approaches to social change. Labor organizing teaches the value of mobilizing around people's immediate perceived needs and interests. By uniting people who share common interests, powerless groups can counter the explicit use of force by elites. Middle-class organizing, on the other hand, provides important lessons about the role of consciousness in shaping perceptions of interests and therefore in shaping behavior. Through largely educational campaigns to alter popular understandings, people begin to redefine their interests and to act differently. In order to reconcile the perceptions of working- and middle-class activists about social change, coalitions must apply the insights of both approaches to organizing.

What is needed is a model of organizing that not only responds to people's immediate needs and interests, but also educates about an alternative society. The conversion movement addresses this intersection between the values advanced by the peace movement and the needs of working people dependent on the military economy. Peace and labor coalitions working for conversion must be sophisticated enough to recognize the interests at stake by all parties in the conversion debate and to build political power for change. But they must add to this a process for introducing new values into interest organizing.

The conversion coalitions in Washington, Maine, and Minnesota represent three distinct approaches to combining interest and education organizing. The first, from Washington, utilizes interest organizing techniques to educate the community about conversion. The second, from Maine, seeks to alter perceptions of interest first as a foundation for economic organizing. The third, the "Minnesota model," pursues interest organizing and education simultaneously but independently, as complementary political processes. None of these are fully developed or conscious "models" of organizing. Rather, they are practical strategic compromises emerging from the process of coalition building.

The case of Washington State Sane Freeze (WSSF) is the best-articulated hybrid model because of the explicit efforts of the former director to apply community organizing within the peace movement. In his words,

> Coming from an Alinsky organization like I did, [my] goal was to build political power by finding common denominator issues. Part of the goal of these organizations is to find those common self interests. . . . My

theory in coming to WSSF was to see if you could take the low income tactics and put [them] in a white, middle-class organization.[41]

WSSF developed a conversion strategy applying interest-based organizing techniques. Labor's interests were straightforward: to keep jobs. The peace organization, on the other hand, sought to alter national policy. Since this is a collective and not an individual goal, it required altering voting behavior. WSSF perceived its interests as a peace organization as creating the will to cut military spending. Conversion provided a program that could advance the interests of both labor and the peace movement. It would free workers to support military budget cuts by providing them with economic alternatives. In this view, the interests of labor and the peace movement in planning to adjust to military budget cuts were different but complementary.

This interest organizing approach was modified over time. The campaign began promoting a direct confrontation with the Boeing Corporation based on a community organizing model. But the unions would not participate in such a campaign, and some in WSSF doubted it could succeed. Instead, they advanced a legislative strategy that could mobilize a broad constituency for conversion. But the purpose of legislation was not to build a more powerful organization that could directly achieve the interests of its members, as interest organizing would imply; the results were intended to be broadly educational. The purpose of the legislation was to convince the state government and the public that conversion is a viable economic alternative. This would hopefully limit attempts to resist federal budget cuts and convince decision makers to assist defense companies to convert.

In sum, what evolved in the Washington case was an organizing strategy that used people's perceived immediate interests as a basis for an educational campaign that would change perceptions of alternatives. Sane Freeze appealed to unions and the peace community with the argument that conversion planning is necessary to renew jobs that are already slated to be cut from the defense sector. These groups supported the campaign because of their currently perceived interests. But community organizing techniques became a means for achieving educational ends—namely, to alter broad perceptions about economic priorities and interests.

In Maine, we see something of the opposite process from Washington. Where WSSF organized around specific interests of some groups in society against others as the basis for broad education about goals, the Peace Economy Project has sought to alter public perceptions of interests first, as the basis for further organizing. Here, the principal organizer began with a peace movement background rather than a community organizing history.

The Peace Economy Project's strategy has been to build a consensus among the various stakeholders in the community. This has meant focusing attention on the benefits of shifting national and local resources to meet social needs. This may challenge the present interests of defense contractors and their unions, and the community could also resist these changes as threatening to the state's economy. Thus, the educational task is first to reorient these groups toward the long-term benefits of deep cuts in the defense budget, which meant shifting their sense of self-interest. Based on this thinking, the project initiated a series of studies to document the negative community impacts of military spending and the positive benefits that would flow from redirecting those resources. All this was geared toward "educating the public and policy makers on the need and possibilities of economic conversion," and "raising the public comfort level" about economic shifts.

As the project began to work with management and labor, it was forced to address the specifics of industrial change and job renewal. Participants in the project from Bath Iron Works and the machinist union demanded this kind of practical detail, and challenged the project to be concrete about its proposals. The project's main response has been to facilitate community planning processes. It also has been working toward an inventory of worker skills and spurred the creation of a state task force to assist with the economic transition. Thus, once a broad community agreed that they shared an interest in economic diversification, then the project could organize around this collective economic interest.

Jobs with Peace in Minnesota has effectively divided its interest-based and educational organizing into two separate, complementary agendas. The organization has participated in many of the typical educational efforts of the peace movement, but it has also assisted with one of the most extensive interest-based organizing campaigns around conversion. Jobs with Peace's principal organizer had experience with both the peace movement and the organizing of disenfranchised groups around self-interests. The organizing in Minnesota reflects this mix of both peace and labor approaches to change.

Educational and interest organizing in Minnesota were mutually re-inforcing. Interest organizing at Unisys provided the demand for change from the company. Political leaders from the mayor to the governor felt compelled to echo this demand. The educational work was designed to make the broader policy case for conversion assis-tance from the government. It sought to convince the public that changes in federal spending are desirable, and that the community should require and assist conversion efforts such as that proposed by the workers at Unisys. The Unisys organizing proved invaluable in this education campaign. It dramatically illustrated the need for public ac-tion for conversion by demonstrating the lack of cooperation from management with the reasonable and creative efforts of citizens. This publicly demonstrated the nature of the problem and justified the organization's call for mandatory corporate planning. IBEW's efforts also provided a context for reaching union members with information about conversion that they would not otherwise have seen. On the other hand, the educational work of Jobs with Peace supported the organizing campaign at Unisys by raising the level of awareness and public pressure for response. This dual effort defined the issue in terms of the long-term benefits of military cuts, where the community and corporations have responsibility for replacing jobs lost in the transi-tion.

We see here, then, three models that blend interest and value organ-izing in different ways. The Washington model proposes that organiz-ing around specific, immediate interests can provide the means for education to change public awareness. The Maine model proposes that a shared definition of the common good can unite a community suffi-ciently to redefine interests. The Minnesota model suggests that sepa-rate pursuit of interest-based organizing can complement educational efforts to produce changes that achieve the goals of both.

Social Conditions and Coalition Forms

The forms taken by peace and labor coalitions differ in each case because of unique social, economic, historical, and organizational con-ditions. Maine, Minnesota, and Washington each present different en-vironments for organizing, as do the aerospace, shipbuilding, and electronics sectors. Some of these factors are beyond the control of organizers. Others are created by the conscious strategies of social actors. In each case, external conditions and social and cultural factors contribute to the outcome of coalition organizing.

Cultural, historical, and economic conditions combine to produce a collaborative approach to organizing in Maine. Maine is unique in that the bulk of military dollars flow to one company that is also the largest private as well as industrial employer in a small state. Just because of its sheer size, state and local governments have inevitably tried to assist BIW. Furthermore, the company's management has strong ties to Maine and retains administrative control over the company despite ownership by an outside investment firm. These decision makers are also invested in ensuring the viability of the local company. These factors combine to form a strong common interest within the community, union, company, and government in planning for BIW's long-term commercial redevelopment.

The configuration of the social movement sector in Maine also contributes to coalition building. Maine is characterized by a historically limited labor movement, but a much stronger environmental movement that overlaps considerably with the peace movement. Faced with bitter strikes in timber and shipbuilding in the 1980s, and with only 15 percent of the work force unionized in 1986, the labor movement had to work in coalition if it was to influence state politics. The environmental movement, however, has been relatively strong in this "vacationland." Maine experienced an enormous growth boom in the 1980s, and polls have found a shift in public emphasis from jobs to environmental preservation. By 1989, given a choice between industrial development and environmental protection, almost two-thirds of the population would preserve the environment.[42]

Many people attribute the willingness of Bath Iron Works and its union to participate at least nominally in conversion planning to a general cultural norm of community responsibility. They argue that companies in Maine must at least publicly state their concern for the well-being of the community and its workers. This is evident when corporate chief executive officer (CEO) Duane "Buzz" Fitzgerald states, "I have a duty to be candid, forthright; and to say that we can protect 11,600 jobs, or that we will succeed in doing so, would be misleading. But I am not misleading people when I say that that is our commitment. We think about it every day."[43]

These circumstances contrast greatly with Minnesota, where confrontational strategies are pursued for both cultural and situational reasons. Minnesota and Maine illustrate the poles of a debate about strategy. Economic and political conditions partly account for this difference. In Minnesota, the conversion issue has become polarized, with management clearly opposed to any union or community participation in new product development or investment decisions. In Maine, the company, union, and community are publicly cooperating. The most important difference is that Unisys is a large, multinational corporation whose decisions are made outside of the local facility, without any clear commitment to the local work force. Then, too, BIW is Maine's largest industrial employer and thus a significant statewide concern. Unisys is a significant employer in St. Paul, but only one of numerous similar companies. Beyond this, top management at Unisys has not shown anything like the personal interest in conversion of top management at BIW.

The contrast between the Unisys and BIW conversion efforts also reflects differing philosophies of organizing. Many of the organizers in Minnesota believe in the need to build power in order to force management to act in the interests of workers and the community. This in part reflects the political situation in Minnesota, but class background and beliefs about organizing are critical as well. Labor's lead in the coalition shaped this strategy. As one labor leader explained,

> I believe that had we been more confrontational and polarized, we would have been more effective. The fight is to be treated as an equal. You do these things so the company can't ignore you. Start with as much confrontation as you can and then come to the table and work out cooperation as an equal. We need to be more confrontational, not less.[44]

The Unisys management in Minnesota had no inclination to allow others to participate in its decision-making process. The alliance between the peace activists and the union served to polarize the issue further. The union's goal in the conversion debate has been to save jobs in St. Paul by somehow convincing management to commit itself to new products that could be produced locally. The goal of Jobs with Peace has been to support the union effort, but also explicitly to alter the distribution of power by forcing the company to include its workers and the community in decision making. These two different goals converged because Unisys's plans have not included saving jobs at its St. Paul plant. Any effort to save these jobs involved challenging the corporation's decision-making process. The company is clearly concerned with protecting its investment decision-making prerogatives, and the peace and community groups are far more explicitly interested in challenging these than is the union. Therefore, the alliance between labor and the peace community was far more threatening to management, who consistently refused even to speak with the community organizations. If the company had been willing to cooperate with its work force, the issue could have cleaved differently, and if so, the union and peace agendas might well have diverged. Thus, the coalition is a result of economic conditions, the strategy taken by Unisys management, and the distinct goals and values of labor, peace, and other activists. It also reflects the philosophy of organizing within Jobs with Peace and the labor community.

The Washington case differs from these two in several important ways. First, the shipbuilding industry in Washington, which was hardest hit in the defense sector at the time of this study, is far less significant in that state's economy than is shipbuilding in Maine or electronics in Minnesota. Washington shipbuilding is dwarfed by the aerospace industry, which had a strong commercial market when the coalition efforts described here developed.

Peace movement cooperation with the Washington State Labor Council was complicated by several factors. Since the labor movement has been strong in the state, it has had less of a need to build alliances than in Maine or Minnesota. Also, the labor movement is divided between several very different economic regions of the state, with distinct relationships to the defense builddown and the economy. The metropolitan region around Puget Sound is dominated by Boeing and has been the center of an enormous development boom in the past decade. The economy of much of the remainder of the west side of the Cascade Mountains depends on the timber industry. This sector has been in a depression despite the urban boom. The area east of the Cascades is largely agricultural except for population centers around the Hanford reservation and Spokane. Eastern Washington unions around Hanford are highly dependent on federal government support through the Department of Energy, making them far more conservative about nuclear weapons and power issues. These divisions are dramatically felt in the Washington State Labor Council, which could not agree on cooperating with the peace movement as the state organizations in Minnesota and Maine did.

Conclusion

The end of the Cold War has fundamentally altered the economic and political system that prevailed in the United States for four decades. An enormous government bureaucracy, corporations, industries, workers, and communities that depended on defense spending, as well as those the military passed by, are now vying to influence the direction of the post–Cold War economy. The form conversion will take and the interests it will serve depend upon the political coalitions that consolidate around particular definitions of the present transition. Conversion of the military economy will only advance both disarmament and the economic security of working people if the labor and peace movements coalesce around a common political agenda.

A labor and peace coalition requires that these movements transcend deep-seated class differences. Working- and middle-class positions in the production process result in divergent experiences of social order and, therefore, of social change. Working-class movements advancing immediate economic needs through interest organizing often find their programs in conflict with middle-class movements pursuing social values through educational means.

The conflict between working- and middle-class movements, however, is not inevitable but is the result of how each class expresses its goals within a society that divides interests from values. Neither movement seeks to advance its goals at the expense of the other. Both seek to protect the fundamental rights of individuals from exploitation, be it economic or military. The challenge for working- and middle-class coalitions is to advance a value-based economy in a society that divides moral and political goals, such as peace, from the mechanisms of the economy.

Peace and labor coalitions can combine the insights of both economic-interest and value-based organizing. Working-class interest organizing and middle-class education organizing each address critical dimensions of the social-change process, and yet alone they fail to respond to the complexity of human motivations or social dynamics. Coalitions are forced to develop a more inclusive approach to organizing for change. Middle-class activists learn to address economic needs and the immediate interests of working people, while working-class participants learn to link their daily struggles to national issues and social values.

Coalition building is a social process, and the forms that coalitions take are highly context-specific. Experimentation and struggle are inevitable as organizations discover the practices and goals that can bring them together. The final form of these coalitions depends upon many factors. The political and social context shapes the opportunities for cooperation. For example, conversion coalitions take different forms when confronting large, multinational firms versus local contractors, when participating organizations are strong or weak, and when pending cuts are large or small relative to the local economy. Organizational characteristics play a critical role as well—characteristics such as the degree of unity within organizations, other organizational priorities, and the history of past conflict and cooperation. Finally, strategies and organizing philosophies determine the form of coalitions. Organizers who pursue cooperation will create different kinds of coalitions than those who advance conflict as a means for change. Coalitions in Maine, Minnesota, and Washington have taken different forms as a result of the unique circumstances in each location.

A peace and labor coalition has the potential to build a political majority for both jobs and peace. Each movement needs the other to attain sufficient political muscle. Moreover, each movement needs the other to expand its political agenda to achieve a more inclusive movement for change. The end of the Cold War provides the best opportunity for a working- and middle-class alliance in a generation. The real potential for conversion to a peaceful, just economy at the present time lies in the ability to use this opportunity to build a labor–peace alliance.

Notes

1. For example see Paul Quigley, "Arms exports: The stop-gap alternative to Pentagon contracts?" in Lloyd Dumas and Marek Thee (eds.), *Making Peace Possible* (New York: Pergamon Press, 1989).

2. For example, see Judith Reppy, "Defense industries in the U.S. and Europe: Shrinking, not converting," paper prepared for meeting of the International Studies Association, March 26, 1993.

3. Current theories emphasize the role of coalitions as a tool for building political power. Social-psychological and game-theoretic approaches to coalitions assume that participants are rational actors maximizing self-gain based on initial conditions and calculations about outcomes. For a review of this literature, see Barbara Hinckley, *Coalitions and Politics* (New York: Harcourt Brace Jovanovich, 1981).

4. John Lofland, Mary Anna Colwell, and Victoria Johnson, "Change theo-

ries and movement structure," in Sam Morullo and John Lofland (eds.), *Peace Action in the Eighties* (New Brunswick, NJ: Rutgers University Press, 1990).

5. Relevant poll data are summarized by John Mueller, "American public opinion and the Gulf War," *Public Opinion Quarterly* (Spring 1993): 80–91, and Dennis Gilbert, *Compendium of American Public Opinion* (New York: Facts on File, 1985).

6. See Gallup poll for 1992 in George Gallup, Jr., *The Gallup Poll* (Wilmington, DE: Scholarly Resources Inc., 1993), and Gilbert, *Compendium of American Public Opinion*.

7. Democratic theorists have long observed the need for learning in democratic life. See Jean Jacques Rousseau, *On the Social Contract* (Indianapolis: Hackett Publishing, 1983); Carole Pateman, *Participation and Democratic Theory* (New York: Cambridge University Press, 1970); Hannah Pitkin, "Justice: On relating private and public," *Political Theory*, 9, 3 (August 1981): 3237–52.

8. AFL-CIO cooperation with government Cold War policies are well documented by Ronald Radosh, *American Labor and United States Foreign Policy* (New York: Random House, 1969).

9. Philip Foner, *U.S. Labor and the Viet-Nam War* (New York: International Publishers, 1989). Union opposition to Reagan Administration policies in Central America are documented by Daniel Cantor and Juliet Schor, *Tunnel Vision* (Boston: South End Press, 1987).

10. In 1979, Representatives Dodd and McKinney's conversion amendments to the public works bill died with the bill in conference committee. This was the first year that the federal government failed to pass a public works bill.

11. Council on Economic Priorities Vulnerability Index, *Research Report* (June 1990).

12. David Holland and Philip Wandshneider, "U.S. military expenditures: Their impact on the Washington economy" (March 1989), preliminary report to the Washington legislature.

13. Leo Troy and Neil Sheflin, *U.S. Union Sourcebook* (West Orange, NJ: Industrial Relations Data and Information Service, 1985).

14. Wilbur Maki, Richard Bolan, and Hossein Ashavi-Pour, "Forging a peace economy in Minnesota," Minnesota Task Force on Economic Conversion (February 1991).

15. Troy and Sheflin, *U.S. Union Sourcebook*.

16. The 6 percent figure comes from the Governor's Task Force on Defense Realignment and the Maine Economy (draft report, April 4, 1991). The 9 percent figure is from the Peace Economy Project cited in Jo Josephson, "Economic conversion: From defense to domestic spending," *Maine Townsman* (May 1991), p. 27.

17. Council on Economic Priorities, *Research Report*.

18. Troy and Sheflin, *U.S. Union Sourcebook*.

19. Interview with a defense worker and conversion activist, January 1991.

20. Lloyd Dumas, "Economic conversion: The critical link," in Dumas and Thee (eds.), *Making Peace Possible*, p. 11.

21. Interview with a peace activist, January 1991.

22. Interview with a defense worker and conversion activist, January 1991.

23. Interview with a defense worker and conversion activist, June 1991.

24. The professional middle-class constituency of the peace movement is well

documented. See Hanspeter Kreisi, "New social movements and the new class in the Netherlands," *American Journal of Sociology*, *94*, 5 (March 1989): 1078–1176; Frank Parkin, *Middle Class Radicalism* (New York: Praeger, 1968), among others.

25. Robert Dubin, "Constructive aspects of industrial conflict," in Arthur Kornhauser, Robert Dubin, and Arthur Ross (eds.), *Industrial Conflict* (New York: McGraw-Hill, 1954), p. 43.

26. Paul Willis, *Learning to Labour* (Westmead, UK: Saxon House, 1978), p. 26.

27. For an overview of definitions of "profession," see I. Waddington, "Professions," in Adam Kruper and Jessica Kruper (eds.), *The Social Science Encyclopedia* (Boston: Routledge and Kegan Paul, 1985), pp. 650–1.

28. Interests are not restricted to material goods, but include such intangibles as fairness and respect.

29. International Brotherhood of Electrical Workers (IBEW), "Tradesman contact book."

30. *Midwest Academy Organizing Manual* (Chicago: Midwest Academy, 1987), p. 10.

31. Meg Campbell, cited in Gary Delgado, *Organizing the Movement: The Roots and Growth of ACORN* (Philadelphia: Temple University Press, 1986), pp. 68–9.

32. Robert Muehlenkamp, Organizing Director of the National Union of Hospital and Health Care Workers, SEIU Local 1199, "Organizing never stops," *Labor Research Review 10*, 1 (Spring 1991): 4.

33. Midwest Academy, *Organizing Manual*, p. 10.

34. Jose La Luz, "Creating a Culture of Organizing," *Labor Research Review*, *17* (Spring 1991): 62.

35. This observation is also made by Mark Kahn in *Middle Class Radicalism in Santa Monica* (Philadelphia: Temple University Press, 1986). Also, in reference to the British Campaign for Nuclear Disarmament, see Richard Taylor and C. Pritchard, *The Protest Makers: The Nuclear Disarmament Movement of 1958–1965 Twenty Years On* (Oxford: Pergamon Press, 1980) and John Mattausche, "The sociology of CND," in Colin Creighton and Martin Shaw (eds.), *The Sociology of War and Peace* (New York: Sheridan House, 1987).

36. Interview with a Seattle peace activist, 1991.

37. Lofland, Colwell, and Johnson, "Change theories and movement structures."

38. Ibid., p. 101.

39. Claus Offe, "New social movements: Challenging the boundaries of institutional politics," *Social Research*, *52*, 4 (1985).

40. "The new radicalism," in Steve Fraser and Gary Gerstle (eds.), *The Rise and Fall of the New Deal Order* (Princeton, NJ: Princeton University Press, 1989), p. 229.

41. Interview with David Fleishman, former director of Washington State Sane Freeze, May 31, 1991.

42. Polls conducted by the *Maine Sunday Telegram*, the University of Maine, and the University of Southern Maine.

43. Cited in Pam Smith, "Swords to plowshares: Economic conversion at BIW," *Maine Progressive* (July 1990).

44. Labor organizer, Minnesota, January 1991.

Part III
Conversion and Public Policy

7

GREGORY A. BISCHAK

Building Job Bridges for Defense Industrial Conversion

Delivering on the promise of job creation through reinvesting defense savings is a major challenge for the federal administration, especially given that more is being cut from the defense budget than is being reinvested in conversion. The lion's share of defense savings continues to be used to reduce the fiscal deficit of the federal government rather than to expand civilian public investment in physical and human resources.

It is estimated that defense cuts will produce layoffs in both the public and the private sectors totaling between 1.8 million and 2 million jobs over the 1993–97 period.[1] These estimates may be conservative since the Office of Management and Budget found that many projected military spending cuts were not specific. The so-called "bottom-up" review of the U.S. defense requirements early in the Clinton administration did not really identify how actual savings would be achieved.[2] It is more than likely that procurement and research and development, as well as operations and maintenance, will be reduced more over time than has been admitted at this writing.

Meanwhile, after taking inflation into account, the balance of the Clinton administration's FY 1994 public investment package for education and training, physical capital, civilian research and development, and other human resource investments showed no net new investment. As a share of total federal outlays, these investments fell for the first time in four years.[3] Given the fiscal constraints of deficit reduction outlined in the president's budget agreement with Congress, it is doubtful whether the federal government can really increase investment in high-tech industry, civilian R&D, human resources, and infrastructure for years. Thus, it seems unlikely that civilian-oriented public investment will even partially compensate for the industrial impact of defense cuts, especially for manufacturing sectors and industrial workers in high-tech, high-skill, high-wage occupations.

Elsewhere, economic growth is being slowed by the cumulative effects of corporate restructuring and large-scale layoffs, the increased reliance on temporary workers to replace permanent workers, the migration of production overseas in both manufacturing and service sector work, the impact of global trade and technological unemployment, and the trend toward public sector downsizing. All of these factors are slowing job creation in the economy and retarding the capacity of the economy to absorb displaced defense workers.

Finally, the Clinton conversion program has been very weak on job retention efforts, let alone new job creation. This is especially true of the Defense Department's Technology Reinvestment Project (TRP), which is attempting to foster defense conversion through a dual-use strategy that is ostensibly geared to developing technologies with both military and civilian applications. As even the most ardent exponents of TRP acknowledge, the program is a long-term effort to reorient defense companies into civilian-related markets, not a short-term job creation program. Meanwhile, displaced defense workers and uniformed and nonuniformed Defense Department personnel have only been offered modest assistance through the usual job retraining and economic adjustment program.

Thus, the central challenge for the administration and the nation is to find the means by which job bridges can be built between declining defense-dependent industries and more slowly developing occupations in new and expanding civilian sectors. Six pillars will have to be built to support such job bridges.

First, public investment in civilian-oriented physical and human resources must be expanded to support near-term job creation efforts and to leverage more private investment in emerging industries and markets. To achieve such an expansionary public investment policy, however, the nation's fiscal policy debate must be recast from the current terms of deficit reduction to a debate that distinguishes between net new public *investments* (which produce a future return) and rising discretionary *expenditures* (which do not). Second, defense firms, especially large prime contractors, require some economic incentives such as an investment tax credit in order to overcome the obstacles and resistance to advance conversion planning and to promote job retention. Third, new high-tech job incubators must be supported through the creation of spin-off enterprises and startup businesses that can exploit new technological opportunities and generate jobs. Fourth, retraining programs should include income support, expanded educational loans, and relocation benefits for displaced workers of all kinds, and should be explicitly linked to public and private job creation efforts so that training leads to real employment opportunities. Fifth, an interagency coordinating and planning body is necessary to coordinate the various programs and to streamline procedures in order to speed access and assistance. And, finally, new sources of finance will be needed to bridge the gap in financing conversion and to assist in the development of innovative enterprises.

Before we examine these proposals in more detail, it is important to clarify the dimensions of the defense conversion challenge by taking a look at the employment and occupational impacts of reductions in the defense budget.

Employment and Occupational Impacts of Defense Cuts

The initial Clinton administration plan was to cut $118 billion ($107 billion in 1993 dollars) in cumulative budget authority from the multiyear defense plan established by the Bush administration in January 1992 for the FY 1994–97 period.[4] Cumulative reductions in military outlays would trim $82 billion ($74 billion in 1993 dollars) from the Bush plan over the same period. The Congressional Budget Office (CBO) has estimated that the Clinton administration's spending plan will cost $131 billion less than the force that former Defense Secretary Richard Cheney had planned to field by 1998.[5] However, as the CBO noted, $50 billion of these savings were derived from lower inflation assumptions by the Clinton administration—assumptions that have proved optimistic. Another $18 billion in savings were to come from a pay freeze on civilian Defense Department employees, but Congress undercut this assumption by giving these employees a raise. Thus, only $63 billion of these projected savings were from reductions in the military's forces and spending. However, the Department of Defense pressed for another $50 billion in Pentagon spending, with at least $30 billion due to higher inflation estimates.[6]

Under these assumptions, there was only a $43 billion to $63 billion cumulative difference between the Bush and Clinton defense spending plans for FY 1994–97. Furthermore, in order to restrain outlays in the later years of the defense plan, the Clinton administration must make relatively large cuts in budget authority, while the actual additional cuts in outlays over and above those proposed by Bush are relatively small. Thus, if all the military budget plans as of this writing are carried out, by 1997, Clinton's procurement cuts may only be $5 billion greater than those that had been scheduled by the Bush administration.

In 1992, defense industry employment stood at slightly more than 2.8 million private sector workers, 1.9 million uniformed active-duty personnel, and 940,000 nonuniformed personnel. The plan that had been put forward by the Bush administration called for over 310,000 fewer active-duty troops, nearly 36,000 fewer civilian DoD workers, and 830,000 defense industry workers.[7] Thus, the FY 1993 Bush plan implied total cumulative layoffs of about 1.2 million defense-related workers over the next five years, bringing defense industry employment down to about 2 million workers, uniformed active-duty personnel down to 1.6 million, and civilian personnel to about 904,000 by FY 1997.

The Clinton administration's defense cuts called for an additional 200,000 direct layoffs among uniformed personnel. Another 95,000 civilian DoD and DoE personnel will probably be affected by the Clinton plan. We should emphasize that these cuts are supposed to come on top of those already outlined by the 1993 Bush plan. Thus, uniformed active-duty personnel would fall to 1.4 million, while nonuniformed personnel would fall to about 809,000.

The military-industrial base will experience additional cuts, as procurement budget levels fall. One should note, however, that few programs are actually being canceled—most of the savings come from trimming around the edges of many different programs.

At this writing, details were not yet available on the composition of proposed budget reductions for the 1995–97 period, as the administration had not revealed the specific results of the so-called "bottom-up" review of defense needs conducted by the secretary of defense. Yet, it is evident that the bulk of the cuts will fall on military personnel and operations and maintenance, while procurement and research and development will be subject to relatively fewer cuts in outlays as compared with the Bush plan.[8] However, defense industry workers will probably suffer additional layoffs of about 289,000 private sector jobs, largely through reduced weapons acquisitions and some cutbacks in purchases of goods and services related to operations and maintenance. Thus, defense industrial employment levels will fall to about 1.8 million workers.

These job impacts represent the gross employment effects of both the Clinton and Bush defense cuts. They do not attempt to account for how many of these job losses will be achieved by normal attrition. Nor do they estimate the rate at which these job losses will be reabsorbed by normal economic growth and job creation. However, there are ample reasons to believe that the lackluster growth rate in the manufacturing economy in general, and the defense-dependent sectors in particular, will make reemployment in the durable goods–producing sectors especially difficult.

Employment Effects by Industry

The estimates presented in Table 7.1 represent the direct and indirect employment effects by industry attributable to the reductions in the nonpay portion of the defense budget over the 1993–97 period. These job losses represent the effects of cuts in the domestic share of defense procurement, research and development, operations and maintenance, military construction, and family housing outlays. Not surprisingly, the largest job losses take place in the military-serving durable goods sectors, such as aerospace and shipbuilding (represented by transportation equipment, excluding motor vehicles), electrical and electronic equipment, nonelectrical machinery, primary metals, fabricated metal products, instruments, and miscellaneous manufacturing. These industries alone account for over 472,000 of the total 1,119,000 jobs lost.

In addition, construction shows large losses, together with business services, miscellaneous services, and wholesale. While most of the losses in the wholesale sectors are attributable to indirect effects from interindustry sales, a large share of the reductions in construction, business services, and miscellaneous services is due to direct job losses from lower defense purchases from these industries. The job losses in other sectors are mostly due to reduced interindustry purchases, al-

Table 7.1

Private Sector Employment Impacts by Industry

Direct and indirect job losses   Job losses, 1992–97

Industry	
Agricultural, forest, etc.	6,170
Mining	8,960
New construction	46,570
Maintenance and repair	660
Food and kindred products	6,160
Textile products	4,300
Apparel	9,000
Paper and allied products	5,900
Printing and publishing	12,970
Chemicals and petrol	18,000
Rubber and leather products	11,100
Lumber and furniture	5,340
Stone, clay, and glass	5,330
Primary metals	15,300
Fabricated metal products	50,200
Machinery, except electronic	22,860
Electrical and electronic equipment	166,000
Motor vehicles	5,260
Transportation equipment	172,220
Instruments and other	20,000
Misc. manufacturing	25,700
Transportation services	63,900
Communications, except TV	22,700
Utilities	8,500
Wholesales	63,270
Retail	12,880
Finance	13,970
Insurance	9,100
Real estate	13,900
Hotels and lodging	15,900
Personal services	12,500
Business services	122,700
Eating and drinking	33,700
Health services	16,700
Misc. services	91,300
Total direct and indirect	1,119,000

Source: G. Bischak and M. Oden, *Armaments and Defense Conversion in the United States after the Cold War* (Geneva: International Labour Office, October 1993).

though the losses in the nondurable goods sectors such as apparel, food and kindred products, and chemicals and petroleum products are due to cuts in the operations and maintenance budgets. Overall, about half of the job losses are due to direct reductions, while the balance are due to indirect effects.

Industrial and Employment Forecasts

In order to provide an economic and employment baseline against which to evaluate the overall impact of these cuts within each major industry group, it is useful to examine government projections for employment growth by industry. An analysis of industrial employment forecasts published by the U.S. Bureau of Labor Statistics (BLS) in 1992 indicated that planned defense cuts would exert a considerable drag on employment growth in the defense key sectors.[9] The BLS forecast, however, is based on the assumption that defense cuts over the period will average about 1.2 percent per year, while the Clinton plan involved reductions of nearly 4 percent per year over the 1993–97 period. Hence, the much more substantial reductions of the Bush and Clinton administrations were not accounted for in the BLS industry employment forecast, making the BLS projections for defense-oriented industries more optimistic.

In addition, the BLS forecast implicitly assumes continued robust growth in the commercial aircraft industry, particularly exports, which have accounted for most of the job growth in domestic aircraft production over the last several years. However, the softening of the commercial aircraft industry worldwide, coupled with the much larger than anticipated defense cuts both domestically and internationally, have generated much greater excess capacity in the industry than reflected in the forecast for aerospace sectors.[10] Moreover, with the contraction of both commercial and defense aerospace markets, the competitive pressures have intensified in commercial aircraft markets, as firms seek more aggressively to pursue commercial opportunities. Nonetheless, the huge development costs for the next generation of commercial passenger jet aircraft, often called the super jumbo, have forced international competitors like Boeing and Airbus to consider possible joint development efforts. Taken together, these factors foreshadow a contraction of the worldwide aircraft industry during the 1990s that is not reflected in the BLS forecast. Reabsorption of defense aerospace workers into civilian operations will therefore be limited.

Prospects are no brighter for the other defense-dependent durable goods industries such as shipbuilding, tank production, and electrical and electronics equipment producers. Clearly, worldwide excess capacity will make the pursuit of arms export markets especially competitive, thereby further depressing future domestic employment growth in these sectors. In the case of electrical and electronic equipment, the BLS forecast suggested a very weak market for domestic producers, which can only be worsened by even deeper defense cuts than evidenced in that forecast. Elsewhere, the overall deterioration of manufacturing job growth in the other durable and nondurable manufacturing sectors will only be exacerbated by deeper defense cuts.

By contrast, the stronger growth forecast for the service sectors makes it likely that the employment losses from defense cuts of this magnitude in these sectors can be more readily absorbed by the growth in employment. However, the fact that the current economic recovery has been so sluggish raises the prospect that job creation might be closer to the low-end scenario forecast by the BLS, rather than the moderate 2.3 percent GNP growth rate examined here. Furthermore, the slow pace of the recovery means that it will take longer than usual to reabsorb those workers who were laid off due to cyclical causes, thus retarding the capacity of the service sector to generate new positions for those laid off by defense cuts over the next year or two. Finally, there is some evidence of a trend in corporate restructuring which is reducing management layers and service overheads.

A later BLS study conducted by Norman Saunders has estimated the projected defense employment losses associated with the Bush and Clinton administration cuts.[11] This study estimated the direct and indirect employment effects using the BLS's input–output model. It found that the impact of planned defense cuts over the 1992–97 period would result in about 1.3 million job losses in defense industry employment. Since these higher estimates include the reductions in defense-related Department of Energy spending and other defense-related functions, the employment estimates seem quite comparable to the somewhat lower estimates presented in Table 7.1, which do not include these other defense spending reductions. Indeed, the distribution of the employment losses among major industry groups is very similar to the estimates presented above. A Congressional Budget Office study provided a somewhat lower overall estimate for defense-related impacts for the Bush administration plan, with total employment losses amounting to only 865,000 for private and public sector jobs.[12] Thus, the estimates presented here lie midway between the CBO and BLS estimates.

The Occupational Effects

The occupational impacts of the Bush and Clinton military budget reductions are depicted in Table 7.2 for the major occupational groups. Predictably, significant dislocation occurs in skilled occupations that are closely linked to the highly dependent military durable goods sectors, especially precision metal workers, inspectors, numerically controlled and combination machine operators, and various other machine tool operators. Semiskilled assemblers are particularly hard hit, with this single occupational group accounting for 9 percent of all the job losses.

Management-related occupations suffer considerable losses, amounting to nearly 111,000 jobs. Characteristically, engineering professions show significant losses, especially in electrical and electronic engineering, mechanical engineering, nuclear engineers, and aerospace/astronautical engineers, with all layoffs in these professions totaling nearly 52,000. Technical occupations involving engineering technicians, drafters, and other technicians also register large losses, amounting to over 56,000 jobs. Scientists of all types suffer losses of over 10,000 jobs. It should be noted, however, that these estimates for scientists, engineers, and technicians probably understate the job losses in these occupations since they are generated using the industrywide average labor force rates, whereas defense requirements are known to be more research-intensive and tend to use relatively more scientists, engineers, and technicians.[13]

The construction trades lose nearly 33,000 jobs, while mechanics, installers, and repairers lose nearly 71,000 jobs. The other occupational impacts are mostly attributable to indirect job losses, rather than the direct impacts of defense cutbacks. The one exception is the clerical occupations, which exhibit huge losses amounting to over 193,000 jobs.

Occupational Growth Forecasts

Forecasts for employment growth by occupation developed by the BLS for the next fifteen years indicate decline in manufacturing and the core defense production occupations, particularly precision metal workers, inspectors, numerically controlled and combination machine operators, and various other machine tool operators.[14] Occupational

Table 7.2

Impact of National Defense Cuts by Major Occupational Groups, 1992–97

Major occupational group	1992–97 effect
Managerial and manaagement-related	110,800
Engineering occupations	54,200
Computer, nataural, mathematical, and social scientists	10,200
Social, educational and religious, lawyers and judicial workers	7,900
Health diagnosing and treating occupations	5,500
Writers, artists, and entertainers	11,700
Technical occupations	56,100
Marketing and sales occupations	63,800
Secretaries, typists, and administrative support occupations	193,500
Service occupations	96,200
Agriculture, forestry and fishing, and related occupations	8,600
Blue-collar supervisory occupations	31,800
Construction trades	35,200
Mechanics, installers, and repairers	68,100
Precision production occupations	61,100
Machine setters, operators, tenders, assemblers, plant, and system occupations	193,700
Transportation and material moving machine and vehicle operators	110,700
Total	1,119,000

Source: G. Bischak and M. Oden, *Armaments and Defense Conversion in the United States after the Cold War* (Geneva: International Labour Office, October 1993).

growth for assemblers is also forecasted to be negative, and, given the reality of deeper cuts and weakness in the commercial aerospace industry, this will only be further depressed. Mechanic, installer and repairer occupations are also forecast to decline in the BLS low-, moderate-, and high-growth scenarios. All of these occupational groups will need well-targeted retraining assistance in order to move into other occupations. However, if there is a serious emphasis on large-scale public investment in high-tech infrastructure, job creation may be generated in fields demanding some of the skills of these workers' skills. Under these circumstances, retraining programs might be crafted to build occupational training bridges between the old and emerging occupational skills requirements.

Robust growth is forecast by the BLS for many of the other occupational groups affected by the defense cuts. However, despite the strong forecast for managerial occupations of all types, there are particular reasons why defense-related managers might find it harder to avail themselves of these opportunities. The most notable factor is that managers who have had a career in the defense industry usually possess skills unique to the defense sector that are not transferable to commercial practices. This well-recognized phenomenon often constitutes a real barrier to occupational mobility into civilian management work. These managers must be retrained to acquire knowledge of marketing in diverse markets characterized by many different types of buyers, as well as the cost and quality control techniques demanded in commercial markets.

Administrative and clerical occupations that also suffer reductions from planned defense cuts will experience broad growth, according to the BLS forecast. However, workers in military firms may find it hard to replace stable full-time jobs due to the growth of part-time and temporary employment in these categories. Sadly, because existing programs do not train workers in high-demand occupations for other higher-skill occupations, these workers may find their employment prospects downgraded.

Again, the more recent BLS study of the employment impacts of defense cuts confirm the estimates presented in Table 7.2.[15] The estimates for some wholesale and retail trade occupations, however, seem to be somewhat at variance with those presented here.[16]

Aside from these occupational impacts, there remains the challenge of providing for the uniformed and nonuniformed military workers being released from government employment. Currently, Congress has established more benefits and programs for these workers than for defense industry workers. Having looked at the employment and occupational impact of projected defense cuts, it now makes sense to consider the extent to which they could be mitigated by a compensatory shift of defense savings into civilian public investment initiatives.

Macroeconomic Policy, Public Investment, and Conversion

President Clinton has retreated from his campaign pledge to "reinvest dollar for dollar" defense budget reductions into the domestic economy and instead earmarked only a small portion of defense savings for a conversion program, devoting the rest to deficit reduction. More generally, Clinton's other campaign pledge, to expand public investment in infrastructure, civilian R&D, and job training, was also sacrificed to the goal of deficit reduction. Together, these two actions represent a significant retreat from the pledge of "Putting People First" by reinvesting in America and realigning national priorities in keeping with the end of the Cold War. Perhaps more important, this retreat may mean that conversion in the larger sense of the word will not be possible, since there will be no shift in public investment away from military to civilian priorities.

As originally presented in his "Vision for Change" state-of-the-union speech, President Clinton's investment program promised a reinvestment of defense savings into an array of economic programs. These public investments were to be concentrated in infrastructure and high-technology-intensive fields, especially in transportation, energy and environmental restoration. In addition, new investments were to be made in human resources and job training. Furthermore, the president argued that redirecting scientific resources to transportation, energy, and environmental needs would stimulate development of new products, production processes, and markets, and provide conversion opportunities for many high-tech military industries. Investments in transportation and environmental protection would likewise generate new demand and conversion opportunities. Not only would these investments compensate for reduced military spending, but they would also improve the nation's competitiveness and enhance the quality of life.

However, the administration's first public investment package for FY 1994 did not augur well for the future of civilian public investment. Indeed, total public spending on education and training, physical capital, civilian research and development, and other human resource investments showed no net new investment after factoring out inflation. According to a report by the Economic Policy Institute, these investments fell as a share of total federal outlays for the first time in four years.[17] Given the fiscal constraints of deficit reduction in the president's budget agreement with Congress, it is doubtful whether the administration could really increase investment in high-technology industry, civilian R&D, human resources, and infrastructure.

Perhaps more distressing, while Washington and Wall Street touted how economic recovery obviated the need for additional public sector initiatives, job creation was being slowed by the cumulative effects of corporate and public sector downsizing, the trend toward using temporary workers in place of permanent workers, the migration of manufacturing and service sector production overseas, the impact of global trade, and technological unemployment. All of these factors slow job creation and retard the economy's capacity to absorb displaced defense workers.

While a shift in federal budget priorities from military to critical domestic needs could minimize the economic repercussions from these shocks, such public reinvestment has been politically resisted. The fiscal deficit of the federal government is the most prominent economic constraint on reinvesting the peace dividend. The conventional wisdom is well known. Excessive levels of public borrowing for chronic deficit financing tend to crowd out private borrowing as the cost of capital increases. Thus, the only remedy is to cut public expenditures so that they come into long-term balance with government receipts.[18]

Indeed, the Clinton economic program is largely based on the dicta of sound government finance. The deficit reduction target of the Clinton administration is scheduled to bring the federal deficit down by 1995, but the federal deficit is also forecast by the Congressional Budget Office to rise after 1996 and to continue to grow to the year 2003. Thus, the best efforts of the Clinton administration only promise to slow the growth of the deficit. Compounding these problems is the fact that even the most optimistic forecasts of the effects of deficit reduction show that it will take five to seven years for the economy to feel the benefits of a lower deficit and more robust private investment. Meanwhile, in the short run, the defense and other discretionary budget cuts will exert a drag on growth, consumption, employment, and investment for the next several years.[19]

Given the shortcomings of the administration's approach, it is no surprise that some have called for more public investment to address the nation's most pressing social, economic, and environmental needs. It has been argued that the deficit could reasonably be ignored in the short run since this investment would lay the foundations for higher levels of economic growth in the future.[20] This alternative approach, grounded in Keynesian public finance, lends support to the argument that it is wise for the nation to invest military savings in areas of national need. According to this view, investing military savings in critical civilian needs could address fundamental economic and social problems while stimulating key economic sectors to produce jobs. Arguably, such public investments should be viewed as wealth-producing assets, rather than as a simple public expense.[21] In the long run, these expenditures would pay for themselves by generating new economic activity and restoring productivity. Thus, according to this view, it is short-sighted to use military savings exclusively to reduce the federal budget deficit while ignoring the nation's most pressing economic and social needs.

While conventional economic wisdom continues to dominate public thinking on this issue, past experience with major military reductions indicates the critical importance of some sort of compensatory macroeconomic policies to promote large-scale conversion efforts. After World War II, the economy greatly benefited from the huge buildup of private savings due to wartime deficit spending and forced savings through the rationing of investment and consumption by government controls. Contrary to the mainstream economic history, the "pent-up demand" that fueled the postwar boom was a direct result of government macroeconomic policies. After the Korean War, government policies provided a different solution, as the share of military spending on new weaponry was dramatically increased during the postwar peace, thereby reducing the need for direct conversion. The Vietnam era provided a different lesson, as the expansion of social spending absorbed a considerable share of the "peace dividend," while relatively modest public sector investment in mass transportation and alternative energy technologies did stimulate some conversion efforts by military contractors.[22]

The contemporary economic benefits of such a compensated shift in federal spending have been examined in numerous economic studies, including a recent study by the Congressional Research Service.[23] Each of these studies has shown that a substantial dollar-for-dollar reinvestment could significantly mitigate many of the employment and occupational impacts of reduced military spending. Indeed, one study of a large compensated shift indicated that many military-serving occupations identified in Table 7.2 could benefit from reinvestment, including managerial occupations, scientists, and many fields of engineering. Even with such a large-scale reinvestment, however, there will still be substantial economic dislocation for the most militarily dependent occupations, such as aeronautical and industrial engineers, and many highly skilled blue-collar trades like precision metal workers, numerical control machine operators, and precision assemblers.[24]

For these reasons, *there needs to be a comprehensive structural economic conversion program that attempts to link targeted industrial and community redevelopment efforts with new sources of finance and to link occupational retraining initiatives with economic development efforts in both the public and private sectors.* It is only through such a coherent approach that job bridges can built between declining industries and occupations and those newly emerging ones.

Building Job Bridges

New efforts in high-speed rail, electric vehicles, environmental technologies, and other fields will take time to gear up to full-scale production and employment levels, thus creating a timing problem for reemploying dislocated defense workers. This situation is being compounded by the commercial restructuring currently under way in aerospace and other fields. The critical matter of expanded public investment has been discussed in detail above. Other policies are also needed to support the job bridges that must be built to span the gap between the rapidly accelerating defense cuts and the slowly developing civilian jobs in high-tech commercial work.

Incentives for Prime Contractors to Convert

By and large, military-serving corporations have been dealing with lower military spending through layoffs, plant closures, mergers and acquisitions, and arms exports. Conversion has taken place in many small to medium-sized firms, and among some larger firms, but the predominant tendency has been either to "cut and run" or to "hunker down and get a bigger piece of a shrinking pie." While the Clinton conversion program offered some assistance to workers and communities, they have for the most part been left to the vicissitudes of the marketplace. The lion's share of the money is being spent on dual-use programs that aim at preserving the defense-industrial base, rather than redeveloping industrial capacity for commercial work.

The defense consolidation/acquisition strategy is reflected in Loral's recent purchases of IBM's defense division, Martin Marietta's purchase of General Electric's defense division and General Dynamics (GD) rocket division, the Hughes buyout of GD's missile division, Lockheed's purchase of GD's combat aircraft division, and FMC's merger with Harsco's armored vehicle divisions. Generally, these strategies have resulted in large-scale layoffs of the work forces of these contractors, as the consolidations and acquisitions have rendered redundant many white- and blue-collar workers.

Corporate civilian diversification is another strategy being pursued by some large defense firms such as Lockheed and Martin Marietta, especially in cases where they have expanded into closely related civilian government markets (see chapter 4). Martin Marietta, for example, has focused on applying its technology to systems it is selling to civilian government agencies. It was recently granted the role of lead contractor in the Federal Aviation Administration's $16 billion program to remodel U.S. commercial air traffic control systems.[25] However, few defense division workers are being shifted into these firms' new civilian operations.

Westinghouse Electric Corporation's electronic systems division has set a goal of achieving 50 percent of its revenues from nondefense work by 1995. It began its diversification efforts in 1989 and now reports that it has developed five separate nondefense projects that employ over one-fourth of the division's work force. These diversification projects involve commercial applications of ground, air, and radar surveillance technologies, transportation automation, electronic controls for security, electric vehicle propulsion, and bar-code mail processing. These efforts attracted a great deal of attention on May 11, 1991, when President Clinton chose the Westinghouse facility in Baltimore to unveil his national conversion plan. Despite this initial success in diversifying its defense division, the company laid off 1,400 defense workers in 1992.[26] Perhaps more indicative of corporate strategy, the mail processing technology is not being produced by the company's permanent employees; instead, it is being staffed by temporary workers in a facility separate from its defense operations.[27]

Corporate civilian diversification strategies are actually more prevalent than is commonly believed. According to a report of a survey conducted by the Winbridge Group of Cambridge, Massachusetts, of over 1,100 senior defense executives, 71 percent of the 148 respondents said they were studying the feasibility of commercializing defense technologies. More than one-third of the firms indicated that they had actually commercialized a defense technology. And 81 percent of those firms that did commercialize defense technologies indicated that they had brought the new product to market within two years. Many other firms, however, reported that they were not pursuing commercialization strategies because of the familiar barriers to moving into civilian work: the defense business fosters high-cost, high-performance management and engineering requirements that create obstacles to the commercial viability of defense technologies; the firms lacked the appropriate staff for commercial work, particularly in marketing; and the efforts by others firms to commercialize were discouraging.[28]

These diversification efforts, however, have produced few cases of large-scale job retention. Indeed, these efforts generally do not create jobs for defense workers, especially when the firm seeks to acquire a commercial firm to diversify its product mix and sales. The most promising opportunities for certain large military-oriented firms are in civilian government markets, but the limitations on new public investments to generate new government-funded markets severely constrain this strategy as a major conversion option for large defense contractors.

Conversion among smaller, less specialized firms in the subcontracting chain is somewhat more common. A number of firms such as Textron Aerostructures of Tennessee, A.M. General in Indiana, Air Industries and Frisby Airborne Hydraulics in New York, and Curtis Universal Joint of Massachusetts have adapted existing products or developed new products to expand civilian business.[29] One medium-sized company, M/A-COM Inc. of Wakefield, Massachusetts illustrates the greater flexibility among subcontractors. M/A-COM produced defense electronics equipment, supplying microwave and radio frequency (RF) components and connectors for the military, and it was 90 percent dependent on military contracts in the late 1980s. But, since the downturn in defense spending, the company has moved aggressively to convert to civilian fields where it has strong technological competence, such as telecommunications and cellular systems, commercial radar, and navigation systems. Success has come quickly, with new markets in cellular communication growing the fastest.[30] While many of these cases of conversion by small and medium-sized firms have succeeded in dramatically reducing the companies' defense dependency, the companies have typically been able to reemploy only a fraction of their work force in civilian activities.

Corporate efforts to move out of defense and into commercial opportunities suggest certain clear lessons. First, firms must develop a corporate strategic plan that identifies the technological opportunities in fields familiar to them and in which they may possess certain market advantages. Second, they should cultivate civilian marketing capabilities through consultants, joint ventures, or acquisitions. Cross-licensing agreements are yet another way that firms might develop marketing and technological partnerships. Third, and perhaps most important, the firms must learn how to control costs and increase quality consistent with civilian market demands. Of particular importance is the need to retrain engineers to meet the cost and quality requirements of commercial markets. Meanwhile, managers used to dealing with only one client—namely, the Pentagon—must undergo thorough retraining to learn how to deal with many customers. Finally, involvement of the work force in the continuous improvements of the manufacturing and services connected to the firms' production and service operations is necessary to compete in the international market. The failure of many corporations to engage the skills of their work force in the conversion is a principal contributor to the large-scale layoffs within military industry (see chapter 2).

Major defense firms may be able to move into some of these emerging new technology markets if they begin planning now to develop new products, retool, reorganize production, develop marketing capabilities, and retrain their managements, engineers, and work force for commercial work. But it is evident that some economic incentives would be extremely helpful—incentives such as preferential awards of civilian government contracts or conversion grants to those firms that engage their work forces in conversion planning and seek to retain jobs among their current work forces. Any incentives should be geared to converting existing capacity and reemploying defense workers in civilian work.

The lack of an explicit emphasis on job retention is one of the main limitations on the Technology Reinvestment Program (TRP) as defense firms' principal means to achieve conversion. Moreover, the Clinton administration's emphasis on dual-use technology development has meant that the TRP will at best only generate jobs in the longer term. If the TRP is to remain the flagship of efforts to convert defense firms, then it should consider making job retention an explicit criterion for TRP grant awards. One possible measure that could promote job retention would be to provide matching federal money to companies that retain or reemploy laid-off workers, counting the wages of these workers as part of the companies' contribution to the match.

Investment in High-Tech Business Incubators

Where large defense contractors choose to shut down plants and lay off workers, rather than convert, new spin-off businesses may offer the best hope to redevelop technology, plant, and the work force for civilian applications. New high-tech job incubators must be created as a means of encouraging spin-off enterprises. Business incubators can help exploit technological opportunities emerging from new areas of civilian investment. Projects like the Calstart initiative in California, which aims to develop a supplier and equipment production base for the electric car market, can help encourage new spin-off enterprises.[31] Job incubators can retain a critical skills base being released by defense industries and can help maintain high-wage jobs in manufacturing. Such job incubators could also provide a foothold for union membership in new and emerging occupations.

Industrial technologies in transportation, communications, energy, and environmental fields are promising areas of new business and job creation, where much activity has been stimulated by patterns of public investment and regulation. Many of these emerging technological fields are more readily developed by smaller, more flexible firms that have no vested interests in existing technologies, particularly in the transportation and environmental arenas. In the case of defense conversion in particular, the lack of commitment on the part of the larger prime contractors makes it especially important that defense-dependent communities and workers explore business incubators and spin-offs as ways to develop new jobs in related fields.

Calstart was started in 1992 with the aim of converting high-tech defense jobs to transportation-related production of components and subassemblies of electric vehicles, new types of buses, and light-rail mass-transit trains. It also aims to capture some of the market needed to supply the infrastructure for electric cars, such as charging stations, battery recycling, and other support services. Calstart is a result of a partnership of over forty business, labor, and governmental organizations, including both defense and nondefense businesses and the International Association of Machinists (IAM) union. Because the state of California enacted the toughest air pollution control laws in the nation, the public and private sectors must develop new and innovative, less polluting transportation technologies, especially in the automobile industry. Indeed, these regulations require that 10 percent of the automobiles sold in California by 2003 will have to be zero-emission vehicles. Calstart estimates that capturing a substantial segment of the market could generate at least 55,000 direct and indirect manufacturing-related jobs by the end of the century.[32]

Initial funding for this consortium came from the federal, state, and local governments, as well as from some of the venture capital firms involved in the consortium. Amerigon Inc., a firm created to design, produce, and sell electric vehicle components and subassemblies to the domestic and international automobile industry, is the leading business in the consortium. While several defense firms are involved in the consortium, most have not committed much in the way of financial resources.

The International Association of Machinists and Aerospace Workers union has been particularly active in Calstart since its inception, and has explicitly linked its conversion and retraining efforts for defense industry workers to the skills base required for Calstart's commercial programs. Moreover, the IAM has developed an innovative labor agreement with Amerigon to establish a high-performance work organization within the production process to ensure continuous improvements in the quality and productivity of the business. In exchange for these measures, labor is assured further jobs gains as the company becomes more competitive in the market, thereby improving workers' job security.

Much of the impetus for these developments has come about through efforts at the state and local levels, rather than through reliance on the federal government. Indeed, eleven states now have regulations similar to California's zero-emission regulatory targets. Federal action, however, will clearly influence the pace of market development for the "clean car." The Big Three auto makers have tried to get the federal government to set goals, and to curb the individual states' authority in setting such regulatory targets. There are indications that the federal government will seek to use its considerable vehicle purchase requirements to help stimulate the domestic market for electric and low-emission vehicles over the next several years. Such direct public investment would be especially powerful if it were coupled to a more aggressive public regulatory regime to accelerate the development of this market. Moreover, additional federal investment in applied research and development will certainly help further both the domestic and the international market potential of Calstart and related businesses.

Targeted industrial research and investment from the public sector could support initial development of a variety of other technologies, including pollution-reducing production techniques and productivity-enhancing research on manufacturing process innovations. Expansion of manufacturing technology centers should also provide specific industrial research support for older primary manufacturers that are often overlooked in the emphasis on high-technology R&D.

In the transportation field, the administration's first investment budget targeted most of the money for developing more conventional highway and auto-related technologies. The Department of Transportation would do well to explore multimodal transportation systems and a wide variety of hybrid auto technologies like solar-electric, natural gas–electric, and hydrogen fuel–electric vehicles. Both high-speed rail and magnetic levitation trains should receive more federal support. In addition, important applied environmental research could readily be increased in such areas as sustainable agriculture, soil conservation, pollution control, acid rain, hazardous waste prevention and treatment, and the health impacts of pollution.[33]

Alternative energy and energy conservation research funding has been crippled by years of less than benign neglect and requires large increases to develop a whole energy-industrial base to succeed the fossil-fueled technologies of the nineteenth and twentieth centuries. While the administration's funding for alternative energy research is a significant improvement over the past, it is a far cry from what is needed to pioneer new technologies.[34] More generally, basic investment requirements for infrastructure repair will grow modestly, at best, perhaps bringing the level of proposed nonmilitary investments back to that of the mid-1970s.[35] Indeed, it is evident that while the Clinton investment program has taken small steps toward a real public investment policy, it is painfully underfunded.

The significance of these investment trends is evident when examining the direct conversion implications of these emerging technologies for absorbing technological and human resources released from the defense sectors. In a study conducted by the Economic Roundtable of Los Angeles, researchers examined the potential for creating transportation jobs for the aerospace industry and its work force in new areas of surface transportation development.[36] The employment potential of new production capacity to supply both Los Angeles' expanding needs for light-rail trains and the international market was analyzed to determine what the size and composition of occupational demand would be for different types of skilled labor. These labor and skill requirements were then matched to those being released from the defense sectors.

Overall, not many direct demands would be created for aerospace workers by investment in light-rail production. However, eight relatively skilled occupations would be in demand. Other defense occupations would require additional training to match the demands for light rail. Nonetheless, the volume of demand for light rail is small compared with the demand that had been generated by defense work, and it is clear that at best it would only absorb a small fraction of the displaced defense workers. However, the report does note that upgrading the light-rail technology to improve the quality of service would probably generate additional demands for aerospace workers' skills. Finally, the study also examined the reemployment potential of fuel-cell production for electric vehicles and found this a promising market. But, again, the study underscored the importance of a proactive federal role in establishing a stimulative regulatory regime for the electric car.

Clearly, no one product or technology will replace the role of defense spending for many defense-dependent occupations, but the combined effect of a realignment of federal investment in areas of national needs could generate significant new activity capable of generating substantial job creation. In California there are government efforts to identify the high value-added industries of the future where the state's manufacturing sectors are well positioned to capture significant market shares, especially in transportation, communications, and energy. This effort, known as Project California, will be linked to the efforts of the state's employment and training panel to retrain workers for new or rapidly growing industries.[37] Project California could serve as a model for a national effort to redevelop and convert the United States' defense industry to the emerging industries necessary to develop a twenty-first-century infrastructure.

Reorganized Job Training Programs Linked to Job Creation Efforts

Evidence on the performance of job training programs for laid-off defense workers as well as workers displaced by foreign trade indicates very mixed results (see chapter 5). The majority of all workers who do enroll in training programs find that the skills developed through retraining are often ill suited to jobs that are actually available. Another disturbing fact is that nearly two-thirds of the former defense workers accepted new jobs that paid less than their previous job. One factor that probably has contributed to the willingness of some former workers to take lower-paying jobs is that the current defense worker retraining programs do not provide income maintenance, or even an extension of unemployment insurance benefits so that they can afford to search longer for more comparable pay. Finally, in the case of the Trade Adjustment Assistance (TAA) retraining program, which is the one program that provides income support, few of the workers found work that required the skills acquired in the program. These results, combined with the slow rate of job creation in the economy, raise profound doubts about the merits of the current job training system. Indeed, these issues have led the Clinton administration to propose a whole new approach to the nation's retraining program.

During its first year in office, the Clinton administration circulated for comment a draft program to revamp the Department of Labor's dislocated workers job training program. The idea was to establish a single worker adjustment system with one standard of eligibility for all types of dislocated workers, including those affected by defense cuts, trade adjustment, and environmental regulations. The program also set up a series of one-stop career centers and a national labor market information system. Initially, the administration had proposed spending up to $4.7 billion on these programs over the 1994–97 period, but later drafts were silent on funding levels. Labor Department economists project that by 1998, nearly 60 percent of the estimated 2.2 million dislocated workers will be served annually by this system.

Beyond the basic employment services previously available to unemployed workers, the program included: outreach to encourage early enrollment in the system; improved career counseling; expanded retraining options, including income support through extended unemployment benefits; relocation allowances; and support services for child care and transportation. Income support under the retraining program would allow for up to eighteen additional months beyond the maximum six months of unemployment benefits currently permitted, but would be restricted to those workers who had been previously employed for two years. This support is aimed at allowing longer term training for permanently unemployed workers. Finally, an amendment to the Worker Adjustment and Retraining Notification (WARN) act would require notice of any layoff of fifty or more workers. It should be noted, however, that there are no provisions for enforcement of WARN by the Department of Labor.

Despite these improvements in recasting the current dislocated worker training programs, the administration's approach still rests on creating a "stand-alone" training program that is not explicitly linked to job creation efforts. Moreover, there is general concern that the program as a whole may be underfunded.

In order to address some of these concerns, Representative Lynn Woolsey (Democrat from California) introduced the Displaced Worker Retraining Act to provide another answer to the structural unemployment problem. This bill would allow wider eligibility than the administration's proposal and would provide more generous benefits for training and educational programs, including vocational, undergraduate, and graduate schooling. In addition, eligible displaced workers would obtain income support for up to three years. Moreover, the bill provides a temporary wage supplement to those workers who are reemployed at substantially lower wages, with the supplement designed to bring the wage to at least 85 percent of the previous level. The bill would also expand relocation allowances and rapid response services to unemployed workers.

Just as important, Woolsey's bill seeks to direct programs to train participants for jobs in growth industries such as environmental products and services, transportation, and telecommunications. As Representative Woolsey has aptly noted, "job training must be linked to job creation." Indeed, this linkage is one of the key differences between Woolsey's bill and the administration's program and calls into question the merits of a simple stand-alone job training effort.

Clearly, both these programs would be an advance over the previous approach to job training, especially since they provide income maintenance, greater relocation benefits, and improved services for the unemployed worker. Yet, at this writing, there has been no visible effort to coordinate the administration's various technology investment programs with these federal retraining efforts. Linking retraining to new federal investments that will generate jobs is a basic prerequisite of a successful conversion.[38] Moreover, without an effective early notification program enforced by the Labor Department, there is little prospect of private sector investment in job redevelopment and conversion. In addition, given the shortfall of the reinvestment initiative and the inevitable mismatch between the skill requirements of jobs being lost and those being created, there will be a need to expand educational assistance. Educational loans should be provided for production workers who may wish to qualify for emerging opportunities in high-tech occupations or to pursue higher education. Educational grants for university–industry consortia also could be used for retraining engineers and managers for work in the civilian sector, particularly in the new emerging technology fields.[39] The National Society of Professional Engineers and the Los Angeles County Private Industry Council have developed a training program to enable engineers to become environmental engineers, linking displaced defense engineers with employment in the emerging environmental field.

Interagency Coordination of Conversion, Training, and Economic Development

Linking reinvestment with retraining and redevelopment efforts will require an interagency coordinating and planning body, preferably housed in the Department of Commerce or the Department of Labor, to carry out this program. Such a body is necessary to coordinate the various programs and to streamline procedures in order to speed access and assistance. In addition, having a civilian-oriented agency take the lead in interagency coordination would place the proper emphasis on conversion to civilian production and would counterbalance undue influence from the DoD, with its focus on maintaining the defense industrial base. Such a body could examine the regional, industrial, and occupational issues stemming from the large-scale shift of resources and help states and localities adjust to these changes.

Another issue with the current and proposed program is the bureaucratic maze created by having these programs strewn across several agencies. Moreover, there are very serious doubts about the merits of leaving most of the authority for administering the conversion program in the hands of the Department of Defense. Many conversion activists have proposed to remedy these problems by creating a "one-stop shopping" center housed in the Commerce Department. Such an approach would help to streamline the application procedures, eliminate bureaucratic red tape, coordinate programs so as to maximize the impact of assistance, and offset the excessive influence of the Defense Department.

New Sources of Finance for Economic
Conversion and Development

Financing economic conversion is a complex issue that has often been either overlooked or treated ideologically. Some want to rely on the dynamics of private market financing to allocate new investment capital for conversion, while others think that pervasive market failures in the allocation of capital by financial markets mean that public finance must carry the load. Another issue is the perception that conversion primarily involves financing relatively risky product development in high-technology fields. Yet, conversion also involves less glamorous efforts by smaller military subcontractors and suppliers that have simply been cut out of finance markets. More broadly, conversion involves reinvesting defense resources and savings into developing a twenty-first-century infrastructure. Thus, the federal funding emphasis on dual-use technologies is a decidedly skewed approach that addresses only one dimension of a manifold problem.

Defense cutbacks and the curtailment of public investment have created many gaps in public and private financing of conversion for large defense contractors, federally funded research labs, and small to medium-sized military manufacturing subcontractors and suppliers.

One possible model to fill some of these gaps is the Michigan Strategic Fund. It is a publicly financed strategic fund that was created by the state of Michigan in 1985 to overcome private sector constraints in business development. The fund first created a Capital Access Program that helped banks overcome the risk and return problems that they face in lending to small and medium-sized businesses. The fund also created new types of private financial institutions that can address financing gaps not being covered by bank lending or traditional venture capital. In particular, it developed the Business and Industrial Development Corporation (BIDCO) to allow the state to become an equity investor in companies, permitting these companies to turn around and generate new types of debt financing through banks and private institutions. The Strategic Fund provided $24 million for these eleven BIDCOs, which in turn have already turned around enough capital to invest $50 million in Michigan businesses. And those investments have attracted another $70 million to those companies. Both the capital-access type program and the BIDCOs have particular relevance to small to medium-sized defense subcontractors that have had difficulty raising investment capital for conversion efforts.

The Seed Capital Program was also developed by the Strategic Fund to invest in and help catalyze the formation of three private seed capital funds that have developed a portfolio of new high-tech startup companies. One financial gap that has been identified through the operation of these seed-capital funds is a lack of other sources of available follow-up capital to supply the credit needs of these startup firms. The program managers found that the seed-capital funds were continuing to invest their capital in these follow-up operations, thereby depleting the investment resources necessary to diversify their portfolio of new startup firms. Efforts to develop new financial resources to address these needs were cut short by the change of governors in Michigan, although there are means to bridge this gap in the private venture capital market.

These Michigan Strategic Fund approaches are potentially adaptable to a national strategy for financing high-technology innovation, business startups, and conversion in the United States.

The Clinton administration moved to create a system of community development banks that might assist in meeting some of these capital needs. Such a role has been played by the capital access program.[40] However, this program would provide only $385 million to capitalize these banks, which is clearly inadequate to address the needs of rebuilding the inner cities, let alone the conversion needs of small business. One idea for funding a more extensive system of community banks to fund public economic development objectives has been put forward by Martin Trimble, of the National Association of Community Development Banks. Trimble has called for an extension of the Community Reinvestment Act to the rest of the financial system, including money market mutual funds, pension funds, institutional investors, and unregulated financial intermediaries.[41]

There are, however, some existing sources of public finance that might be usefully applied to the conversion financing problem. For instance, Tom Schlesinger, director of the Southern Finance Project, has noted that among the original missions of the twelve Federal Reserve District Banks was a regional economic development function that has not been widely used.[42] Given the Federal Reserve's deep pockets, proponents of conversion would do well to advocate a regional role for the Federal Reserve in financing conversion.

A missing ingredient in this public policy debate is the potential role of investment banks and state and local bonding authorities in financing large-scale infrastructure development. The lack of new federal bonding authority to finance new infrastructure development has meant that conversion in the broader sense of the word cannot take place, nor is it possible for the administration to leverage other sources of private and public sector infrastructure investment through traditional debt and equity finance to fund its investment program.[43]

Meanwhile, trends in the institutional investment community have also created obstacles to financing conversion. Herb Whitehouse, president of Whitehouse Fiduciary Advisors, has argued that the investment criteria of institutional investors are biased against investment in smaller businesses and conversion ventures. He has called for appropriate asset allocation rules to promote diversification by institutional investors into these areas of the economy.

Clearly, new sources of finance for enterprise development will be needed to assist in the development of innovative enterprises, including employee ownership, middle-management buyouts, and community redevelopment projects. The Clinton plan puts very little money in community redevelopment assistance and provides little for financing new business development. These are some of the issues that must be addressed if the conversion process is to create new jobs.

Conclusion

As the nation embarks on the conversion of the Cold War military system, the role of public sector economic intervention will have to be fundamentally redefined. There can be little doubt that the dynamics of the private market cannot alone redirect the economic and technological resources being released from the defense sectors. Indeed, the administration's recognition of this fact led to the creation of a whole new set of defense and nondefense industrial policy initiatives that should provide some resources to facilitate industrial restructuring of all kinds. However, the lack of substantial net new civilian public investment leaves open to question whether the public sector role once defined by the Cold War will be replaced by a new regime defined by real public investment needs, or by retrenchment along habitual lines.

Such profound restructuring in the defense economy, as well as in the civilian sector, will require new institutional innovations to create job bridges to the emerging industries and occupations that are capable of providing the high-skill, high-wage jobs so necessary to ensuring the quality of life. In addition, revitalizing the civilian economy will require investments in new technologies that are essential for creating environmentally sustainable production and transportation systems.

A successful conversion process will only generate a sufficient quantity and quality of new jobs, however, by ensuring the participation of all the major stakeholders in the planning process and safeguarding against the tendency to address public policy only to the vested interests of the existing industrial system. Moreover, market failure in the financial sector requires that new institutions be created to cover those gaps in financing the conversion process, particularly for community-based efforts and smaller businesses. If we fail in this effort, the nation will lose the opportunity to revitalize the civilian economy and create the basis for sustainable economic development. Moreover, failure to convert successfully will create resistance to further reducing our military budgets and block the chance to develop a more enduring basis for international peace and security.

Notes

1. These estimates are drawn from Michael Dee Oden and Gregory A. Bischak, *Armaments Industry and Defense Conversion* (Geneva: International Labour Office, October 1993, forthcoming monograph).

2. See "Secretary Aspin announces bottom up review results," News Release, Office of the Assistant Secretary of Defense (Washington, DC: September 1, 1993).

3. See Todd Schafer, "Still neglecting public investment: The FY 94 budget outlook" (Washington, DC: Economic Policy Institute, August 1993).

4. These cuts are derived by comparing the last complete defense budget submitted by President Bush in January 1992 for FY 1993, which includes the multiyear defense plan for 1993–97. It does not consider the defense plan submitted by President Bush in January 1993 for FY 1994 because none of the details were outlined for this plan. The Clinton plan is drawn from National Defense Budget Estimates for FY 1994, May 1993, Office of the Comptroller, Department of Defense, Washington DC, Table 1–2, p. 5.

5. See "Effects of alternative defense budgets on employment," *CBO Papers* (April 1993), p. 6.

6. See "A needless gift to the Pentagon," the *New York Times* editorial (December 27, 1993). Also see Clay Chandler, "1995 budget gives additional $10 billion to Pentagon for raises," *The Washington Post* (December 23, 1993): A-8. Foreshadowing of this is found in Barton Gellman, "Pentagon may seek $20 billion more," *The Washington Post* (August 13, 1993), and Eric Schmitt, "Plan

for new military doesn't meet savings goal," *The New York Times* (September 15, 1993): A-21.

7. These estimates are drawn from four sources: Troop and civilian reductions are taken from *News Briefing, Defense Budget Plan, FY 1993*, Office of the Secretary of Defense (January 29, 1992), Appendix on Manpower (End Strength), 1987–97, and from *National Defense Budget Estimates for FY 1993*, Office of the Comptroller, Department of Defense (May 1992). The Clinton DoD personnel numbers are taken from *National Defense Budget Estimates for FY 1994*, Office of the Comptroller, Department of Defense (May 1993). Defense industry estimates were developed by the author using static input–output modeling techniques to estimate the industry-by-industry impacts of changes in national defense spending.

8. The gross employment and occupational impacts of the baseline Bush-Cheney FY 1993 multiyear plan and the Clinton scenario are modeled using a static input–output analysis. We used the employment level for 1992 spending as the base year to compare with the last year of the Bush plan and with employment levels generated by the last year of the Clinton plan. See Oden and Bischak, *Armaments Industry and Defense Conversion*, for complete methodology. The employment impacts of these defense plans estimate the direct and indirect effects of the demand changes. These estimates, however, do not include the induced effect of job losses stemming from reduced consumer spending. We did not include the induced effects because these losses should be offset by more general measures to promote economic growth. Finally, the outlay data reflect the specific changes in spending within particular accounts for military personnel, operations and maintenance, procurement, research and development, military construction, and other expenses. Because no detailed budget accounts are available on the composition of spending for the 1995–97 period, we have had to project out the composition of spending in FY 1994 to cover the years 1995–97. We used these budget forecasts for the scenarios to analyze the employment impacts of changes in defense spending over the period. However, we excluded atomic energy defense-related DoE budgets due to a lack of detailed data on the purchase patterns related to nuclear weaponry and testing. Instead, we used a slightly narrower budget definition (called the 051 budget function by the Office of Management and Budget). Furthermore, we used outlay data to model the economic and employment impacts since it is the change in outlays that measures the actual spending impact on the economy. Nine translators were developed by the authors to distribute the spending by major accounts into the proper industrial proportions of purchases involved in defense-related operations and maintenance (O&M), procurement, research and development, and military construction. Four separate translators were developed to distribute the O&M purchases by industry for each of the armed services and defense agencies. These industrial proportions are based on the analysis developed in Margaret I. Sheridan, Paul H. Richanbach, and David L. Blond, *The Defense Translator* (Alexandria, VA: Institute for Defense Analysis, 1984).

9. See *Outlook 1990–2005*, Bureau of Labor Statistics, U.S. Department of Labor, *BLS Bulletin, 2402* (May 1992): 56–60, table 5, based on the moderate-growth scenario.

10. Boeing announced major reductions in production due to cancellations or

delays of aircraft orders by airlines. See "Press release by Boeing commercial airplane group" (January 26, 1993); also see "Pratt & Whitney's news release" (January 26, 1993).

11. See Norman Saunders, "Employment effects of the rise and fall in defense spending," *Monthly Labor Review* (April 1993): 3–10.

12. "Effects of alternative defense budgets on employment," p. 28.

13. See Ann Markusen and Joel Yudken, *Dismantling the Cold War Economy* (New York: Basic Books, 1991), pp. 140–6.

14. *Outlook 1990–2005*, pp. 62–92.

15. See Saunders, "Employment effects."

16. Again, the differences seem to be attributable to the way in which the trade margins were estimated by Saunders versus the technique used by the author.

17. See Schafer, "Still neglecting public investment."

18. See Congressional Budget Office (CBO), *Federal Debt and Interest Costs* (May 1993), ch. 6; also *The Economic Effects of Reduced Defense Spending* (February 1992): pp. 12–20.

19. Ibid.

20. See, for instance, Jeff Faux and Max Sawicky, *Investing the Peace Dividend* (Washington, DC: Economic Policy Institute, 1991). More generally, an open letter to President Bush, the Congress, and Federal Reserve Chairman Alan Greenspan by one hundred of the nation's leading economists in March of 1992 made the case for more economic stimulus and investment to solve both short-term and long-term economic problems facing the nation.

21. A sophisticated version of this argument has been advanced by economist Robert Eisner (*How Real Is the Federal Deficit* [New York: Free Press, 1986]), who argues that conventional measures of the deficit overstate its magnitude because it does not distinguish between capital investments made by government and current expenditures. According to Eisner, proper accounting for such investments would dramatically lower the estimates of the deficit. Yet, critics have noted that not all government investments have discernible paybacks and therefore it might be difficult to treat all such fixed investments as capital outlays.

22. See Greg Bischak, "Peace Dividends . . . Past and Present," *The New Economy* (Washington, DC: The National Commission for Economic Conversion and Disarmament), *14*, 3, 2 (1992): 4.

23. See the most recent of such studies, conducted by DRI for the congressional Research Service on behalf of the House Committee on Government Operations. This study found that for every $1 billion shifted from defense to state and local government expenditures, there was a net increase in employment of nearly 6,300 jobs. See CRS memorandum of February 1, 1993. Also see an earlier study by Roger Bezdek, "The economic impact—regional and occupational—of compensated shifts in defense spending," *Journal of Regional Science*, *15*, 2 (1975). Also see *Converting the American Economy: The Economic Effects of an Alternative Security Policy* (Lansing, MI: Employment Research Associates, 1991).

24. *Converting the American Economy*, p. 29, table 11.

25. *After the Cold War: Living with Lower Defense Spending* (Washington, DC: Office of Technology Assessment, 1992), p. 203.

26. See "Companies in profile," in *IEEE Spectrum, Special Issue on Conversion* (December 1992): 42.

27. See Miriam Pemberton, "Where are the jobs?" *The New Economy, 20* (Fall 1993): 14.

28. The Winbridge Group, Inc., *The Commercialization of Defense Technology: A Survey of Industry Experience* (DRI/McGraw-Hill, and the Fraser Group Inc., November 1991), p. 2.

29. See National Commission for Economic Conversion and Disarmament, "Successful conversion experiences" (Washington, DC: 1992), pp. 7–10.

30. See "Companies in profile," *IEEE Spectrum*.

31. See James Raffel, "Calstart, California's innovative conversion consortium," *The New Economy, 15* (Summer 1992): 4–5.

32. Ibid.

33. See American Association of Environmental Engineers Ad Hoc Committee on Research, "Environmental engineering, establishing research priorities," *Journal of Water Pollution Control Federation, 61,* 4, 1990, pp. 454–9.

34. See Worldwatch Institute, *State of the World, 1993*, Washington, (DC) pp. 101–38, 180–200.

35. GDP forecasts taken from CBO, *The Economic and Budget Outlook: Fiscal Years 1994–98* (January 1993), table 1.3. The baseline for nondefense infrastructure investment is taken from *Budget of the United States, Fiscal Year 1994* (April 1993), p. 72; the net additions (excluding investment tax credits) are calculated based on data presented in *A Vision for Change for America*, Executive Office of the President of the United States (Washington, DC: U.S. Government Printing Office, February 17, 1993), pp. 135–9, table 5. Historical data on the relative investment rate in nonmilitary public investment as compared with GDP are taken from David Alan Aschauer, *Public Investment and Private Sector Growth* (Washington, DC: Economic Policy Institute, January 1991), pp. 5–9.

36. See *Creating Transportation Jobs, Aerospace Industrial and Workforce Capabilities for Surface Transportation Manufacturing* (Los Angeles: Economic Roundtable, January 1993).

37. See James Raffel, "State Retraining Programs," *The New Economy, 18* (Spring 1993).

38. See Elizabeth Mueller et al., *Retraining for what? Displaced defense workers come up against EDWAA* (Project on Regional and Industrial Economics, Rutgers University, September 1993).

39. See "Employment of engineers: What is the national society doing about it?" *Industry Engineering* (National Society of Professional Engineers, Los Angeles), April–May 1993.

40. See Andrew Taylor, "Remodeled community plan approved by committee," *Congressional Quarterly* (November 13, 1993): 3108–9.

41. See *The New Economy, 20* (Fall 1993): 10.

42. Schlesinger made these observations at the National Technology Conversion Conference in October 1993. See ibid.

43. See an address by Felix Rohatyn before the J.F. Kennedy School of Government on "The American economy and the rest of the world: Two sides of the same coin," November 30, 1993.

8

JAMES RAFFEL

Economic Conversion Legislation: Past Approaches and the Search for a New Framework

Despite the end of the Cold War, military spending remains high in historical terms. According to the comptroller of the Department of Defense, military spending in FY 1993 totaled $240.6 billion. Adjusted for inflation, in 1962, the year of the Cuban Missile Crisis, the United States spent $230 billion on the military.[1] Recently, Senate Budget Committee Chairman Jim Sasser (D-TN) described the current situation around the defense budget: "We are now into an era of military pork barrelling in this country. We are not responding to external threats. We are responding to internal threats of job losses as a result of cutting the military budget. That is what it is about."[2]

A comprehensive fiscal and structural conversion program is essential to move beyond the pork barrel politics of Capitol Hill. Numerous economic studies confirm that civilian investments generate more jobs and growth than military spending. In 1993, for example, the Congressional Research Service (CRS) found that for every $1 billion cut from the military and reinvested in the domestic economy, the economy gained more than 6,200 more jobs than it lost.[3] Clearly, as Seymour Melman, Lloyd J. Dumas, and other leading conversion scholars have long argued,[4] cutting the defense budget need not lead to massive job losses if this structural change to the economy is properly managed through reinvesting defense savings in sectors of the economy that generate wealth and growth as well through a series of initiatives to help workers, communities, and businesses. Indeed, the larger point is that continued military spending *undermines* the productive capacity of the nation's economy, endangering future levels of growth and prosperity.

The conversion movement deserves significant credit for alerting the nation to the dangers of excessive military spending. Yet, to date, it has not succeeded in getting Congress to pass legislation that would move the nation's economy beyond its Cold War moorings, although for nearly thirty years the movement rallied behind a substantial conversion bill that could have made a major contribution to that goal. The bill, which ultimately evolved into the Defense Economic Adjustment Act, represented a potential tool for moving the nation away from a military-led industrial policy toward a fiscal and regulatory program emphasizing meeting human needs and sustaining economic growth.

While the Defense Economic Adjustment Act has undergone many changes from its introduction in 1963, the bill has always placed a paramount emphasis on planning, and for good reason. The notable differences between the military and civilian economies indicate that such planning is crucial if defense firms are to enter commercial markets successfully, a point supported by experience. Melman pointed out in *The Permanent War Economy* that planning also serves the vital political function of assuring defense-dependent workers in particular that "new markets and new jobs are in the offing to secure their economic future."

Melman, however, never assumed that planning alone could build a constituency for conversion. Conversion planning, he wrote, "cannot come to life except as a major part of the population discards the ideological controls that harness it to the war economy."[5] Unlike any other event since the end of World War II, the demise of the Soviet Union presents a fundamental challenge to the consensus in the United States for maintaining a large military budget. With this challenge comes the opportunity to advance an alternative vision for organizing a substantial portion of our economy and society.

A New Approach?

Powerful military and corporate interests have successfully blocked efforts to promote a comprehensive economic conversion program that would generate substantial civilian jobs and growth through reorienting budget priorities and advanced alternative use planning. As a result, conversion advocates have pursued reforms in existing adjustment programs, which, while useful, do not engage the fundamental challenge of demilitarizing the economy and civilian job creation.

During the debate over the North American Free Trade Agreement, an impressive coalition of labor, environmental, human rights, social justice, and public policy organizations nearly succeeded in defeating the treaty. A similar coalition is needed if progressives are to advance an economic agenda emphasizing conversion and civilian job creation. Putting together a substantial coalition to press for conversion and a program to generate sustainable civilian jobs that address the sources of dislocation brought about by defense cutbacks, trade and environmental regulations, as well the needs of other economically disadvantaged Americans will likely require a new legislative vehicle. While long-term goals and strategies need to be addressed and reconciled, conversion opportunities in environmentally benign transportation, energy, and environmental technologies present immediate opportunities for coalition building.

As an important new paper points out, conversion activists have worked with peace groups, environmentalists, and trade unions, even middle management at defense firms, as well as organizations working on industrial retention and community development on various components of the vast challenge of demilitarizing the nation's economy.[6] While several of these constituencies achieved major victories around specific projects, contradictory goals (particularly around cutting the military budget, environmental sustainability and traditional economic growth) and different methods of political organizing have hindered the development of a significant political movement around sustainable civilian job creation (see chapter 6). Although President Clinton's 1994 state-of-the-union address rejected further cuts in defense spending to pay for domestic programs, it is clear that his administration, unlike its predecessor, sees a strong role for government in administering the wind-down in military spending. That view provides important political openings that conversion advocates need to exploit in advancing an alternative agenda.

Early Conversion Legislation

The first bill introduced in Congress emphasizing conversion planning was the National Economic Conversion Act (S. 2274), introduced by

Senator George McGovern (D-SD) on October 31, 1963. Ten senators cosponsored the bill, which called for creating the interagency National Economic Conversion Commission in the White House, chaired by the secretary of commerce.[7] The bill required the commission to prepare a study of the "appropriate policies and programs to be carried out" by the federal government to promote economic conversion. One key aspect of this study required the commission to consider potential areas of the economy where federal funds could be invested to create new nonmilitary market opportunities for defense-dependent workers, communities, and firms.[8] Another key provision of S. 2274 required firms that assigned 25 percent or more of their employees to defense work to set up Industrial Conversion Committees. These committees were charged "with planning for conversion to civilian work arising form possible curtailment or termination," of defense contracts subject to more specific regulations issued by the National Economic Conversion Commission.[9]

Shortly after McGovern introduced the bill, the *Washington Post* editorialized that "Senator McGovern is espousing simple prudence in urging Congress to create a National Economic Conversion Commission," adding that "reductions and shifts [in defense spending] are occurring all the time and are not contingent on reaching a disarmament agreement with the Soviet Union." In addition, the editorial specifically endorsed mandatory industrial conversion committees, noting that the "need for an approach like this does not have to be labored; every member of Congress is familiar with the desperate protests that come from the constituency whenever the end of a defense contract is even rumored."[10] Although the Senate held hearings on this legislation, the war in Vietnam and a rising defense budget inspired by the conflict soon overwhelmed this early effort to promote conversion planning.[11]

As the United States disengaged from the conflict in Indochina, economic conversion and reinvestment became major political issues. The Johnson administration, confronted by the growing contradictions of its fiscal guns and butter policies, identified areas of domestic investment following the end of the Vietnam War in its last Economic Report of the President in January 1969.[12] In 1970, the subcommittee on Executive Reorganization and Government Research to the Senate Government Operations Committee circulated a questionnaire to a wide range of industry leaders on whether the United States should establish an interagency economic conversion commission, as called for in S. 1285, The National Economic Conversion Act,[13] to develop policies to respond to the consequences of lower defense spending. Senator Abraham Ribicoff (D-CT), the subcommittee chair, wrote an introduction to the report that in many ways remains a valid description of the challenges facing the nation today.

> [P]rivate industry is not interested in initiating any major attempts at meeting critical public needs. Most industries have no plans or projects designed to apply their resources to civilian problems. Furthermore, they indicated an unwillingness to initiate such actions without a firm commitment from the government that their efforts will quickly reap the financial rewards to which they are accustomed.
>
> . . . Eventually, the manpower released by current cutbacks in the defense industry may be reemployed as our economy continues to grow. But in the meantime, individuals and companies are suffering. And our environment and cities are suffering also, as the talents and know-how that could be utilized to attack these problems lay idle.
>
> . . . In light of the lack of initiative on the part of private industry to develop its own products and programs in the realm of civilian programs, what is needed is a strong federal role in conversion and in the use of industry resources for public programs. Not only could such a role prove beneficial to our cities and the environment, it would also provide companies with a profitable alternative to layoffs in the event of a major defense spending cutback. Such a cutback may become possible with either an end to the Vietnam War or a strategic arms limitation agreement with the Soviet Union.
>
> . . . Without a strong Federal role in conversion, the consequences of the current relatively minor cutback in defense spending, combined with the overall lack of initiative on the part of our Nation's industries can mean that an end to the hostilities in Vietnam may bring either a huge rise in the development and production of supersophisticated, overdesigned and unnecessary military hardware or else a real depression, concentrated in the geographical areas currently most dependent on defense production.
>
> . . . The irony is that without an increased Federal role in conversion, we may reach the point where our superweapons symbolically turn against us, destroying what they are designed to protect.[14]

In addition to the interagency task force, another key provision of S. 1285 required defense contractors to define their "capability for converting manpower, facilities and any other resources now used for specific military products, or purposes, to civilian uses." Trade unions, industry associations, and professional organizations were encouraged to "make appropriate studies and plans to further the conversion capabilities of their membership." All firms holding multiyear defense contracts employing more than forty-nine workers or 25 percent of their work force were subject to these provisions.

In testimony before the Senate Labor and Public Welfare Committee, Walter P. Reuther, the president of the United Automobile Workers, acknowledged his "fullest sympathy" for the bill in general and this provision in particular, but added that its goals "are not likely to be achieved unless an effective mechanism is embodied in the Bill to overcome the foot-dragging by defense contractors who prefer the easy profits of military-business-as-usual." In particular, he noted that the bill's conversion planning provision was "aimed at the right direction, [but] is not sufficient in itself to assure that corporations engaged in defense production will plan seriously for conversion to civilian production."[15]

As a result of Reuther's testimony, Senator McGovern introduced new legislation the following year, S. 4430, the National Economic Conversion Act. This bill required contractors to deposit 12.5 percent of their profits from defense and space work into a trust fund to finance the implementation of conversion programs developed by the firm and to pay benefits to workers who might be adversely affected by the transition. If the contractor successfully converted to civilian work, the firm could reclaim all of the funds remaining in its account with interest and free of all taxes.[16]

Although this bill did not pass, many of the ideas raised at the time around federal involvement in conversion and insuring management participation in conversion through incentives remain significant concerns today. Subsequent conversion bills were introduced in the 1970s and 1980s. By the 101st Congress, The Defense Economic Adjustment Act (HR. 101) sponsored by Representative Ted Weiss had incorporated many of the ideas considered earlier and evolved into a more substantial bill.

The Defense Economic Adjustment Act

The Defense Economic Adjustment Act (HR. 101) established the Defense Economic Adjustment Council (DEAC) within the executive branch.[17] One of DEAC's key responsibilities was to prepare and distribute a "Conversion Guidelines Handbook" that would provide an outline of the numerous issues associated with defense conversion. The bill also required the Defense Department to notify DEAC one year in advance of a pending or proposed change in defense spending that would lead to defense industry job losses. Each community "substantially and seriously" affected by defense cutbacks was to be eligible for federal economic adjustment assistance, with priority going to communities "most vulnerable economically" to defense cutbacks. DEAC would have been required to disseminate information regarding federal assistance to the appropriate alternative use committee (discussed below).

One of the most controversial provisions of the Weiss bill, however, called for the creation of mandatory alternative use committees (AUCs) at every defense facility employing more than 100 workers. These committees were to have at least eight members with equal representation of labor and management (or base command, if the facility was a government military installation). Local governments were eligible to send nonvoting representatives to serve on these AUCs, although nonvoting members could not exceed 50 percent of the total voting members.

AUCs were: (1) to evaluate the assets of the facility and the resources and needs of the local community in terms of physical property, the skills and experience of the local work force, and the economy; (2) to develop and review once every two years a detailed plan to convert the facility to civilian production in the event of a contract cancellation or termination or denial of an export license; (3) to provide retraining and reemployment counseling services or ensure that such training was done by other agencies for all affected employees; and (4) to dissolve itself and return all assets to management after the conversion was completed. The conversion plans adopted by the AUCs would be designed to maximize job retention at existing facilities. The bill also required that the plan spell out a strategy for completing the conversion process within two years. Finally, another controversial provision required management to pay for the operation of AUCs.

The Weiss bill specified that all workers employed by a defense contractor for at least six months prior to layoff as a result of a contract termination or reduction were eligible to receive income support for up to two years at 90 percent of the first $20,000 in salary and 50 percent of the next $5,000 above that level, plus full credit toward a pension and maintenance of health insurance. Workers could also receive reimbursement for reasonable relocation expenses if they found work in other geographical areas. The bill required managers and engineers to enter retraining programs as a condition of receiving these benefits.

Another key provision of the bill established the Economic Adjustment Fund to pay for this program. Contractors would be required to pay a 1.25 percent tax on the value of their defense contracts into this fund. In addition, the government was to estimate the projected savings that would result from canceling or cutting back a defense contract and deposit 10 percent of those savings into the fund.

The Weiss Bill and the FY 1991 Defense Authorization Act

Economic conversion received renewed attention on Capitol Hill in 1988, when the first Base Closure Commission made its recommendations for closing domestic military bases. In January 1989, Melman and then–House Speaker Jim Wright (D-TX) met for over three hours to discuss conversion. According to an article by David Beers in *Mother Jones*, Wright came away from the meeting deeply impressed: "Melman had done more thinking on the subject [of defense conversion] than any other. . . . he's also very persistent. His idea that each defense procurement dependent plant must have a conversion plan made sense to me." In the same article, Beers wrote, "Suddenly Weiss was no longer Don Quixote: Wright liked Melman and Melman was Weiss' idea man. A few other members had related bills in the works; Wright told all the pertinent Demo[crat]s to begin creating a compromise that he could take to the floor."[18] While Jim Wright's political career ended soon afterward, Majority Leader Richard Gephardt pursued the issue the following year.

Along with Weiss, Representatives Nicholas Mavroules (D-MA), Sam Gejdenson (D-CT), and Mary Rose Oakar (D-OH) were among the other members of Congress working on conversion-related legislation at the time. The Mavroules Economic Conversion Act (HR. 699, introduced on January 27, 1989 in the 101st Congress) called for expanding job training programs and unemployment compensation for laid-off defense workers, to be financed by earmarking a percentage of savings from defense budget cuts. The bill also made funds available for community economic adjustment planning and required the secretary of defense to provide one year's advance notice of a major contract cancellation and notice of base closures and realignments.

The Gejdenson Economic Diversification and Defense Adjustment Act (HR. 2852, introduced on July 11, 1989 in the 101st Congress) borrowed elements from the Weiss and Mavroules bills by requiring the secretary of defense to provide six months' advance notice of a weapons system contract cancellation. The bill called for $200 million to be made available for worker training and community development grants. Communities receiving these funds would have been required to establish diversification alternative use committees consisting of labor unions, defense and nondefense businesses, local and regional governments, local education institutions, and private nonprofit agencies. These committees would have: (1) developed and reviewed detailed plans for diversifying a region's defense-dependent economy through nondefense economic development; (2) developed and reviewed plans for the alternative civilian use of a major defense facility in the event of a contract termination or reduction; and (3) evaluated the resources of the facility and the resources and requirements of the local community. The plans developed by these committees were required to specify the skills used by defense industry workers and which of those skills could be used by nondefense businesses. They were also to provide a timetable for achieving concrete results.[19] Another bill, sponsored by Representative Mary Rose Oakar, incorporated community economic development, job training, and unemployment benefits.[20]

Maggie Bierwirth, who at the time was responsible for conversion issues for Representative Gejdenson, recently published an account of how the congressional working group viewed these various approaches:

> Early discussions . . . focused on whether the Weiss bill's requirements for facility-based advance planning by alternative use committees [were] feasible. . . . Some of the congressional working group members questioned whether companies would be willing or able to comply with the advance planning requirement, going to the trouble and expense of conducting production analyses and marketing studies of new products, unless the defense market had already dried up. . . . Gejdenson empha-

sized the importance of getting the program written into law, generating successes, and increasing funding in the future when the program's value had been demonstrated. . . . Mavroules felt strongly that it was critical to go forward with a proposal of modest proportions, for which a majority of Congress could be mustered with relative ease, rather than risk losing everything by advancing an ambitious proposal with slim support. Weiss understood that the 1.25 percent tax on defense contracts would not be part of the consensus legislation, but he wanted to include extended unemployment benefits as well as job training.[21]

According to Bierwirth, all the members of the congressional working group agreed on the necessity to extend unemployment benefits for defense workers because "even if diversification plans could be implemented quickly in the communities that needed them, the transition period from defense to new industries could easily take longer than the six months in which workers would receive regular unemployment benefits." However, the working group doubted that the Ways and Means Committee "would agree to single out defense workers for benefits without examining the broader question of extended unemployment benefits for all workers, a controversial and time consuming process with enormous potential impact on the federal budget." So, according to Bierwirth, the working group decided to advance the worker training and community adjustment provisions through, respectively, the Education and Labor and Banking Committees so that conversion advocates "could focus their efforts on the more ambitious and riskier extended unemployment provision, which would be offered as an amendment, regardless of how it fared in the Ways and Means Committee."[22]

While Bierwirth's account offers valuable insights into the congressional process that conversion advocates must take into account when adopting a legislative strategy, it leaves out one significant detail: *Representative Weiss remained committed to conversion planning.* He described the two amendments he hoped to offer in a letter to members of the House seeking their support:

> One of these amendments will provide adjustment assistance to civilian workers dislocated due to the curtailment or termination of a defense contract, or the realignment or closure of a military installation. This assistance would include a 26 week extension of Unemployment Insurance and maintenance of health insurance for up to one year. Workers

would be eligible for these benefits only if they are participating in a certified retraining program. . . . These benefits are . . . consistent with aid extended to other categories of workers who are victims of circumstances beyond their control.

Another amendment will give local governments, community members as well as workers and managers of defense facilities employing 100 or more (both private contractors and government installations included) the opportunity to form local Community Adjustment and Diversification Committees. These Committees will be made up of the facility's workers and management, and would develop plans for the facility and its workers in case defense cuts lead to the realignment or termination of a contract or the closure or realignment of a military installation. . . . The amendment requires management of defense facilities to participate on a planning committee *ONLY if the local government, community members, or facility workers request that they participate.* And, if the facility's management forms its own adjustment committee, it need not participate in one formed by the other parties.[23]

Neither of these amendments was permitted by the Rules Committees. In a letter to an advocacy group, Weiss's legislative assistant expressed bitterness about the process, claiming that Majority Leader Richard Gephardt (D-MO) went back on his word to Representative Weiss by not coming out in favor of at least one of his amendments before the Rules Committee.[24]

While Ted Weiss supported the Mavroules amendment, it was far from the comprehensive conversion initiative he had championed:

A genuine and comprehensive policy of economic conversion includes advanced planning. It would have plans for the conversion of the facility drawn up before contract reductions are announced. If this is done, then when the contract is cut back, a facility will be able to convert, retrain its workers and start production without the massive employee layoffs and community disruption which often [occur] with contract cancellations.[25]

In September 1990, Congress included an amendment to the FY 1991 Defense Authorization Act, establishing the $200 million Defense Conversion Adjustment (DCA) Program. The legislation required the Defense Department to transfer $150 million to the Department of Labor's Job Training Partnership Act (Title III) program to train dislocated defense industry workers. The Department of

Defense was also required to transfer $50 million to the Commerce Department's Economic Development administration's Title IX Sudden and Severe Economic Dislocation program for communities responding to military base and plant closures.

The same section of the authorization included a Sense of Congress calling for increased funding for the Export-Import Bank to help converting businesses capture civilian export markets. In addition, the bank was to consider, where appropriate, several conversion-related provisions as part of its application process for export financing. In particular, applications from companies or "groups of workers" that either were "substantially and seriously affected by defense budget reductions," or were "in transition from defense to nondefense production," were to receive preference.[26] Although the provision was nonbinding, it represents one indication of how far Congress traveled on this issue of export financing for civilian versus military products within just two years.

Implementing the 1991 Program

Although the Defense Conversion Adjustment Program was far less substantial than the proposals outlined in HR. 101, the Bush administration's opposition to using DoD funds for conversion-related activities significantly delayed its implementation. This delay caused considerable hardship for defense-dependent workers and communities. Since the DCA money was not available as Congress intended, the Labor Department spent $6 million of its own money to aid more than 6,000 workers in St. Louis and Dallas–Fort Worth who had been laid off as a result of the A-12 cancellation in January 1991. Jim Van Erden, a Labor Department official, told the Chicago *Tribune* in March 1991 that Labor had written at least three letters to the Department of Defense asking for reimbursement, adding that "If that money [Labor's share of the $200 million] had been here, we would not have used the discretionary pot," to aid the laid-off A-12 workers.[27] Using the discretionary funds meant, in effect, taking money away from other deserving laid-off workers.

The House Armed Services Investigations Subcommittee held a remarkable hearing on the implementation of this program on May 15, 1991. In a prepared statement, Christopher Jehn, who at the time was the assistant secretary of defense for force management and personnel, prepared a statement for the subcommittee that said that the "Defense [Department] has not yet decided whether to transfer the $200 million to the Departments of Commerce and Labor."[28] At the hearing, however, in response to strong opening statements from several members of Congress, the DoD representatives promised to release the funds. Bierwirth identified the "unusual amount of constituent activity [that] had been generated to turn up the heat on the DoD to release the money," as a reason why the transfer occurred.[29]

Despite this apparent victory, bureaucratic delays (in part the result of the Bush administration's continued opposition) continued. The Department of Labor received an initial $50 million in May 1991; the Commerce Department received its share of the funds in January 1992. At the end of 1993, according to Labor Department documents, approximately $102 million had been spent to serve more than 38,000 workers nationwide. Both the $50 million made available to the Economic Development Administration (EDA) through the amendment plus an additional $80 million subsequently transferred as part of the FY 1993 Defense Authorization Act (see below) were obligated by the end of 1993.

Before Congress adopted the Defense Conversion Adjustment Program, Representative Weiss said that whatever conversion program emerged, "I would hope . . . it maintains some of the basics: advanced notification, retraining, subsidization of training, and decentralization of decision making as to what alternative program they are going to be going into."[30] While Congress and the Clinton administration have endorsed a variety of "conversion" programs since the FY 1991 act, the nation still lacks a comprehensive program.

FY 1993 Defense Authorization

Three conversion-related program categories were created by Congress in the FY 1993 Defense Authorization Act to assist the major constituencies affected by cutbacks in military spending.[31] These programs provide over $750 million in transition and training benefits for laid-off military personnel and civilian workers, nearly $215 million in economic adjustment assistance to defense-dependent communities, and over $870 million for defense industry and technology programs. Most of these conversion and adjustment initiatives are managed by the Department of Defense and the Veterans Administration.

The lion's share of the defense industry and technology programs is intended to promote dual-use technologies—that is, those technologies that ostensibly have both military and civilian applications. The major objectives of these dual-use programs are to preserve the defense industrial base, promote spin-offs from defense technologies to civilian use, and increase the use of civilian high technologies for weaponry in order to reduce costs. Many of the programs within this category ultimately became the Technology Reinvestment Project (described below). The "other initiatives" referred to in Table 8.1 were nine programs previously authorized; the only new effort was the $4.9 million "National Center for Advanced Gear Manufacturing Technology."

In addition, Congress authorized and appropriated $75 million for retraining and employment adjustment services under Title III of the Job Training Partnership Act (JTPA). Certain members of the armed forces, civilian DoD and DoE employees, and defense industry workers are eligible to participate in the program, which is known as the Defense Diversification Program. Unlike the 1991 program, the Pentagon was not required to transfer these funds to the Department of Labor, although the legislation permits such a transfer, which in fact occurred in March 1993. However, the legislation built on the 1991 program by providing $80 million for community adjustment administered through the Commerce Department's Economic Development Administration. In addition, the Pentagon's Office of Economic Adjustment (OEA) received a $79.9 million appropriation for FY 1993. OEA was required, however, to spend $50 million to support an initiative at the Philadelphia Naval Shipyard. Obviously, it made no sense to allocate almost two-thirds of the agency's budget to one project when many efforts nationwide needed support. More fundamentally, the priorities of the appropriators are not an effective substitute for the sectoral planning needed to make conversion possible in the shipbuilding industry and throughout the economy.

The Authorization Act restructured OEA by permitting it to make grants for implementation as well as for planning. While the language of the act makes clear that Congress did not wish to undermine EDA, these changes at best will build yet another bureaucracy within the Pentagon that already exists elsewhere. Actually, this strategy probably has more to do with reconciling the different priorities of the House and the Senate than with developing a coherent long-term plan. One positive feature of the authorization, however, is that it requires OEA to set aside $2 million for grants to communities seeking to reduce

Table 8.1

Funding for Conversion-Related Programs in the FY 1993 Defense Authorization Act

	$ in millions	
Program	Authori- zation	Appro- priation
Defense industry and technology base programs:		
Program for Analysis of the Technology & Industrial Base	5	—
Center for the Study of Defense Economic Adjustment	2	—
Defense Dual-Use Critical Technology Partnerships	100	97
Commercial-Military Integration Partnerships	50	48.5
Regional Technology Alliances Assistance Program	100	97
Defense Advanded Manufacturing Technology Partnerships	25	24.3
Defense Manufacturing Extension Programs	100	97
Defense Dual-Use Assistance Extension Program	200	97
Defense Procurement Technical Assistance Program	12	16
Defense Manufacturing Engineering Education Program	30	29.1
Other defense industry and technology base programs	70	67.7
Other initiatives		296.8
Subtotal	694	870.4
Community adjustment and assistance programs:		
Office of Economic Adjustment	52	79.9
Defense Conversion Commission		5
Impact Aid	58	50
Economic Development Administration	80	8
Subtotal	190	214.9
Personnel assistance programs:		
Temporary early retirement authority	254	254
Temporary health transition assistance	76	76
Guard and reserve transition initiatives	40	40
Separation pay and civilian health benefits	72	72
Troops to teachers and teacher's aides	65	65
Rnvironmental education and retraining programs	20	20
Job training and employment and educational opportunities	84	84
Service member occupational conversion and training	75	75
National Guard Civilian Youth Opportunities pilot program	50	50
Other programs of the commission on national and community service	30	20
Job placement assistance and career training		0.21
Civilian community corps demonstration program	30	20
Subtotal	796	756.2
Grand total	1,680	1,841.5

their defense dependency before cuts occur. A related section authorized an additional $2 million for OEA to conduct a pilot program to improve economic adjustment planning. The pilot program funded four studies of local economies responding to various challenges related to reduced defense spending, including a base closure, a closure of a major weapons laboratory, and cutbacks by a defense contractor.

Congress provided substantial funds in the FY 1993 Authorization for the DoD and DoE military and civilian personnel. The largest sum, $254 million, was appropriated to encourage early retirements among those with at least fifteen years in the service. Much smaller amounts will fund early retirement for selected civilian DoD employees and members of the reserves. The term of transitional health policies has been extended from one year to eighteen months for both civilian and military personnel, although the service member will still be required to pay both the employer and employee contributions.

Two small job training programs were created. The "Troops to Teachers" program provides training stipends and subsidizes the beginning salaries of former service members and civilian DoD and DoE personnel who enter the teaching profession. Part of the program has also been extended to laid-off defense industry scientists and engineers; the program pays half their certification costs, requiring the contractor to pay the other half, but does not offer the beginning salary subsidy. In addition to eligibility for the JTPA program, Congress revived an old program that pays half the costs of training departing GIs to employers who agree to provide them with permanent employment.

The Omnibus Budget Reconciliation Act and the FY 1993 Conversion Program

In constructing this program, Congress had to work within the limitations of the Budget Enforcement Act of 1990. A key provision of this legislation established spending ceilings on defense and nondefense discretionary spending. In addition, the law stated that if Congress appropriated less money than was permitted by these "caps," the resulting savings were required to go to deficit reduction. In other words, funds from one category could not be transferred to another. For conversion programs, this meant that DoD funds could not be transferred to civilian agencies, although two small transfers did in fact occur. While numerous domestic organizations and labor unions mounted a significant lobbying campaign to "take down the walls" between discretionary spending categories, Congress rejected an initiative to do so in a March 1992 vote. The walls between categories came down for the FY 1994 budget, although the overall cap for discretionary programs remains in effect.

The Budget Enforcement Act had a long-term negative influence over the effort to establish a comprehensive conversion program. The legislation had the effect of establishing the Pentagon as the lead agency for conversion for FY 1993. However, the Clinton program borrowed heavily from the architecture of that authorization. Thus, a temporary mechanism designed to promote deficit reduction contributed to a military-led "conversion" program.

Early Notice and Conversion Planning in the FY 1993 Defense Authorization Act

Two of the most significant conversion provisions of the FY 1993 authorization involved program initiatives to provide firms and workers with six months' advance notice of major contract reductions or terminations and to encourage contractors to plan for conversion and diversification.[32] Unfortunately, DoD's inadequate implementation of both programs greatly undermined their effectiveness and underscores the dangers inherent in expecting the Pentagon to manage the nation's conversion programs.

The FY 1993 Defense Authorization Act included a provision (section 4471) that required the Department of Defense to provide notice to contractors involved with projects valued at $500,000 or more of contract terminations or reductions equal to or exceeding 10 percent from the previous year's funding level for a particular program. Contractors, in turn, had two weeks to inform at-risk workers. Workers receiving notice were then eligible for JTPA job counseling through rapid response services. Under the original law, the Department of Defense had one month after the president submitted his budget in February to provide notice to the contractors. This process would be repeated in the fall following enactment of the appropriations act. In other words, this legislation permitted workers to consider conversion planning or retraining options in April, six months before an appropriations act made the actual cuts. Obviously, workers involved with projects Congress decided not to terminate or reduce would no longer be eligible for JTPA benefits.

The FY 1994 authorization act (see below) undermined the early notification provisions in two ways (section 1372). First, the Defense Department was given 180 days after the budget submission and enactment of the appropriations act to get the notices out to contractors. This means workers who were involved with projects slated for major reductions/terminations in February would not get notice until the middle of August, just six weeks before passage of the appropriations act. The act also raised the threshold for notification from 10 to 25 percent, meaning that fewer workers and companies would receive these notices.

In its initial effort to implement the 1993 act, the Department of Defense opted for the 25 percent threshold, violating both the letter and the spirit of the law. Raising the threshold for notification was no small detail, since it meant that thousands more workers would not be notified. A memo prepared by the Office of Undersecretary of Defense for Acquisition indicates that as many as eighty-two major weapon system procurement programs may be cut by 25 percent or more; no comparable calculations were made public for the 10 percent figure.

Calculations prepared by Greg Bischak, executive director of the National Commission for Economic Conversion and Disarmament, revealed several significant contract reductions among major defense contractors that would fall below the 25 percent threshold. For example, the DDG–51 Destroyer, produced by Bath Iron Works in Maine, will be cut by about 18 percent, the Air Force's F–22 ATF aircraft will be cut by nearly 17 percent, and the troubled C–17 cargo jet will be cut by nearly 16 percent. Meanwhile, the upgrades on the F–16s for the Air National Guard will be trimmed by 11 percent. There can be little doubt that a complete list starting at the 10 percent threshold would double or triple the number of contractors and subcontractors that would have to be notified.

The Department of Defense and Congress likely opted for the higher threshold in order to reduce the bureaucratic requirements for the department. However, while this might make the department's job easier, it makes conversion planning more difficult for the affected contractors and workers. Restoring the original language would complement a key provision of the administration's proposed *Reemployment Act of 1994*. (This is the administration's proposal for restructuring the Job Training Partnership Act.) In particular, that bill contains a provision (section 116) permitting states to fund projects that "provide services to assist in the conversion or restructuring of businesses in order to avert plant closings or substantial layoffs." That program would work well with the notice requirements originally specified in section 4471. Without these changes, workers must rely on the dubious and inadequate sixty-day notice specified under the WARN act.

Conversion Planning

Another section of the FY 1993 authorization of interest to conversion activists required the secretary of defense to "prescribe regulations to encourage defense contractors to engage in industrial diversification planning." At a hearing on conversion sponsored by the Research and Technology Subcommittee of the House Armed Services Committee on May 25, 1993, featuring representatives from the AFL-CIO, the International Association of Machinists and Aerospace Workers, and the United Auto Workers, Subcommittee Chair Patricia Schroeder made note of this provision of the law. The topic emerged when two of the witnesses testified in favor of mandatory alternative use committees.

That same day, Schroeder sent a letter to then–Defense Secretary Les Aspin inquiring about Defense Department's progress toward implementing this provision of the law. Schroeder's letter also inquired about "what consideration is being given to writing [the] regulations in such a way that would encourage the participation of defense industrial workers in this [diversification] process."

The Department of Defense had in fact failed to comply with either the letter or the spirit of the law. DoD officials say that no guidelines will be forthcoming. Instead, officials say that the Pentagon's initial effort to comply with this regulation came in a memo by Undersecretary John Deutch on expanding reimbursement for independent research and development and bid and proposal (IR&D/BP) costs to cover dual-use technologies. According to DoD officials, the trade associations for defense contractors argued that more subsidies were the way to promote conversion, not the issuance of more guidelines. Beyond the well-known shortcomings of the dual-use approach, it is obvious that simply giving more no-strings subsidies to defense contractors is no way to promote conversion.

The Clinton Administration's Defense
Reinvestment and Conversion Initiative

On March 11, 1993, President Clinton traveled to a Westinghouse defense facility in Linthicum, Maryland, to announce a five-year defense conversion program.[33] At that event, which came just before the Pentagon was to recommend to the Base Closure and Realignment Commission the closure of domestic military bases, the president said, "I know today that the world's finest makers of swords can and will be the finest makers of plowshares and they will lead America into a new century of strength, growth and opportunity."[34]

As of early 1994, the administration's five-year package called for spending approximately $21.6 billion from 1993 to 1997. Within the program, the administration plans to spend approximately $7.7 billion for assistance to defense workers, personnel, and communities. This figure includes spending by the Labor Department for retraining dislocated workers.

As of this writing, the administration has two bills pending before Congress to reshape the Job Training Partnership Act, the nation's program for retraining workers. One of the most important features of the Reemployment Act of 1994 is that it would serve all dislocated workers, regardless of the reason for layoff, thus eliminating over time programs to serve workers impacted by defense cuts, trade, and environmental regulations. While this approach could lead to more efficient service, organized labor wants to maintain several of the separate programs, including Trade Adjustment Assistance, which would be consolidated into one program under the administration's plan.[35] A separate bill would provide support for workers in long-term retraining programs, thus in principle fulfilling a key long-time objective of conversion advocates. The support available to workers through this program, however, is not as generous as the provisions contained in the Weiss bill.

Another component of the administration's program calls for spending $6.7 billion on a variety of "dual-use" technology initiatives. "Dual-use" technologies are those that supposedly have both military and commercial applications.[36] The Technology Reinvestment Program (TRP), which is perhaps the administration's best-known conversion program, is included within this category. Also included here are procurement reform efforts aimed at promoting greater commercial-military integration. Considering the well-known differences between military and commercial economies, however (to say nothing of the history of procurement reform initiatives), the potential of the dual-use and procurement reform efforts to achieve real success in civilian markets is highly questionable.

Washington has recently backed away from some of its claims regarding the job creation potential of dual use and the TRP. Dorothy Robyn, a staffer on President Clinton's National Economic Council, told an industry journal that "the major reason for undertaking dual-use programs is for national security, and secondarily to ease economic adjustment problems," adding that "these are not jobs programs."[37] The director of the TRP, Lee Buchanan, went further by saying, "There were a lot of people that were under the impression that dual-use really means a technology previously of DoD interest and now totally a commercial interest—*that's really defense conversion and that's not what we're talking about.*"[38]

The final component of the package is $7.1 billion on civilian-oriented investments referred to as "New Federal High Technology Investments." This last category includes: (1) Cooperative Research and Development Agreements between DoE labs and private industry; (2) renewable energy and conservation Research and Development; (3) the Transportation Department's Intelligent Vehicle Highway System; (4) the Commerce Department's Information Highways and various programs carried out by the National Institute for Standards and Technology (NIST); and (5) the Environmental Technology Program administered by the Environmental Protection Agency.

While the administration deserves credit for recognizing the need for federal leadership in administering the military spending winddown, the program does little to promote short-term job retention and creation, focusing instead on long-term, defense-led R&D initiatives and adjustment programs. In the absence of a vigorous reinvestment initiative, reorienting the initiative to make better use of various existing and proposed programs administered by the Commerce and Labor Departments could lead to a more effective approach.

To date, the TRP's aggressive outreach program has not been matched on the civilian side. Without such an effort, the programs identified as "new federal high-technology investments" stand little chance of promoting conversion or regional redevelopment, as the relevant agencies are designed to serve other purposes. For example,

NIST's Advanced Technology Program (ATP) serves a valuable purpose by providing cost-shared funding to companies to develop high technologies that may have enormous economic benefits. Yet ATP's criteria for evaluating proposals do not consider conversion or job retention or creation.

Better coordination and outreach would substantially improve the situation. Federal agencies charged with reinvestment should conduct an aggressive outreach program for local administrators of retraining and community adjustment programs. Such outreach would help connect worker and community programs—which are more focused on conversion—with job-creating civilian investments. Creative use of existing EDA planning grants and Labor Department job retention grants could encourage more proactive and comprehensive approaches to conversion and job retention.

One of the Clinton administration's proposals to rework the nation's programs for dislocated workers could also be used to advance conversion and jobs. The Reemployment Act contains provisions permitting states to fund projects that work to upgrade skill levels of workers facing layoff or that assist in conversion efforts seeking to avoid plant closures or substantial layoffs. States' rapid response teams could present this information to employers and workers as a means to avert layoffs. The new profiling system set up by the bill to survey workers' skills, interests, and goals could identify likely candidates for such training. A more aggressive and complementary approach would be to use the Labor Market Information Service to track federal procurement spending that might generate employment opportunities for laid-off workers. Through effective coordination with federal procurement spending, these programs could help create new opportunities in the civilian sector.

Worker retraining and community adjustment programs are not designed to create jobs. Increased funding for new initiatives in transportation, energy, the environment, and infrastructure programs contained in the administration's conversion program under "federal high-technology investments" is the critical component of an effective conversion program. However, the austere fiscal climate dominating discussion of the federal budget suggests that creating a low-cost, general-purpose, federally sponsored capital fund for civilian business development could provide vital assistance to commercial business enterprises seeking commercial and venture capital that is otherwise either prohibitively expensive or simply not available. Such a fund should be open to all civilian enterprises, rather than just defense firms seeking to exit a declining industry, to ensure both social equity and the emergence of new businesses not linked to military purposes.

The FY 1994 Program

Following President Clinton's March 11 announcement, it came as no surprise that conversion figured prominently in the FY 1994 Defense Authorization Act. Despite several notable victories, however, the package that emerged once again proved disappointing (Table 8.2).

Conversion and Arms Sales

In early 1993, several of the nation's largest defense contractors decided that, rather than considering commercial work, seeking more money from Washington to subsidize weapons exports represented a valid approach to conversion.[39] The idea originated in February 1993 with a letter sent by the Aerospace Industries Association (AIA), a trade association, to then–Defense Secretary Les Aspin. CEOs from several large firms, including Martin Marietta, Bath Iron Works, Raytheon, Grumman, Rockwell International, and Lockheed signed the letter, which argued that "this program would certainly be an appropriate part of any conversion or transition program."

Although AIA could not find a single member of the House of Representatives to introduce an appropriate amendment into the House version of the defense authorization, Senator Dirk Kempthorne (R-ID) successfully introduced language into the Senate bill earmarking $25 million to establish a $1 billion program to underwrite exports to the North Atlantic Treaty Organization (NATO) countries, Israel, Australia, South Korea, and Japan. An amendment offered by Senator Jeff Bingaman (D-NM) to eliminate the program failed 63:37. The House, however, overwhelmingly endorsed an amendment offered by Representatives Tom Andrews (D-ME) and John Kasich (R-OH) banning the use of conversion funds to finance arms exports.

The final version of the authorization combined the two amendments. While the program received a $25 million authorization, none of these funds are permitted to come from the administration's conversion program. The Andrews-Kasich and Kempthorne amendments

Table 8.2

The Clinton Administration's Program

Budget authority[a]	\$ in millions					
	1993	1994	1995	1996	1997	1993–97
I. Assistance for defense workers, personnel, and communities						
Dod personnel assistance and community support[b]	1,020	1,265	1,192	1,192	1,192	5,861
DoE worker community transition program	92	200	125	100	100	617
DoL workforce security program[c,d]		125	195	195	195	710
DoC Aid through EDA[c]		80	140	140	140	500
II. DoD dual-use technology						
TRP[e]	465	554	625	650	675	2,969
Other dual-use initiatives[b]	417	887	804	804	804	3,716
III. New federal high-technology investments (conversion opportunities)[f]		907	1,734	2,054	2,444	7,139
IV. Other industry assistance programs						
National shipbuilding initiative		50	50			100
Grand total	1,994	4,068	4,865	5,135	5,550	21,612

[a]According to the administration, these estimates reflect: (i) funding above the 1993 level and new programs that contribute to defense conversion, and (ii) the portion of existing programs restructured and redirected to conversion efforts.

[b]Figures presented for 1996 and 1997 remain at the 1995 level because estimates for these years are not yet available.

[c]Funds were previously transferred from DoD to these agencies that are not reflected in the total.

[d]Portion of the overall investment increase that could be expected to be used to assist displaced defense workers.

[e]In addition to the \$465 million in TRP funding, the 1993 TRP solicitation included \$7 million in separately budgeted SBIR funds.

[f]Includes investment programs providing direct conversion opportunities and 50 percent of programs that provide some conversion opportunities.

were not mutually exclusive, since the AIA program would be financed with funds earmarked for research and development and would not take away funds from the administration's conversion program. However, no funds were actually appropriated for the program and to date, it has not been implemented.

As a result of the hearing on May 25, 1993, the House included a provision in its version of the defense authorization, calling on the secretary of defense to encourage contractors to plan for conversion and diversification. The committee report to the authorization went further by "direct[ing] the department [DoD] to encourage its major defense suppliers to consult closely with workforce representatives in formulating such diversification plans through such mechanisms as labor–management product development committees."[40] This language was sponsored by Representative Elizabeth Furse (D-OR). Despite an intense lobbying effort by nonprofit organizations, religious groups, peace groups, and some labor unions, however, this language was dropped in the final authorization.

The $261 billion defense authorization for FY 1994 provided little insight into how the nation will resolve competing budgetary priorities in the aftermath of the Cold War, as funding for most major weapons systems was not seriously cut. The $2.5 billion "conversion" package in the Defense Appropriations Act included over $1 billion for programs that have little or no relation to conversion (see Table 8.3). Perhaps more distressing was Capitol Hill's move to offload the Defense Department's economic liabilities onto hard-pressed domestic agencies, notably the Commerce Department's Economic Development Administration. While Congress increased EDA's budget by more than $100 million, the agency was directed to spend $80 million on conversion programs that were previously funded by the Department of Defense. In light of the devastating budget cuts borne by EDA throughout the 1980s, the lack of DoD funds for community conversion initiatives will complicate efforts to rebuild the agency. In addition, no new money was forthcoming either from the Defense Department or from the Labor Department for retraining laid-off defense industry workers; that funding issue has emerged around the administration's proposed job training bills.

Several notable conversion programs were included in the FY 1994 authorization. An initiative by the House Armed Services Committee to promote the nation's commercial shipbuilding industry, by provid-

Table 8.3

Conversion Funding in the FY 1994 Defense Authorization Act

	$ in millions	
Program	Authorization	Appropriation
Defense technology conversion and reinvestment		
TRP dual-use partnerships	624	474
Shipbuilding initiative	197	80
Other technology initiatives	1,397	1,227
Subtotal	2,218	1,781
Personnel transition		
Training and placement programs	(48)	15
Occupational conversion and training	25	6
Separation pay and health benefits	100	100
Transition and relocation assistance	67	67
Temporary health transition assistance		12
Other conversion initiatives		77
Temporary early retirement	319[a]	319
Regional clearinghouse	(10)	—
Subtotal	192	596
Community assistance		
Office of Economic Adjustment	70	39
Junior ROTC	73	73
Subtotal	143	112
Total authorized	2,550	
Grand total	2,930	2,490

Notes:
[a]Program did not need explicit authorization for FY 1994.
To be supported out of unobligated funds appropriated to DoD and DoL in FY 1993 for conversion.
Numbers may not add to sum due to rounding.

ing export subsidies and loan guarantees for modernizing shipyards, received $80 million. The authorization also includes some measures developed by the Senate Democratic Defense Reinvestment Task Force aimed at rationalizing the process of redeveloping military bases.

Another substantial advance for conversion, not contained in the defense authorization, was the administration's decision to create an Office of Economic Conversion Information within the Commerce Department. The need for a single source of information regarding federal conversion programs was first recognized by Senator Barbara Boxer (D-CA), who introduced legislation outlining the functions of the office earlier in the year. Representative Lynn Schenk (D-CA) introduced comparable legislation in the House. One key provision of the Boxer bill, not mentioned in the administration's announcement, called for the Office to conduct outreach activities nationwide to allow all major stakeholders the opportunity to comment on and evaluate the effectiveness of federal conversion programs. This legislation would expand and institutionalize the office's functions. In April 1994, Representative Paul Kanjorksi (D-PA) introduced an amendment to legislation reauthorizing the Economic Development Administration that would institutionalize and expand the office's functions as part of a larger economic development initiative.

Within the "conversion" package, however, there are ample grounds to question some of the priorities established by Congress. While each of the armed services declined to fund the Junior Reserve Officer Training Corps program from their personnel accounts, the Department of Defense received $73 million in conversion funding for this dubious program, nearly double the $39 million allocated to the Office of Economic Adjustment. A $76.8 million allocation for "other conversion initiatives" mostly goes to projects of doubtful merit, although some funds were set aside for ocean thermal power plantships, methanol plantships, and other interesting projects. A major issue that flows from Congress's propensity to earmark such funding for their districts' constituencies is how the Advanced Research Projects Agency will manage a competitively awarded set of grants for such projects. This issue has caught the attention of Representative George Brown (D-CA), the chair of the House Science, Space and Technology Committee. At this writing, Brown is considering issuing a subpoena of DoD documents outlining which projects received earmarked funding.

Toward an Effective Conversion
Legislative Reform Agenda

The administration has requested $4.9 billion for "conversion" in FY 1995. Of this total, $2.6 billion would be funded by the Department of Defense. Most of these funds are devoted to dual-use technology programs. While much of the program closely resembles the initiatives of previous years, the chances for reforming this package have been vastly improved by better cooperation between labor unions and the peace, social justice, and religious communities.

Two important labor-led coalitions committed to advancing economic conversion emerged in 1993. The Call to Action, which emerged out of a conference at the University of Connecticut in June 1993, consists of New England's six AFL-CIO state presidents, Region 9A of the United Auto Workers, and various UAW and IAM locals. A conference sponsored by the Industrial Union Department of the AFL-CIO, led to the formation of another coalition, the Workplace Economic Conversion Action Network (WE*CAN). Both the IAM and the UAW are involved with WE*CAN, as are several peace and conversion and nonprofit groups, including the National Commission for Economic Conversion and Disarmament, Peace Action, the Council on Economic Priorities, and NETWORK: A National Catholic Social Justice Lobby and the Work and Technology Institute.

At this writing, the conversion, religious, peace, and social justice groups within the Economic Conversion Working Group and the Call to Action were working to convince the federal government to adopt the following agenda:

1. *Provide adequate early notification of contract reductions and/or terminations for defense industry workers* by restoring the language contained in the FY 1993 Defense Authorization Act (section 4471) and repealing language in the FY 1994 Defense Authorization Act (section 1372).

2. *Establish a fund to finance market feasibility studies for identifying market opportunities in near-term product development areas for converting defense firms.* Many small to medium-sized businesses, as well as reuse projects at bases slated for closure, need limited financial assistance to conduct market feasibility assessments of the potential demand for possible alternative civilian products. Without this information, companies are not able to raise funds from commercial banks or venture capitalists for financing the overall project. A $10 million dedicated program managed by the Pentagon's Office of Economic Adjustment could help leverage substantial amounts of private capital by enabling more companies to seek private funding for commercial efforts. Ideally, such a program would be administered by the Commerce Department, but the politics of Capitol Hill make the prospect of transferring Pentagon money to a civilian agency extremely unlikely.

3. *Commercial shipbuilding.* The House Armed Services Committee is seeking $50 million for MARITECH, an initiative to support the revitalization of the U.S. commercial shipbuilding industry. The Senate authorized $40 million. The coalition supports the higher figure.

4. *Loan guarantees.* Small to medium-sized converting businesses often lack access to capital to pay for the retooling, restructuring, and retraining necessary for civilian production. The House Defense Authorization (section 1113) would make the loan guarantee authority for converting businesses outlined in section 2524 of Title 10 USC mandatory and would condition these loans on the extent to which projects led to job retention. Without the $50 million for this program recommended by the House, many opportunities to save jobs through conversion will be lost. While the Senate Armed Services Committee opposed using TRP funds for this purpose, separating legislation endorsed by the Small Business Committee would authorize $100 million for this purpose, with the funds most likely coming from the Department of Defense.

5. *Expand the grant selection process of the Technology Reinvestment Project to include job creation and retention as criteria and make trade unions eligible to apply for funding.* Expanding TRP's grant selection criteria and potential applicants is crucial for making the program support the goals of job creation and retention. Despite the program's increasing military orientation, the sizable funding that this program will continue to receive makes it critical to push for worker involvement and significant commercial orientation.

Alternative Use Committees and Labor–Management Cooperation

While Ted Weiss did not live to see major portions of the bill he introduced enacted into law, Representative Jerry Nadler (D-NY) introduced a bill during the 103d Congress containing much of the language from the Defense Economic Adjustment Act calling for mandatory alternative use committees (AUCs). The reluctance of Congress to address this controversial issue, however, suggests that greater labor–management cooperation around industrial conversion efforts is not likely to be secured through this approach. Nonetheless, conversion advocates scored a major victory in early 1994 when the state of Connecticut passed landmark legislation related to alternative use planning, corporate accountability, and job creation. On the federal level, the issue of labor–management cooperation has been rolled into a larger effort around labor law reform.

In May 1994, the Connecticut General Assembly passed two major conversion-related bills. Insuring that state economic development funds are used in the public interest, especially to promote job creation and retention, is the goal of An Act Concerning Economic Development Program Accountability. The Act Concerning Defense Diversification requires Connecticut defense companies receiving state financial assistance to establish alternative use committees. A Call to Action: Labor's Agenda for Economic Conversion in New England, a coalition of New England's six AFL-CIO state chapters and defense-dependent union locals, played a decisive role in securing passage of these bills.

The Act Concerning Defense Diversification specifically requires Connecticut firms with DoD contracts exceeding $1 million that receive state economic development aid to establish alternative use committee. Representatives from labor and management will serve on these committees to prepare plans aimed at reducing or eliminating the facility's defense dependency; community representatives may also be invited to participate. Specifically, these plans will include: alternative civilian products that can be produced and marketed and retraining resources necessary to produce such projects in order to avoid dislocation of the current work force. The state's Department of Labor will monitor implementation of this program.

The Act Concerning Economic Development Program Accountability requires the state's Department of Economic Development and other grant-making agencies to outline the public policy objectives underlying its financial assistance programs. The goals listed in the act include:

- Retaining existing businesses and jobs;
- Expanding the level of economic activity by existing businesses;
- Expanding employment opportunities with existing businesses;
- Attracting new jobs;
- Providing jobs for underemployed workers, laid-off workers, and those on public assistance;
- Increasing, enhancing, and updating the capacity of business;
- Increasing, enhancing, and updating workers' skills and training.

The legislation requires businesses with twenty-five or more employees seeking economic development assistance of $250,000 or more to explain how the funds will be used to meet these objectives, particularly around job creation and retention. There is also language in the bill encouraging businesses to consult with workers and local officials in preparing proposals. As part of the process for selecting projects to be funded, grant-making agencies are required to consider whether proposals serve the public interest, whether these goals can be realistically achieved, and the extent to which the business has worked with community and employee representatives. The legislation encourages businesses to establish labor–management committees to promote the public policy objectives outlined above in carrying out the program.

After approving an economic development project, the state and the firm are required to sign a statement outlining the public policy objectives the grant will meet, particularly around job creation and retention. This statement will include an acknowledgment by the firm that it is receiving aid in expectation that it will be used to produce such benefits. A copy of this statement, as well as subsequent annual company reports to the state outlining progress toward achieving the public policy goals, will be made available to the mayor of the city where the company is based, as well as to the firm's unions. This process will enable key stakeholders to monitor implementation of individual programs. In addition, grant-making agencies are required to maintain a log of all pending requests for economic development assistance that would list the companies seeking aid, a brief summary of the proposed project, and instructions on how the public could get additional information about a project.

The Dunlop Commission and Labor
Law Reform: Cooperation or Coercion?

On the federal level, labor–management cooperation is one of many issues around labor law reform currently under consideration by the presidentially appointed Commission on the Future of Worker–Management Relations. The commission, which is chaired by former Labor Secretary John T. Dunlop, recently released a set of findings on worker–management relations in the United States. The administration plans to use the findings to help labor and management groups reach consensus around changes to existing labor law, a process that will be difficult at best, considering the vastly different agendas of these two groups. Despite the presence of several commissioners who either are from or are sympathetic to organized labor, a determined lobbying effort by corporations, along with an administration with a mixed record on labor issues, has many union advocates concerned about the final shape of a reform package.

One of the commission's key findings is that union representation elections are a highly confrontational activity for workers, unions, and firms, and many new collective-bargaining relationships begin in a highly adversarial atmosphere. In addition, the study found that roughly one-third of workplaces that vote to be represented by a union do not obtain a collective-bargaining contract.[41] A recent *New York Times* article indicated that the AFL-CIO leadership was interpreting that finding as evidence that current law should be changed so that a facility would be unionized if a majority of workers signed cards asking for representation.[42] At the hearings, corporate groups made their opposition to this step clear.

A key issue that faced the commission involved reforming labor law to promote greater worker–management cooperation. In recent times, an increasing number of labor, government, and industry figures have come to believe that traditional strategies for organizing mass-production industrial work—outlined first by Frederick Winslow Taylor in the early part of the century—may be contributing to job losses and declining U.S. competitiveness. For its part, the commission found that,"where employee participation is sustained over time and integrated with other policies and practices, it generally improves economic performance"[43] (see chapter 2). However, while corporate performance tends to improve with the introduction of labor–management "high-performance work systems," such cooperation may take a variety of forms, not all of which are equally beneficial to workers.

A recent paper prepared by Eileen Appelbaum and Rosemary Batt for the Economic Policy Institute (EPI) distinguished between *lean production* and *team production* high-performance work systems.[44] The authors explained that while both models rely on "similar applications of information technology and similar quality tools to improve performance," they differ "in the extent to which front-line workers have responsibility for continuous improvement and in the extent to which workers or their representatives participate in joint decisionmaking processes off the shop floor and at the plant and corporate levels."

Lean production, a system adopted by firms competing for the Commerce Department's Malcolm Baldrige Quality Award, emphasizes management's role in improving the operation of a company. While companies that win Baldrige awards tend to address some human resource issues, the EPI study argues that firms adopting lean production systems often do take into account key issues for workers, including employment security, wage growth, due process guarantees, conflict resolution procedures, and employee voice. Barry Bluestone and Irving Bluestone, two labor economists, recently argued that, "while companies in the nonunion sector can do a great deal to ensure employment security and to de-Taylorize jobs," they cannot "provide workers with true contractual empowerment. The underlying weakness of the nonunion work force lies in its total dependence on the goodwill and the personal philosophy of managers."[45]

Team production, in contrast, makes labor and management partners *throughout all levels of the enterprise.* In these high-performance work systems, unions often negotiate agreements on gainsharing, employment security, and guarantees of the union's own security and ability to organize and represent the interests of new and continuing members. The General Motors Saturn plant in Tennessee, which is run jointly by GM and the United Auto Workers, is the most famous example of a team partnership. According to a 1989 Labor Department study, there are at least six reasons why union involvement improves the likelihood of successful labor–management cooperation:

- Unions help weed out the bad plans for cooperation up front.
- Unions help institutionalize the process, which keeps companies from unilaterally reverting to old practices.
- Unions provide a mechanism for addressing problems that may emerge, without throwing out the entire process.
- Unions give employees a meaningful voice in cooperative endeavors.
- Unions can play a critical role in educating workers to make informed decisions essential to the functioning of the process.
- Unions "have provided a creative power and tension to the process that simply does not exist in a nonunion setting."[46]

Labor–management cooperation is more likely to be attractive for workers in instances where unions can negotiate gainsharing agreements and guarantees of the union's own security and ability to organize new members. In other instances, however, "cooperation" may be a company tactic to speed up hourly employees and undermine unions and the collective-bargaining process by negotiating changes to working conditions and the skill content of jobs. Oftentimes unions also need to develop their own capabilities to be full joint partners in good faith cooperation efforts.

Conclusion

While the term "economic conversion" has entered into mainstream political discourse, the nation still lacks a comprehensive program for economically disengaging from the Cold War. To date, Congress has been content with enacting legislation that offers limited assistance to defense-dependent workers, communities, and businesses. While some of these programs have considerable merit, they fall far short of the reorientation of federal fiscal priorities crucial to the nation's long-term economic health.

The level of cooperation between conversion advocates and labor organizations around a common reform agenda represents a major accomplishment. However, advancing a larger agenda around the need to build a more socially just, environmentally sustainable economy in the post–Cold War era is the more daunting, yet urgent, task.

To win on Capitol Hill, conversion advocates should foster dialogue among the environmental, labor, and human rights organizations similar to that which emerged during the debate around the North American Free Trade Agreement. The debate must look beyond the retraining, community development, and other adjustment programs currently touted by the administration, toward more fundamental issues such as shortening the length of the work week and maintaining real income levels through shared productive gains, nonmonetary benefits to encourage greater work sharing and other issues. Considering the strength of the vested military-corporate interests that to date have blocked substantial programs toward reorienting federal budget priorities, greater efforts at dialogue and coalition building are essential to develop the necessary political clout to advance a more comprehensive agenda.[47]

Notes

1. Office of the Comptroller of the U.S. Department of Defense, *National Defense Budget Estimates for FY 1994* (Washington, DC: The Pentagon, May 1993), table 7–2, "Federal Outlays, FY 1945–1994," pp. 128–9. These figures are in constant 1987 dollars.

2. See the *Congressional Record* for March 23, 1994.

3. The CRS study considered a scenario whereby $3 billion was cut from the military budget and reinvested in a variety of state and local economic development projects, including education, infrastructure, and public works. The study found that the economy gained more than 18,000 jobs than it lost. See "The employment effects of shifting three billion dollars from defense to state and local government-related activities," Congressional Research Service, February 1, 1993 (study prepared by DRI/McGraw-Hill). A more comprehensive scenario was considered by Marion Anderson, Greg Bischak, and Michael Dee Oden, *Converting the American Economy* (Lansing, MI: Employment Research Associates, 1990). The ERA study found that an annual average transfer of $70.5 billion from the military budget to education, infrastructure, and other critical needs would generate an annual gain of nearly 477,000 more jobs on average over a four-year period; in other words, the study found that every $1 billion transferred from military spending to civilian investment would create a net gain of 6,800 jobs. Moreover, the gross national product was shown to grow by an average of $17.6 billion annually.

4. The depletionist literature is vast. Basic sources include works by Seymour Melman, *The Permanent War Economy* (New York: Simon and Schuster, 1974), *Profits without Production* (New York: Alfred A. Knopf, 1983), and *The Demilitarized Society* (Montreal: Harvest House, 1988); Lloyd J. Dumas, *The Overburdened Economy: Uncovering the Causes of Chronic Unemployment, Inflation and National Decline* (Berkeley: University of California Press, 1986), and (with Marek Thee) *Making Peace Possible: The Promise of Economic Conversion* (Oxford: Pergamon Press, 1989). More recent works include Greg Bischak (ed.), *Towards a Peace Economy in the United States* (New York: St. Martin's Press, 1991), and (with Kevin J. Cassidy) *Real Security: Converting the Defense Economy and Building Peace* (Albany: State University Press of New York, 1993); and Ann Markusen (with Peter Hall, Sabina Dietrick, and Scott Campbell), *The Rise of the Gunbelt* (New York: Oxford University Press, 1991), and (with Joel Yudken), *Dismantling the Cold War Economy* (New York: Basic Books, 1992).

5. Melman, *The Permanent War Economy*, p. 296.

6. See Greg Bischak, "National economic conversion strategic options," paper presented at the Conversion Organizer's Retreat sponsored by Center for Economic Conversion, Washington, DC, June 17, 1994.

7. Other representatives to the commission included the secretaries of defense, agriculture, labor, and interior, the chairs of the Atomic Energy Commission and the Council of Economic Advisors, the director of the Arms Control and Disarmament Agency, and the administrator of the National Aeronautics and Space administration.

8. This provision of the bill referred to "possible schedules of public and

private investment patterns resulting from various degrees of economic conversion and the anticipated effects upon income and employment of such patterns."

9. There were other provisions to S. 2274 as well. The bill required the commission to convene the National Conference on Industrial Conversion and Growth "to consider the problems arising from a conversion to a civilian economy, and to encourage appropriate planning and programming by all sectors of the economy to facilitate the Nation's economic conversion capability." Finally, the bill required the commission to consult with state governors to "encourage appropriate studies and conferences at the State, local and regional level, in support of a coordinated effort to improve the Nation's economic conversion capability."

10. "Defense Dislocations," *The Washington Post*, December 2, 1963.

11. See Melman, *The Permanent War Economy*, pp. 292–6, for an account of this early legislation.

12. See Greg Bischak, "Peace Dividends . . . Past and Present," *The New Economy*, 3, 2, 14 (Spring 1992): 4, for a discussion of this remarkable document.

13. This bill was sponsored by Senator George McGovern and had thirty-one cosponsors.

14. Senator Abraham Ribicoff, chairman, Subcommittee on Executive Reorganization and Government Research, "Introductory statement," in "National Economic Conversion Commission: Responses to subcommittee questionnaire," submitted by the Subcommittee on Executive Reorganization and Government Research to the Committee on Government Operations, U.S. Senate, on S. 1285: A Bill to Establish a National Economic Conversion Commission and For Other Purposes, September 1970, pp. 1, 4.

15. Walter P. Reuther, "Swords into ploughshares: A proposal to promote orderly conversion from defense to civilian production" (statement and testimony of Walter P. Reuther, president of the UAW, to the Senate Committee on Labor and Public Welfare, December 1, 1969), p. 15.

16. See "S. 4430–Introduction of the National Economic Conversion Act," *Congressional Record 116*, 173 (Friday, October 2, 1970), for the text of the bill and Senator McGovern's remarks.

17. The secretaries of commerce, labor, health and human services, house and urban development, transportation, defense, and energy were to serve on the council. Other members included the director of the Office of Management and Budget, the administrator of the General Services administration, the chair of the Council of Economic Advisors, six representatives from business and six representatives from organized labor. The bill also created the Office of Economic Adjustment within the executive branch to provide staff support to the DEAC.

18. David Beers, "Brother, can you spare $1.5 trillion," *Mother Jones* (July/August 1990): 32.

19. See the Economic Diversification and Defense Adjustment Act.

20. The summary of the Oakar bill taken from Maggie Bierwirth, "Capital Hill and conversion: A summary of recent congressional action," in Gregory A. Bischak and Kevin J. Cassidy (eds.), *Real Security: Converting the Defense Economy and Building Peace*, p. 191. In her summary of the Gejdenson bill, Bierwirth does not mention its provisions dealing with "diversification alternative use committees."

21. Ibid., pp. 192–3.

22. Ibid., p. 194.

23. Dear Colleague letter from Ted Weiss, August 9, 1990. Emphasis in original.

24. Letter from Jennifer Brown, legislative assistant to Representative Ted Weiss, to Greg Bischak, Executive Director of the National Commission for Economic Conversion and Disarmament, September 14, 1990.

25. See the *Congressional Record*, September 12, 1990, p. H7470.

26. See section 4303 of The National Defense Authorization Act for FY 1991, p. 384.

27. David Evans, "Pentagon holds back job retraining funds," *Chicago Tribune*, March 20, 1991.

28. Statement of the assistant secretary of defense for force management and personnel, Christopher Jehn, before the Investigations Subcommittee of the House Armed Services Committee, May 15, 1991, p. 4.

29. Bierwirth, "Capitol Hill and conversion," p. 196.

30. Beers, "Brother, can you spare $1.5 trillion."

31. This section is adapted from Greg Bischak, Miriam Pemberton, and James Raffel, "1993 conversion legislation: An update," *The New Economy*, *3*, 4, 16 (Fall 1992): 4–5.

32. This section adapted from Greg Bischak and James Raffel, "Defense Department drags feet on conversion law," *The New Economy*, *4*, 2, 18 (Spring 1993): 1.

33. This section adapted from James Raffel and Greg Bischak, "Federal conversion programs: An update," *The New Economy*, *5*, 1, 21 (Winter 1994): 6–7, 14.

34. "Remarks by the president to Westinghouse employees," Westinghouse Electric Corporation, Baltimore County, Maryland, March 11, 1993.

35. See "Remarks of AFL-CIO president Lane Kirkland to the Interstate Conference of Employment Security Agencies, Washington DC, March 10, 1994," for a summary of organized labor's views on the administration's proposal. Also see Frank Swoboda, "Clinton to unveil $3.4 billion retraining program," *The Washington Post*, March 8, 1994, p. C1. Swoboda reported that "business groups have made it clear they will openly oppose the bill if Congressional Democrats attempt to use the legislation to toughen current law requiring advance notice of plant closures. Some Democrats and labor groups want to extend the notification period from 60 to 180 days."

36. For more on the shortcomings of the dual-use approach, see Greg Bischak, "Dual use technology: A barrier to conversion," *The New Economy* (Fall 1992): 3; also Ann Markusen and Joel Yudken, *Dismantling the Cold War Economy*, pp. 244–7. For a recent statement of the administration's view of its program, see "Reforming the Pentagon: An inside job" (interview with John M. Deutch, undersecretary of defense for acquisition), *Technology Review* (April 1994): 31–6.

37. Stephen C. LeSueur, "U.S. crafts loan support for small defense firms," *Defense News* (June 20–26, 1994): 4.

38. Pamela Lessard, "Confusion over TRP continues, a frustrated Buchanan concedes," *McGraw-Hill's Federal Technology Report* (May 12, 1994): 3 (emphasis added).

39. This section adapted from James Raffel, "Deja vu all over again: Congress finishing work on DoD budget for FY 1994," *The New Economy*, 4, 3, 19 (Summer 1993): 3–4.

40. *National Defense Authorization Act* for FY 1994, pp. 353–4. This was section 1341 of the bill.

41. "Fact finding report on the future of worker–management relations released today," Department of Labor Press Release, June 2, 1994, USDL # 94–277.

42. Louis Uchitelle, "A call for easing labor–management tensions," *The New York Times*, May 30, 1994, p. 17.

43. U.S. Department of Labor Press Release, June 2, 1994.

44. See Eileen Appelbaum and Rosemary Batt, *High Performance Work Systems* (Washington, DC: Economic Policy Institute, 1993).

45. Barry Bluestone and Irving Bluestone, *Negotiating the Future: A Labor Perspective on American Business* (New York: Basic Books, 1992), pp. 154–5.

46. See U.S. Department of Labor, Bureau of Labor–Management Relations and Cooperative Programs, "Labor-Management Cooperation: 1989 State of the Art Symposium," *BLMR Reports*, *124* (1989): 17–20, as cited in ibid., p. 173.

47. See Greg Bischak, "The search for a new framework," *The New Economy*, 5, 1, 21 (Winter 1994). See also Seymour Melman, *What Else Is There to Do: Neglected Prospects for Major Job Creation in U.S. Manufacturing* (Washington, DC: National Commission for Economic Conversion and Disarmament, October 1993).

9

JONATHAN M. FELDMAN

Public Choice, Foreign Policy Crises, and Military Spending

The end of the Cold War has raised public expectations that military budgets can now be safely reduced and civilian expenditures expanded. In a Gallup poll taken in October 1991, exactly half of the population said that too much was being spent for national defense and military purposes, while only 10 percent said too little was being spent. The public wanted most of the savings realized by cuts in the defense budget to be used for domestic problems rather than for deficit reduction. In total, 67 percent said most of the money saved should be used to address domestic problems, 16 percent said most should be used to reduce the federal budget deficit, and 15 percent said most of the money should be used to reduce taxes.[1]

Do such citizen budget preferences translate into federal actions to cut military funds and use them for alternative civilian purposes? Public choice theories suggest that citizen preferences on the nature and level of social goods have been and will continue to be translated into action by the government. Voters are the demand agent, using their votes to express policy preferences. The executive and legislative branches of government are the supply agent. Both the relatively slow rate of military budget reductions and the fact that the peace dividend has so far been minimal raise questions about how well public choice theory explains the behavior of the federal government in the early post–Cold War period.

The author would like to thank Lloyd J. Dumas, Ted Goertzel, Robert Krinsky, Ann Markusen, Thanos Mergoupis, and Michael Dee Oden for their comments on drafts of this chapter.

Public Choice: The Economics and Politics
of Public Goods Distribution

The public choice model developed in "the theory of social goods" argues that a political process is used to govern demand and supply of social goods. According to public choice theory, national defense is a social good where both nonrival consumption (consumption by one does not reduce the availability of the good to another) and non-excludability (the good is available to everyone) go together.[2] Under these conditions, the ordinary market mechanism will fail. Thus, a different distribution system is needed to link benefits and costs as well as demand and supply. With ordinary (private) goods, consumers reveal preferences and "the value they assign to successive marginal units of consumption" through direct purchases.[3] But, because social goods are provided without exclusion, consumers need not reveal their preferences. If one person pays for a social good, this will not prevent others from benefiting. People can get away with using the good for free. How then are costs levied and preferences revealed?

Consumers use their votes on tax and expenditure decisions: "(1) to tell the government what social goods should be provided; and (2) to furnish it with the fiscal resources needed to pay for them."[4] Votes on taxes and expenditures will reveal consumer preferences about what level and kind of social goods are desired. In elections, voters are presented with a choice among different budget proposals. Supply and demand as well as costs and benefits become linked because the electoral process is a rational system:

> To serve as an efficient mechanism of preference revelation, the voting process should link tax and expenditure decisions. Voters are then confronted with a choice among budget proposals which carry a price tag in terms of their own tax contribution. This price tag will depend on the total cost for the community as a whole as well as on the share to be contributed by others.[5]

Voters' public support of social goods is contingent upon a belief that others must also contribute in line with the adopted tax plan. The theory asserts that military spending levels will be determined by the "public choice between public and private goods, and on another level, by perceptions concerning the marginal value of military expenditures relative to the benefits provided by other public goods."[6] Votes are the indicators of demand and the underlying preferences for particular social goods. Politicians become the agents for supplying these goods.

Public choice theory is often joined with democratic theory to explain how social goods are distributed. The normative expectation that is derived from democratic theory is that governments will respond to public opinion. In the extension to public choice theory made by Anthony Downs, it is assumed that both politicians and voters act in their own self-interest. People will vote for those candidates who best represent their interests. Politicians will offer programs to supply this demand through campaign propositions and support for legislation that meets the needs of the constituent as potential voter. Politicians who follow this maxim will receive the most votes and gain office or stay in power.

In *The Logic of Congressional Action*, Douglas Arnold argued that lawmakers "have a strong aversion to proposals that impose particular costs on their constituents because they believe that voters might blame them for these costs." Congress is accountable to the public because "legislators regularly attempt to anticipate how specific roll-call votes might be used against them and regularly adjust their votes in ways designed to forestall electoral problems."[7]

Public Choice: Empirical Evidence

Some social scientists have worked within the public choice paradigm to explain the level of military expenditures in terms of citizen preferences. Using regression techniques and interviews, they have tried to test some of the claims of the public choice model. Those working within the public choice school view both public preferences for military spending and public interpretations of foreign policy opinions as "rational." They attempt to prove that Congress has been responsive to such rational choices. In their view, public opinion is not manufactured by government.

Benjamin Page and Robert Shapiro believe that when public opinion can be defined clearly on issues of central concern, foreign policy is about as congruent with popular sentiment as it is with domestic policy.[8] Bruce Russett argues that military spending levels are responsive to public opinion, finding that there is a strong, positive relationship between public opinion in one year and changes in defense spending levels in the following year.[9]

Russett and Thomas Hartley tested the hypothesis that changes in military spending are influenced by changes in public support for, and opposition to, changes in military spending. The authors related the change in total U.S. military spending to the change in Soviet military spending (lagged by two and three years), the change in the difference between Soviet and U.S. military spending (lagged by three years), the change in the deficit (lagged one year) and the change in the percentage of potential voters responding in polls that the United States spends too little on defense.

Examining the period from 1965 to 1990, Hartley and Russett concluded that the greatest influence on the change in U.S. military spending was the change in Soviet military spending lagged three years, but that "increases in the percentage of the public that believes that government is spending too little on the military result in increases in military spending." They also found that "if the percentage of public opinion opposing increases in military spending rises, then actual spending tends to come down." Specifically, all things being equal, they discovered that for "every 1% change in support for (or opposition to) increased [military] spending" there was "about a $.33 billion increase (or decrease) in defense spending." This level was considered small but not insignificant because "swings in public opinion were as large as 25% during the late 1970s and early 1980s." Beyond this, the authors found that the deficit variable was statistically significant, but the difference between Soviet and U.S. military spending was not. Finally, they concluded that "public opinion may in fact be exogenous to policy on military spending."[10]

Larry M. Bartels examined the question of how voter preferences translate into changes in military expenditure. He found that votes by congressional representatives on a series of defense budget roll-call votes in the first year of the Reagan administration's military build-up were related to opinions expressed by voters during the 1980 presidential campaign.[11] In January of 1980, about a year before the election of Ronald Reagan, 49 percent of the public felt that too little was being spent on national defense. Pollsters suggested that public support for increased defense spending had soared to the highest point recorded by their surveys in more than a decade because of concern over Soviet military actions in Afghanistan. Support for such spending was bipartisan; 74 percent of Carter supporters, 78 percent of Reagan supporters, and 60 percent of Anderson supporters wanted to increase defense spending.[12] Political scientists have argued this period was an exceptional one.

Bartels argues that both congressional action and the presidential election were vehicles for translating public opinion in support of increased defense spending into policy outcomes. One study he cites found that the defense spending issue contributed 7.6 percentage points to Reagan's margin of victory.[13] The Congress responded to the shift in tide. The Democratic House "approved 94 percent of the President's first term requests for new arms."[14]

In a regression model of congressional decision making, Bartels used House votes on a series of measures related to the FY 1982 defense appropriations process as his dependent variable. Support for military spending was measured by the National Election Study (NES) sample of congressional districts. In 1980, 107 of 108 districts included in the survey had mean constituency opinions favoring increases in defense spending. Bartels examined the effects of six predictor or independent variables designed to measure constituency opinion, economic interests, partisanship, and presidential influence.

The most significant contributor to congressional votes on defense appropriations was constituency opinion, with every one-point change in mean constituency opinion (on the NES seven-point scale) producing an estimated change in congressional defense appropriations preferences of almost $13 billion in the same direction. Did representatives with greater benefits (measured in annual per-capita outlays by the Defense Department) than costs (measured in annual federal tax payments) vote for increased military spending? Bartels found these effects significant.

There was a $7.7 billion *increase* in congressional support for defense appropriations for every $1,000 per-capita increase in *military outlays*. On the other hand, every $1,000 increase in per-capita *tax burdens* was associated with a $4.1 billion *decrease* in support for defense appropriations. Bartels linked regional defense spending to public choices which then shape congressional action, arguing that economic interests also substantially affect congressional voting indirectly through their impact on constituency opinion.[15] These results contradict earlier findings that claimed that regional concentrations of defense spending do not influence congressional policy.[16]

Public choice advocates argue that the president joins Congress as an agent responsive to citizen opinions. Ronald Hinckley, a national security official in the Reagan administration, observes that opinion polls are a central tool used by presidents to make decisions.[17] Polls were reportedly used by aide Michael Deaver and by Nancy Reagan to persuade Ronald Reagan to alter his military spending proposals.[18] In sum, public choice models in the tradition of "democratic theory" suggest that the public is getting what it wants because the Congress and president respond to citizen opinion.

Some empirical work has challenged the assumptions of public choice. For example, Higgs examined whether senators responded to public preferences on ten defense-related votes in 1987. His model made two basic assumptions: that constituency preference exists and that legislators know what it is. But, since a state's two senators serve the same constituency, when these senators vote differently, "one of them is *necessarily* voting against the [majority] constituency preference." Same-state senators voted differently about 37 percent of the time.[19] But, while Higgs concluded that his model showed evidence that senators may vote based on ideological preference, it is not clear how particular votes were linked to specific polls or preferences. It is conceivable that voters had conflicting preferences, which senate vote splits reflected.

Public Choice and Public Accountability

How strong are the systems that make government accountable to public opinion? In theory, the public's distaste for tax increases that outweigh the benefits of military spending will create a ceiling on defense budget levels. But that depends on the accountability and responsiveness of government agencies to public preferences. Of course, accountability requires that the government act as servant and representative of opinion without distorting the flow of information to the public. Yet, the record shows that the impact of these factors in creating accountability systems has been mixed.

The First World War: A Test Case
for Public Choice

The First World War provides evidence that contradicts the claims of public choice theory regarding government responsiveness to citizen opinion. Conclusions as to how responsive government was to public choices regarding support for or opposition to the war hinges on whether or not there was a clear enough public preference to which the Congress and president could respond. Journalist and war critic Randolph Bourne argued that support of the mass citizenry for the war was fragmented: intellectuals joined "the richer and older classes of the Atlantic seaboard" as primary supporters of the war while "farmers . . . small business men and workingmen" were apathetic toward the war.[20]

Before the outbreak of the war, public opinion reflected the different loyalties of immigrants with ties to the competing European powers. Eastern elites supported intervention on the side of the Allies against Germany. Many of the eastern bankers and lawyers most active in diplomacy and commerce were of British descent themselves. They had linkages to London banks and were sympathetic to British legal institutions. At the same time, there was considerable pro-German sentiment among Americans in the Midwest, most of whom were of German descent. Support for the war and conflicts within public opinion extended to the working class. German-Americans marched at a Bavarian *Volkfest* and telegraphed their congratulations to King Ludwig of Bavaria on the first day of the war. The same day, there was a clash in the streets of Chicago between marching Slavs and marching Germans. President Woodrow Wilson "saw public opinion . . . as an angry beast that would drag prudent leaders into war."[21]

One historical accounting of the period, however, notes that "support for the war among workers and farmers was spotty, and necessitated a dual policy of concessions to pro-war organizations such as the American Federation of Labor, and suppression of antiwar organizations and periodicals."[22]

Once Wilson decided to enter the war, public choice could no longer be considered an exogenous variable, independent of government action. The war was promoted by the coordinated action of government authorities. In discussing what allowed the war effort to proceed, Bourne argued that it was "coercion from above . . . rather than patriotism from below."[23] Wilson created the Committee on Public Information, whose mission was to manage public opinion on a massive scale. Government claims on society led to the enlistment of a wide variety of institutions for the war effort: "for the first time the industrial economy, the educational system, the entertainment and information industries, indeed the whole country, had to be mobilized for war."[24] A dozen propaganda films were sponsored by the federal government during the war. Other feature films were also used for propaganda purposes.[25]

This attempt to alter opinion went beyond manipulation. The Committee on Public Information ran advertisements in the press which called on readers to report peace supporters to the Justice Department. Publications opposed to the war were barred from the mail, and the Sedition Act passed in May 1918 made it a criminal offense to say anything "scornful or disrespectful" of the uniform, flag, Constitution, or government.[26] The Wilson administration met the challenge of war opposition by attempting to destroy socialist and left-wing labor organizations and publications. It also attempted to coopt working-class opposition from the ground up by making concessions to labor and organizing "pro-war liberal groups to win the confidence of rank and file pro-socialist workers and reformers."[27] Randolph Bourne observed that: "in wartime there are literally no valid forces moving in another direction. War determines its own end—victory, and government crushes out automatically all forces that deflect, or threaten to deflect, energy from the path of organization to that end."[28]

In sum, the First World War revealed serious splits in domestic public opinion, although a large portion of opinion was initially mobilized by an elite in support of the war. After the war began, the government placed serious constraints on opinions against the war, making government fiat more important than any attempt at accountability to the abstract ideal of popular will.

American Involvement in the Vietnam War

The belief that our country entered the Vietnam War because of accountability to popular will is clearly mistaken. It seems clear that the August 1964 incident in the Tonkin Gulf used to justify U.S. military action in Vietnam was also used to manipulate public opinion.[29] This incident led to an 85 percent approval rating of American military action and a congressional resolution opposed by only two senators. The president was given an almost free hand to further expand military action in Vietnam. One problem with linking military activity in Indochina to public preferences was that significant actions in the war were not even made known to the public. For example, some 3,500 secret bombing raids against Cambodia took place in 1969 and 1970.[30]

One public choice argument suggests that the public accommodates tax increases in times of war or national emergency. "Public expenditures in capitalist democracies tend to increase in response to major wars and then remain at the higher levels after the wars since the public has learned to tolerate higher levels of taxation."[31] In other words, citizen preferences will allow public spending to reach high levels as voters pay more for wars. Even public choice advocates point out that the Vietnam War was something of an exception. It was followed by a sharp decline in military spending as a percentage of GNP. The Vietnam case also shows that the public does not necessarily "ratify" a war policy by willingly paying higher taxes. "Neither the Korean War nor the Vietnam War was a sufficiently credible threat to American security to justify increases in taxation."[32]

Much of the Vietnam War was funded by deficit financing and subsequent inflation, rather than increased taxation. Nevertheless, public reactions to rising war costs and casualties do seem to have slowly affected government policy. When rising inflation forced President Johnson to call for a 10 percent tax surcharge, support for the war dropped sharply. The first big casualty lists had a similar effect. President Johnson responded to the drop in the polls by telling his staff that "the weakest chink in our armor is American public opinion. Our people won't stand firm in the face of heavy losses, and they can bring down the government."[33]

Before the Tet offensive in March of 1968, 61 percent of respondents to a February 1968 Gallup poll called themselves "Hawks" while 23 percent self-identified as "Doves." But by March, 41 percent were Hawks and 42 percent Doves. In January of 1969, 30 percent of the public thought the country was spending too little on defense and 15 percent thought it was spending too much. By July of 1969, 21 percent thought the country was spending too little and 59 percent thought it was spending too much.[34] After the withdrawal from Vietnam, military budgets were cut and in the mid-1970s most people thought that the level of U.S. military spending was about right.[35] These changing polls reveal that public preferences regarding military spending levels are not stable.

The Tonkin Gulf incident reveals that the government is able to create facts or crises which then trigger opinion. On the other hand, military spending levels and support for the war do appear to be related. But in contrast to some public choice models, the mechanisms that trigger changes in state action and government accountability to such preferences do not appear limited to the strictly economic costs of war. The mobilization of the antiwar movement and the changing nature of the conflict itself shaped public opinion. For example, one study showed a strong correlation between the number of protesters and the percentage of the population disapproving of the war from 1965 to 1968.[36]

A more detailed analysis linked the development of Senate opposition to the Vietnam War not only to public opinion, but also to cumulative war costs and antiwar demonstrations.[37] Therefore, public choices were themselves products of other variables. But, consistent with public choice theory, citizen votes were used to ensure accountability. Citizens used votes in congressional elections to register views on the war, "replacing pro-war representatives with antiwar freshman ones, and changing the minds of continuing representatives in part by the threat of electoral defeat if they did not shift their positions."[38]

Defense, Tax Preferences, and Accountability

Even if the Vietnam War was a case of changing opinion and matching government action, accountability systems appear to weaken just before and in the early stages of a war or threat-based military buildup. Part of the reason seems linked to the political mobilization by the state in support of war. This is significant because such threats or perceived foreign policy crises are a major fuel for defense budget escalation.[39]

There are two major reasons why the accountability of public opinion regarding wars and budgets can be delayed or displaced. First, "ordinary citizens usually have little to do with making foreign policy decisions, especially critical ones, but they can act as executioners if the decisions go badly."[40] The public's ability to play a serious and continuous role in foreign policy is limited by its lack of information. At the beginning of conflicts, a surge of patriotism sweeps the country. That emotional reaction, combined with the fact that the costs of the fighting are not yet obvious, results in high public support, as was the case in Vietnam.[41]

Costs suggest a second factor: political leaders have often short-circuited the constraints of tax accountability by delaying, concealing, or displacing the tax burdens of military spending. This has played an important role in the public's views of military budgets. The government has often financed wars or military expenditures through deficits. For example, the Reagan military buildup was financed without tax increases. The war was financed by deficits which in the short term gave Reagan the political space he needed to raise military budgets. The Reagan administration sponsored the largest peacetime buildup in U.S. history and increased real military spending nearly 40 percent between 1981 and 1986. During those same years, the administration borrowed more than $1 trillion, more than doubling the national debt.[42]

There may be an important indirect link between public opinion, electoral accountability, and pressures to reduce the military budget. While the economic problems in 1991 and 1992 that cost Bush the election may have been generated by factors other than military depletion, his failure to move aggressively to support civilian industrial policies and a peace dividend probably complicated his position. Such an assessment seems reasonable given that macroeconomic studies show the overall benefits of military spending reductions matched by compensated civilian investments.[43] Even if Bush was ideologically committed to defense spending and his political base was tied to defense-dependent regions, one could argue that the military-driven deficit financing reduced his room to maneuver in terms of offering a stimulative fiscal policy in the year prior to the election.

Studies indicate that economic conditions affect the level of support a president is given: "Changes in inflation and the growth of the gross national product (GNP) are reflected in polls and at the ballot box. People apparently do not respond to their own personal hardships or well-being but judge the national economy and the president's ability to cope with these national problems."[44] After the Persian Gulf War, Bush's poll ratings dropped steadily from March to the end of 1991, as domestic economic problems returned to the fore. By the fourth quarter of 1991, bad economic news had lowered Bush's ratings to only slightly above those of the other U.S. presidents.[45]

While tax ceilings may have been weakened as a source of accountability for military expenditures, tax requirements for federally provided goods and services still serve as a constraint on state managers. Unless labor, business groups, and other mobilized publics support a sacrifice in wages or profits through taxes, increases in military expenditures will be limited. Michael Oden's analysis of military expenditure trends from 1952 to 1987 showed that increases in federal tax revenue as a proportion of gross national product had a strong positive association with the military share of real GNP.[46] It is not clear whether the Reagan era trends of deficit financing weakened this association.

Government Responsiveness to Public Preferences

Are all sectors of government equally accountable to public opinion regarding military budget choices? There is evidence that the president and Congress will respond to public choice, but federal bureaucracies may well be hostile to public debate about military budgets. We need to account for how diverse departments of the executive branch respond to public choices. Both theoretical and empirical work suggests a clear breakdown in bureaucratic responsiveness to public opinion.

There is a long tradition that argues that military bureaucracies will act to extend their power and thereby seek to influence public opinion. Thomas Paine, in *Rights of Man*, wrote:

> [W]ar is the common harvest of all those who participate in the division and expenditure of public money, in all countries. It is the art of *conquering at home:* the object of it is an increase of revenue; and revenue cannot be increased without taxes, a pretence must be made for expenditures . . . in reviewing the history of the English Government [one would have to conclude] that taxes were not raised to carry on wars, but that wars were raised to carry on taxes.[47]

Later, the economist Joseph P. Schumpeter would explain the domestic face of war. He described the military elite of ancient Egypt: "created by wars that required it, the machine now created the wars it required."[48]

In this tradition, Seymour Melman argued that in a "state-managed military economy," bureaucrats will follow the principle of managerialism in which the primary goal is to acquire more power and status and thereby extend managerial control. He wrote that "an increase in the number of people controlled is both a persistent objective and a conclusive test of managerial success." This managerial drive leads state managers "to maintain and enlarge the military-industry and military organizations of the United States," explaining an 80 percent defense budget increase from 1960 to 1970.[49]

Melman's views have been echoed in refinements of public choice theory. Particular government bureaus (such as the Pentagon) can be the sole provider of a public good. Their goal, however, is not to maximize profits, but to maximize budgets. Doing so enhances the economic opportunity, power, and prestige of the bureau's managers.

One view of public choice directly mirrors the managerial language deployed by Melman, noting that public officials "have strong incentives not only to retain their positions but to upgrade them, thereby augmenting their salaries and position of authority."[50]

The economic incentives for bureaucratic behavior are based in part on the opportunity costs associated with life outside the bureau. Once occupations are selected, changing them while maintaining income becomes difficult. The specialized skills of military bureaucrats may result in lower earnings in an era of shrinking military budgets. These wage losses may likely occur if displaced bureaucrats can only find *civilian* employment. But Pentagon managers frequently gain jobs in the defense industry and defense industrial managers gain jobs in the Pentagon.[51] Large defense contractors sell to the Pentagon, an unusual client who demands military goods that are typically specialized and differentiated from civilian goods. As a result, the contractors need to "have marketing teams that are familiar with the inner workings of the Pentagon and the services. No one does this job better than former military men, who are attractive hires for the military-oriented firm."[52]

Military managers may thus push to increase budgets (or slow their decline) to maintain present bureaucratic employment, to extend the scope of alternative defense industrial employment, or to gain status in the larger professional world. This last option has been noted by public choice theorists: a policy maker can "augment his/her income prospects once out of office by using the power of the office to confer rents upon particular constituents. For many officials this augmentation occurs directly through expanding the size of their organization because salary or prestige and organization size often go hand in hand."[53]

Such revisions to public choice theory appear to narrow the impact of public opinion on bureaucratic outcomes. One of the leading students of political bureaucracies argues that many federal agencies become independent of the shifting sands in congressional elections and political currents. This occurs through formalized decisions, the use of technical expertise to justify decisions, and the monopolization of information necessary for effective oversight.[54] Yet, the foreign policy bureaucracy has not always been sheltered from shifting political currents. Some observers argue that the civil service has been manipulated by politicians:

During the communist-scare campaigns launched in the late 1940s and 1950s, the Foreign Service was accused of disloyalty and individual diplomatic officers were pilloried for expressing inconvenient opinions on the true nature of international conflicts. The diplomatic corps has never recovered.[55]

Frederick Malek, who served as White House personnel director during the Nixon administration, actually issued a manual for political appointees detailing procedures for evading the civil-service laws. The guide could be used to intimidate or even eliminate federal employees who did not accept Nixon's political agenda and his interpretation of the law.[56] The erosion of bureaucratic autonomy may reflect "accountability" to the public's selection of Richard Nixon as president of the United States. But the erosion of Nixon's support and his resignation linked to criminal activities suggest that such bureaucratic manipulation need not reflect public choices.

Are foreign-policy bureaucracies more pliable before state rather than grass-roots political pressures? Can public choices affect bureaucracies directly? Philip J. Powlick provides some evidence for a breakdown in foreign-policy officials' responsiveness to public opinion. In sixty-eight interviews with National Security Council and State Department officials from May 1988 to January 1989, 58 percent of his respondents said that public opinion was "always a factor" or a "delimiting constraint" in decisions. But officials were just as likely to resist public opposition to policies: 17 percent reacted to public opposition to policy by "doing nothing," and 38 percent reacted by trying to "educate" or "inform" the public about policy.[57]

It should also be noted that some empirical work models the impact of bureaucratic inertia or momentum on military spending levels.[58] In some cases, a variable measuring bureaucracy is added to an equation containing a model of public opinion. Or bureaucratic resistance can be measured by equations in which spending levels are said to be the lagged response to public opinions.

In either case, the interaction between bureaucracy and militarism requires more detailed qualitative and historical analysis. Some sociologists trace the bureaucratic resistance to defense cutbacks to defense planning during the Second World War.[59] Quantitative changes from year to year cannot easily measure as complex and omnipresent a variable as political power.

The Limits of Public Choice as a Causal Variable

Even public choice advocates acknowledge that other factors, such as the level of Soviet military spending and the economic costs and benefits of militarism, may shape either the level of defense spending or congressional action. Beyond this, the production function for national security is unknown, and conjectures about its nature are likely to be heavily influenced by ideology and fashion.[60] Therefore, it is difficult to interpret the quantitative associations made by public choice advocates between increases in defense spending and public desires.

The establishment of a relationship between public opinion, desired defense levels, and actual procurement levels is also complicated by the existence of an "overkill" capacity in strategic nuclear weapons programs. In 1988, the amount of nuclear weaponry aimed at Soviet cities was sufficient to destroy them fifty times over. Reducing the budget for this capacity by 75 percent ($54.6 billion) would have left an overkill capacity of twelve. It is hard to see what the utility difference between such capacities was, or how these could possibly be measured.

Some scholars believe that public opinion itself is affected by such external events as foreign policy crises. Oden argues that neoclassical public choice models do not adequately account for this.[61] Choice may be affected by external events, but opinions of these events change over time as well. The president's response to a foreign policy crisis seems to be heavily influenced by public perceptions of how he has responded or might respond to changing events.[62] Theodore Lowi argues that the presidency is caught in a constant struggle for mass approval.[63]

Can a president, seeking to respond to public preferences, manipulate public opinion through skillful use of international conflicts and the media? Is public opinion really an exogenous variable, independent from external influences?

Nincic argues that public opinion is influenced by political leaders:

> [F]oreign policy decision-makers must be manipulators of domestic politics, and the more ambitious the external goals, the more likely it is that their pursuit will leave domestic traces. Consequently, the conduct of foreign policy affects the domestic societal sources from which it flows and, by extension, the political matrix in which these sources are embedded.[64]

According to Frey and Lau,

> When a government's popularity is high (expected vote ≥ 52%), it pursues its ideological goals; when low, it manipulates the policy variables at its disposal to increase its popularity. The latter were assumed to be the key macroeconomic variables amendable to government intervention . . . the popularity of an incumbent government is linked to the economic health of the economy, and its policies to affect the economy are linked back to its popularity.[65]

In addition to macroeconomic stimulants, foreign policy crises are used to increase popularity. One survey of the use of U.S. force overseas found that it was

> significantly more likely to occur following negative dramatic events—scandals in the White House, strikes, and other signs of domestic disarray. It is also more likely to occur when economic conditions are worsening. A rise in the misery index significantly increases the likelihood of a use of force.[66]

The Bush Administration and Media Manipulation: Turning the Tide against the Peace Dividend?

Does media manipulation or distortion of information by media corporations and the executive branch alter public opinion, which then supports or opposes military campaigns and budget levels? "Foreign policy," writes Nincic, "is especially vulnerable because, government control of information being greatest there, political authorities can conceal or misrepresent reality without being challenged—particularly if the media is made an instrument of such deception."[67] Short- to medium-term changes in opinion have been linked to the role of the media, experts, and popular presidents, although long-term changes in opinion may be more autonomous and rooted in demographic, social, and technological factors.[68]

The Bush administration provides a useful case study for testing whether the executive branch can successfully manipulate public opinion. Bush used both macroeconomic policy and foreign-policy crises as part of an attempt to increase public support for his administration. On September 3, 1992, two months before the presidential election, the

New York Times reported: "President Bush put his authority over foreign policy to work on behalf of his political campaign today, handing nearly $8 billion in contracts and grants to hardpressed farmers and arms workers."[69]

As president, Bush made himself more available to the press and increased targeted media briefings during foreign-policy crises. He spoke about foreign policy more often than most presidents, using military spectacles to generate attention from the media. "Bush's speaking almost always accompanied a major use of force."[70] The military spectacle became an important means to define what was "topical," and the topicality of an event is a driving force behind media coverage. Leaders strive to create benchmarks to manipulate the focus of the media's attention and to define what are significant policy actions and issues. These benchmarks can include a dramatic foreign-policy move near election day, because recent developments often disproportionately affect opinions of how successful an administration has been. Foreign-policy crises can be used to outmaneuver political opponents.

Each military intervention during the Bush presidency provided a base for favorable coverage from the mainstream media. Public opinion surveys, however, indicated mixed results. After the U.S. invasion of Panama, the press praised Bush's transformation from his earlier "wimp" image.[71] One poll after the invasion revealed that Bush's job approval rating had increased by twelve points. Yet, other domestic problems, including a deteriorating economy and a highly controversial budget standoff with Congress, kept his ratings relatively lower than they otherwise might have been.

The ebbs and flows of Bush's presidency were linked to foreign-policy diversions. Bush's poll ratings increased with the Panama invasion, fell the following month, and then dropped further. His summit with Soviet leader Mikhail Gorbachev led to increased popularity, but his poll ratings fell again the next month. The Persian Gulf crisis made his polls shoot upward once more; then the budget fight caused them to plunge. When the Persian Gulf crisis turned into the Persian Gulf War, Bush's ratings skyrocketed. One study concluded that Bush's relatively high ratings, beginning in the summer of his first year, were exclusively associated with international events. But the rise of domestic problems ultimately brought his standing in the polls close to the average of other presidents.[72] The brief duration of the Gulf War was partially motivated by public opposition to a drawn-out conflict as in Vietnam. Yet, the short duration of the war allowed economic problems to resurface quickly and begin to dominate the public agenda.

The contingent nature of the political capital generated by the war spectacle was reflected in the instability of opinion poll trends. One solution to the fleeting quality of crises might be to direct and organize a series of crises. Bush, in fact, did this. The frequency with which force was used in his first years of office was considerably higher than other presidents, including his rhetorically hawkish predecessor, Ronald Reagan.[73] In sum, Bush's military campaigns "once made him the most popular President of the twentieth century, but his natural state without war was political collapse."[74]

Bush's electoral loss to Bill Clinton might provide one measure of the limits of executive branch manipulation in influencing public opinion. In fact, we noted earlier that past military expenditures of the Reagan/Bush era shrunk the resources available for civilian macroeconomic stimulus to influence the election. Yet, despite Bush's electoral loss, media manipulation and foreign-policy crises did seem to play a role in shifting support away from major cutbacks in military spending.

Clinton, the first post–Cold War president, pledged to turn the United States from a "defense to an economic giant" on the night of his election victory. But during his campaign, Clinton promised to reduce military spending only $60 billion below the Bush "base force" plan— only a 5 percent cut. Trying to overcome his past as a Vietnam dissenter, Clinton limited defense cuts to curry favor with Sam Nunn, chair of the Senate Armed Services Committee. In fact, one of Clinton's leading campaign advisers referred to his proposed military budget as "the Sam Nunn defense plan."[75]

Prior to the Gulf War, there were numerous stories in the print and electronic media about the prospects of using savings from military budget reductions made possible by the end of the Cold War. These newly released financial resources were commonly labeled the "peace dividend." The press coverage seemed both to reflect and to enhance public opinion and expectations. But a primary theme in the mainstream media's coverage was that the peace dividend would be small, and whatever financial resources were freed from the military budget should be used to reduce the federal budget deficit. Media reports also typically ridiculed, or at best ignored, groups advocating peace dividend investments in affordable housing, infrastructure, and environmental repair.

Many scholars argued that the mainstream media's coverage of the Gulf War strengthened the hand of the Bush administration and weakened opposition to his policies. The administration and the Pentagon restricted media access to the Gulf War through a controlled press pool. This could have (and should have) been challenged by the media, but instead the mainstream press went along with the Pentagon's censorship and propaganda during the war. Press censorship and media bias facilitated Pentagon objectives and helped thwart diplomatic responses to the Persian Gulf crisis. However, there have been no real ethnographic studies of how media bias influences voter decision making on military budgets. This would require detailed interviews tracing citizen responses back to media influences.[76]

Polls are at best a crude approximation of public sentiment. Walter Lippmann in *The Phantom Public* expressed these limitations by noting that public choices in polls and votes are usually subject to qualifications. "It would take us hours to express our thoughts, and calling a vote the expression of our mind is an empty fiction."[77] Polling data can be used, however, to reveal general trends in public sentiment. They provide evidence of the rising support for cuts in the immediate post–Cold War period and less support for cuts since the Gulf War.

One polling series traced reduced support for defense cuts from 1991 to 1993. It appears that international conflicts have strengthened popular support for military institutions and that fears about economic instability and recession (in the absence of an effective conversion program) have weakened support for defense cutbacks. A Gallup Poll published in April 1993 found that the military was the institution in American society in which Americans had the most confidence. It headed a list of fifteen institutions and was followed by the church or organized religion, police, television news, the presidency, the U.S. Supreme Court, public schools, and banks.[78] This follows a trend found in the period from 1981 to 1987, when confidence in the military increased from 50 to 61 percent.[79] Such confidence may also be linked to the Gulf War. One survey in the *Washington Post* described opinion polls that revealed that the U.S. military, U.S. defense industry, U.S. soldiers, George Bush, Israel, Saudi Arabia, and the news media all gained respect because of the conflict and war.[80]

While further research is needed, the polls may mean that continuing international crises, and the widespread legitimacy of military institutions, are important factors that qualify support for defense cuts.

Consider an April 1993 poll that asked citizens to compare the views associated with President Clinton and General Colin Powell, former chair of the Joint Chiefs of Staff. Clinton was linked to cuts in defense spending "by 126 billion dollars over five years," with savings from cuts used "to reduce the budget deficit and redirect funds to address America's economic needs." Powell was linked to "proposed cuts of 60 billion dollars over five years" and warnings against larger cuts which "would limit America's ability to respond to crises abroad." Thirty-eight percent thought the views linked to Clinton were best, while 60 percent thought those linked to Powell were best. The hesitancy to support military cuts appears to be based on fears of continuing security threats and economic instability.[81]

Social Movements, Interest Groups, and Public Choice

Has the peace movement influenced public opinion? Paul Joseph, author of *Peace Politics*, argues that the peace movement has been effective. He writes that there was about a fifteen-percentage-point shift in the direction of positions generally favored by the peace movement between 1981 and 1984, a time of the movement's peak activity. It is significant that this shift occurred before the rise to power of Mikhail Gorbachev.[82] But other observers argue that the impact of the peace movement has been limited:

> By 1985, the American peace movement [had] achieved major success in raising the consciousness of the American people about the special destructiveness of nuclear war. But this awareness was not accompanied by formulated programs for halting and reversing the war system juggernaut whose activities now dominate public life.[83]

The nuclear freeze campaign proposed a halt in the production and deployment of new nuclear weapons so as to "freeze" existing nuclear weapons arsenals. It was particularly effective in galvanizing public attention, becoming "the largest social movement in American history."[84] Yet, increased fear of nuclear war, more than any particular attraction to the freeze itself, made the proposal popular.

With the end of the Cold War, the peace movement expanded its educational agenda, with a number of groups calling for a 50 percent reduction in arms expenditures (although such calls were not necessarily linked to a comprehensive framework such as a disarmament treaty). Many peace groups, joined by the religious community and labor unions, have conducted public education campaigns in support of economic conversion policies. These campaigns are more than ad hoc protests and have begun an educational process that addresses issues, such as military dependency, that lie behind the arms race.

A major constraint on the ability of the peace movement to influence the media and public debate is the enormous disparity between the financial and personnel resources available to peace groups and those available to the Pentagon and its allies. In 1971, a survey revealed that "the Pentagon was publishing a total of 371 magazines at an annual cost of some $57 million, an operation sixteen times larger than the nation's biggest publisher." An update in 1982 found that the Pentagon was publishing 1,203 periodicals. One of the largest nonprofit organizations challenging the Pentagon has been the American Friends Service Committee (AFSC). In 1984–85, the AFSC's "main office information-services budget . . . was under $500,000 with eleven staff people."[85]

It seems quite clear that the peace movement helped speed the Vietnam War, thus constraining a major source of defense expenditures. Since then, it has won key legislative battles in campaigns to slow deployment of the MX missile and to pass congressional resolutions in support of a nuclear freeze. Yet, after passing the freeze resolution, the House of Representatives approved funding for MX and Trident missile development, and for the first phases of the Strategic Defense Initiative. It also approved deployment of the cruise and Pershing II missiles in Europe. And all of these moves contradicted the spirit, if not the letter, of the freeze resolution.[86] Generally speaking, one might argue that the peace movement has been able to marshal a constituency that is sympathetic to reductions in military budgets and particular weapons systems, but has had very limited leverage in determining the rate at which overall cutbacks are made.

Conclusion

Government policy on defense spending and related military engagements that trigger such spending are not simply variables dependent on public choices. Rather, there is an ongoing process in which the public and government limit and influence each other. There is evidence that public choices do affect the level of military spending, but public choice theory must be supplemented by a broader framework because it does not capture all of the forces determining the level of military expenditures. Public choice theory does not address whether the *level* of defense spending matches public choices or military managers' interpretations of them. Although spending may increase in response to changes in public opinion, *the rate and amount of increase* cannot be logically linked to public desires because of the absence of a clear production/preference function and the problems of military overkill.

The limitations of public choice theory become clearer once we examine its potential relevance for the politics of the peace dividend. Here, *the central problem* is the rate and amount of decrease in military budgets. The accumulated budget deficits created by the Reagan and Bush arms buildup have now helped trigger the accountability structures that are pressuring politicians to reduce military spending. Although the public has desired to shift priorities from defense to new civilian expenditures, this transition has been far from easy. Public choices here have not been readily translated into policy.

By his January 25, 1994, state-of-the-union message, President Clinton said he would make no further defense cuts, particularly to fund civilian programs. He said that "defense conversion will keep us strong militarily and create jobs for our people at home."[87] In other words, we would have "conversion" without either disarmament or a peace dividend.

Despite the slow rate of military cuts, independent forces have been successful in expanding civilian budgets. But increasing entitlements and health-care budgets are not the same thing as a peace dividend. A real peace dividend would require using military cuts to finance new investments in housing, mass transportation, alternative energy, and environmental renewal. It would also tap the new flow of civilian wealth that can be generated by the conversion of defense firms. This kind of conversion is rooted in reduced military budgets.

Why has public preference for a peace dividend not produced a stronger government response? Polls themselves represent attitudes, and attitudes are often a weak proxy for political will. Voters are also sending Congress conflicting messages. On the one hand, they want Congress to reduce the deficit. In fact, "the opposition to government deficits has remained steadfast and stable as far back as public opinion polls are available."[88] On the other hand, an important segment of the public would like a peace dividend.

Different constituencies have different preference functions, with some groups clearly having a greater stake in larger or smaller military budgets. Both peace groups and military contractors have preferences that are stronger than those of more disinterested publics. In addition, such preferences are shaped by a larger political calculus of the tactics needed to respond to a shifting political terrain. Defense contractors facing the end of the Cold War may settle for stable rather than growing budgets. Peace groups may reduce the size of cuts they ask for to build political alliances in Congress. This shift will affect their grassroots education campaigns and the preferences of those with whom they are in communication.

Revisions to public choice theory acknowledge that voters can be divided into groups with different preferences for competing policies. The existence of such multiple preferences will affect the ability of legislators to carry out popular will. Under certain conditions, there simply is no one policy that is preferred by the majority to all others. For example, with three people and three policies, if for person one, the policies are ranked $A > B > C$; for person two $B > C > A$; and for person three $C > A > B$, then there is no policy that wins out over both of the other two in a majority vote. This situation becomes more and more likely as a policy has more and more effects (or dimensions).

Interestingly enough, in this case, whoever controls the voting process controls its outcome. For example, suppose we have three policies, A, B, and C, with effects on military budgets, budget deficits, and international stability. Say A is best for military budget reductions, B is best for reducing the budget deficit, and C is best for increasing international stability. Suppose further that there are three senators who rank these policies the same way as persons one, two, and three ranked them above. Then, if policy A is put to a vote against policy B first, the majority of the senators will vote for A. If A is put to a vote against C first, then C will win. But if C were put to a vote against B first, then B would have won! The sequence of the voting determines the winner. Thus, voting rules and agenda setting can actually play an important role in determining voting outcomes.[89]

Discussions that link various policy dimensions must be matched by comprehensive planning efforts that also link issues. The political process and complexity involved in economic changes may create a situation in which various elements of the destination activity will come on line at different times. Such "piecemeal" economic programs can create serious problems. For example, policies designed to facilitate manufacturing conversion without promotion of new civilian markets may result in firms moving into civilian production in the absence of sufficient demand to make their new products economically viable.[90]

Comprehensive education efforts show how policies can be linked in theory. Comprehensive planning efforts link various policies in practice. But comprehensive education and planning are mutually supportive and may well be necessary conditions for each other. Public education efforts that claim that various policies such as arms cuts and economic stability through conversion can be combined gain credibility when planning efforts move in this direction. Conversely, educational and lobbying efforts that attempt to show how policies can be linked may affect actual planning that links policies. In this case, labor unions might educate their members about the advantages of using a peace dividend for worker retraining and industrial development.

The linkage of policies through the implementation of comprehensive planning has been blocked by several factors. These factors have facilitated the separation of government policy on military budgets (and budget deficit reduction) from proactive civilian planning and peace dividend policies. These forces explain why public choices to shift resources from the military to civilian expenditures are difficult to carry out. First, the Reagan-initiated deficit wave helped create pressure for defense cuts, but has made the peace dividend a hostage of the past military buildup:

> [T]he deficits have had the effect of sharply constraining discussion about new domestic programmes—even amid growing recognition that such programmes are needed to reverse economic decline. This, indeed, seems to have been the intent of the [Reagan] administration in creating the deficits in the first place.[91]

Second, the military has found new ways to finance operations despite budget cuts. Although there are serious constraints on each, both the $53.5 billion subsidy from allies during the Gulf War and a burgeoning arms trade (which increased the contracts of the U.S. Army for foreign military sales from $2 billion in 1986 to $12 billion in 1991) have divorced levels of military activity from the public purse.[92] Such actions represent economic barriers to achieving a conversion-based peace dividend.

Third, the congressional planning for expanding new peace dividend missions has broken down because of archaic political structures and competing fiefdoms. This makes it difficult to coordinate diverse federal policies required by conversion with matching disarmament initiatives. When Congress has attempted to link policy goals in budget planning, it has been thwarted by complexes of power disinterested in such coordination. "Agencies and committees work with private interests to form 'iron triangles'—little fiefdoms that cut their own deals and are less beholden to party leaders."[93]

Finally, the institutions of civilian planning in the United States are rather weak. Sociologist Gregory Hooks notes that

> in the course of World War II and afterward, the Pentagon captured the federal government's most important planning tools. This planning capacity built upon the legacy of the New Deal, but at the same time it destroyed the institutional foundations necessary for New Deal reform and civilian planning.[94]

The discrepancy between public choice and government action does not mean that a peace dividend and civilian planning are impossible. The level of military expenditures is not driven by public choices alone. Now that the Cold War is over, the pressures to reduce the military budget at some significant rate have been overwhelming, although resistance to cuts is also great. And even critics who argue that government economic planning has been limited tend to acknowledge that crisis situations will provoke a civilian planning response by government. The disruption caused by layoffs of millions of defense workers and defense firms threatened by military cuts has helped trigger government programs to support conversion, although these are rather weak at present.

While the resistance of Congress and pressures to save weapons systems in politically important regions have slowed cutbacks, in real terms the military budget is declining. The power of the military-industrial complex has slowed the rate at which cutbacks occur, but it has not succeeded in preventing cuts. Public choice models do not explain how the resistance to cutbacks, the rate of military cuts, and resistance to conversion are rooted in regional, firm, and industrial military dependency. But, used in conjunction with macroeconomic and institutional analyses, they can show the direction of long-term policy trends.

The relationship between public choice and military budget levels has direct bearing on the future course of conversion politics and organizing. Revisions in public choice theory account for bureaucratic resistance to military budget cutbacks and multiple preferences, but cannot easily explain the role of the media in shaping the terms of debate. This "media framing" influences choices and the desired combination or ranking of preferences. The Gulf War illustrated how military managers and their allies in Congress can manipulate "new threats" overseas to slow the rate of defense cutbacks. But it is not clear whether socially desirable outcomes would occur if military spending simply followed public opinion and leaders just followed polls.

The space for more deliberative dialogue about the opportunity costs of large-scale military budgets and requirements of multidimensional policies needs to be expanded. This dialogue would reveal the false tradeoffs that opinion polls assume exist between jobs and economic security or international threats and economic conversion. A new foreign-policy regime involving military budget reductions, arms conversion, and a multilateral disarmament process would require the extension of education and political power by groups with a stake in an expanded civilian economy. This extension could be based on popular campaigns linking topical media events to face-to-face organizing. Such campaigns could promote local economic models of a peace economy and find support in new economic institutions responsive to citizen participation. But the extension of such power is far from the concerns that have motivated the development of public choice theories until now.

Appendix: Changing Support for the Peace Dividend

Public opinion on the question, "Should federal spending on military and defense programs be increased, decreased, or kept about the same?"

	Increased	Decreased	Same
January 1981[a]	61	7	28
October 1984	17	22	54
January 1985	19	26	53
January 1986	17	26	53
November 1987	13	38	45
January 1988	18	26	53
January 1989	14	24	58
January 1990	13	36	48
March 1991	16	15	65
October 1991	10	36	52
January 1992	8	45	46

(continued)

[a]In January 1981 the question read, "If you had a say in making up the federal budget this year, which programs would you like to see increased and which reduced? Should federal spending on military and defense problems be increased, decreased, or kept about the same?

Source: News release from *New York Times*/CBS News Poll (New York, January 25, 1992), p. 10.

Notes

1. George Gallup, Jr., *The Gallup Poll: Public Opinion 1991* (Wilmington, DE: Scholarly Resources Inc., 1992, p. 202.

2. In the market, exchange is contingent upon the "exclusion principle." For one person to pay a price for a given good, another person, who does not pay, must be excluded from consumption of the good. Exchange depends on property rights, which require exclusion. With exclusion, the market can be used as an "auction system" where consumers bid for a product and reveal their preferences to the producer. The producer, under the constraints of a competitive market, uses these signals to produce according to consumer preference. This system works in the private market because those who pay also benefit. That is, "benefits are internalized and consumption is *rival.*" Thus, when a person purchases or consumes a product, only he or she (or an immediate social circle) will benefit, not the public at large. Exclusion of the public from consumption is feasible because "the goods are handed over when the price is paid, but not before."

In contrast to exchanges of private goods in the market, social goods require a different system of distribution. The consumption of these goods can be "nonrival" because if one person partakes of consumption benefits, this "does not reduce the benefits derived by all others." As each consumer is added, marginal cost is zero. Prices should reflect marginal cost but it is hard to place a cost on additional users. Therefore, it is inefficient to use the market to ration the good.

In some cases, exclusion of social goods (such as "national security") is not possible because the functioning of society depends on allowing the general public to have access to the good or its benefits. In other cases, excluding the public from the good is not desirable. It is possible for consumption of social goods to be rival because in conditions of scarcity consumers will be competing for access to limited goods, like parking spaces, seats on buses, and budgetary "porkbarrel" programs. However, for most social goods, exclusion is "impossible or too costly." The private market should not supply goods where exclusion is difficult because it will be hard to link charges to individual users. See Richard A. Musgrave and Peggy B. Musgrave, *Public Finance in Theory and Practice*, 3d ed. (New York: McGraw-Hill, 1980), pp. 55–6.)

3. Musgrave and Musgrave, *Public Finance in Theory and Practice*, pp. 57, 61.

4. Ibid., p. 61.

5. Ibid.

6. Michael Dee Oden, *Military Spending, Military Power, and U.S. Postwar Economic Performance* (Ph.D. dissertation, Department of Economics, The New School for Social Research, 1992), p. 108.

7. Douglas Arnold, *The Logic of Congressional Action* (New Haven, CT: Yale University Press, 1990) pp. 4, 9.

8. Benjamin Page and Robert Y. Shapiro, *The Rational Public: Fifty Years of Trends in Americans' Policy Preferences* (Chicago: University of Chicago Press, 1992).

9. Bruce Russett, *Controlling the Sword: The Democratic Governance of National Security* (Cambridge, MA: Harvard University Press, 1990). pp. 99–101.

10. Thomas Hartley and Bruce Russett, "Public opinion and the common defense: Who governs military spending in the United States?" *American Political Science Review*, *86*, 4 (December 1992): 910–11.

11. Larry M. Bartels, "Constituency opinion and congressional policy making: The Reagan defense buildup," *American Political Science Review*, *85*, 2 (June 1991): 457–74.

12. George Gallup. 1981. *The Gallup Poll: Public Opinion 1980* (Wilmington, DE: Scholarly Resources Inc., 1981), pp. 46, 191.

13. Warren E. Miller and J. Merrill Shanks, "Policy directions and presidential leadership: Alternative interpretations of the 1980 presidential elections," *British Journal of Political Science*, *12*, pt. 3 (July 1982): 349.

14. Joshua Cohen and Joel Rogers, " 'Reaganism' after Reagan." In *Socialist Register 1988*, ed. by Ralph Miliband and John Saville (London: Merlin Press, 1988), pp. 387–424.

15. Bartels, "Constituency opinion and congressional policy making," pp. 463–4.

16. Cobb had found that there was "almost no evidence that concentrations of defense spending had an influence on 'the jingoism scales'." See Stephen A. Cobb, "Defense spending and foreign policy in the House of Representatives," *Journal of Conflict Resolution*, *13*, 3 [September 1969]: 358–69). See also Stephen A. Cobb, "Defense spending, foreign policy voting, and the structure of the U.S. House of Representatives," read at the 1972 Meetings of the Southern Sociological Society at New Orleans; and Stephen Cobb, "The United States Senate and the impact of defense spending concentrations," in *Testing the Theory of the Military-Industrial Complex*, ed. by Steven Rosen (Lexington, MA: Lexington Books, 1973), pp. 197–223. Russett, on the other hand, did find that there was support for the hypothesis that concentrations of military spending affected voting by U.S. senators (Bruce Russett, *What Price Vigilance?* [New Haven, CT: Yale University Press, 1970]).

17. Ronald H. Hinckley, *People, Polls, and Policymakers: American Public Opinion and National Security* (New York: Lexington Books, 1992) p. 4.

18. Russett, *What Price Vigilance?*, p. 108.

19. Robert Higgs, "Do legislators' votes reflect constituency preference? A simple way to evaluate the Senate," *Public Choice*, *63*, 2 (November 1989): 177–9.

20. Randolph S. Bourne, *War and the Intellectuals: Essays by Randolph S. Bourne*, ed. by Carl Resek (New York: Harper and Row, 1964), p. 5.

21. Richard J. Barnet, *The Rockets' Red Glare* (New York: Simon and Schuster, 1990), pp. 144–6.

22. James Weinstein, *The Corporate Ideal in the Liberal State: 1900–1918* (Boston: Beacon Press, 1968), p. 233.

23. Bourne, *War and the Intellectuals*, p. 37.

24. Barnet, *The Rockets' Red Glare*, p. 157.

25. William Albig, *Public Opinion* (New York: McGraw-Hill, 1939), pp. 368–9.

26. Barnet, *The Rockets' Red Glare*, pp. 157–8.

27. Weinstein, *The Corporate Ideal*, pp. 236–7.

28. Bourne, *War and the Intellectuals*, p. 41.

29. Robert Y. Shapiro and Benjamin I. Page, "Foreign policy and the rational public," *Journal of Conflict Resolution, 32*, 2 (June 1988): 233.

30. William Shawcross, *Sideshow: Kissinger, Nixon, and the Destruction of Cambodia* (New York: Pocket Books, 1979).

31. Alan Peacock and Jack Wiseman, *The Growth of Public Expenditure in the United Kingdom* (Princeton, NJ: Princeton University Press, 1961).

32. Ted Goertzel, "Militarism as a sociological problem: The political sociology of U.S. military spending, 1951–1983," in *Research in Political Sociology*, vol. 1, ed. by Richard G. Graungart and Margaret M. Braungart (Greenwich, CT: JAI Press, 1985), p. 128.

33. Stanley Karnow, *Vietnam: A History* (New York: Viking, 1983), p. 481.

34. Herman and Chomsky contend that the Tet offensive did not trigger increased opposition to the war. The offensive led to an initial wave of support for the president and was followed by a slow drift to the Dove position. Barnet cites a "a poll taken in the midst of the Tet offensive" which "showed that 53 percent of the respondents wanted a more vigorous prosecution of the war even at the risk of fighting Russia or China." Herman and Chomsky make an interesting point about how elite opinion after Tet changed media reporting: "the Tet offensive not only reduced Washington to gloomy despair and convinced U.S. elites that there was no realistic hope of a military victory in Vietnam at a cost acceptable to the United States, but also changed the character of media reporting and commentary, which mirrored the changes in elite opinion." See Edward S. Herman and Noam Chomsky, *Manufacturing Consent: The Political Economy of the Mass Media* (New York: Pantheon Books, 1988), pp. 217, 219–20; and Barnet, *The Rockets' Red Glare*, p. 343.

Elite opposition to the war (supported by majority opinion) also affected media coverage. Max Frankel, the executive editor of the *New York Times*, explained how coverage of opposition to the war changed over time: "As protest moved from left groups, anti-war groups, into the pulpits, into the Senate . . . as it became majority opinion, it naturally picked up coverage. And then naturally the tone of the coverage changed. Because we're an Establishment institution, and whenever your natural community changes . . . , then naturally you will too" (Todd Gitlin, *The Whole World Is Watching: Mass Media in the Making and Unmaking of the New Left* [Berkeley: University of California Press, 1980], p. 205).

35. Ted Goertzel, "Public opinion concerning military spending in the United States: 1937–1985," *Journal of Political and Military Sociology, 15*, 1 (Spring 1982): 64.

36. Irving Louis Horowitz, *The Struggle Is the Message* (Berkeley: The Glendessary Press, 1970), p. 20.

37. Paul Burstein and William Freudenburg, "Changing public policy: The impact of public opinion, antiwar demonstrations, and war costs on senate voting on Vietnam War motions," *American Journal of Sociology, 84*, 1 (July 1978): 99.

38. Andrew Katz, "Who ended the Vietnam war?" Manuscript (Gambier, OH: Kenyan College, Political Science Department, 1988).

39. Goertzel, "Public Opinion." See also Robert Higgs, "U.S. military spend-

ing in the Cold War era: Opportunity costs, foreign crises and domestic constraints," *CATO Institute for Policy Analysis*, no. 114 (Washington, DC: Cato Institute, November 30, 1988).

40. Barnet, *The Rockets' Red Glare*, pp. 11–12.

41. Miroslav Nincic, *United States Foreign Policy: Choices and Tradeoffs* (Washington, DC: Congressional Quarterly Press, 1988), p. 248. The ability to engage in military conflicts with minimal loss in life has helped create public support for post–Cold War engagements like the Persian Gulf War. "Despite strong indications that the public would have supported more protracted diplomacy and other nonviolent measures to remove Iraq from Kuwait, a direct, swift, and seemingly successful military operation with little direct human cost to Americans was able to decisively reverse the public's disinclination to support a war" (Paul Joseph, *Peace Politics* [Philadelphia: Temple University Press, 1993], p. 119).

42. Cohen and Rogers, " 'Reaganism' after Reagan," pp. 397, 401–2.

43. Marion Anderson, Greg Bischak, and Michael Oden, *Converting the American Economy: The Economic Effects of an Alternative Security Policy* (Lansing, MI: Employment Research Associates, 1991). See also Roger H. Bezdek, "The 1980 economic impact—regional and occupational—of compensated shifts in defense spending," *Journal of Regional Science*, 15, 2 (1975): 183–98.

44. Paul Brace and Barbara Hinckley, *Follow the Leader: Opinion Polls and the Modern Presidents* (New York: Basic Books, 1992), pp. 24–5.

45. Ibid., 148–9.

46. Oden, *Military Spending*, 135.

47. Thomas Paine, *Rights of Man* (New York: Penguin Books, 1984), p. 77.

48. Joseph Schumpeter, *Imperialism and Social Classes* (New York: August M. Kelley, 1955), p. 33.

49. Seymour Melman, *Pentagon Capitalism* (New York: McGraw-Hill, 1970) pp. 20, 83.

50. William H. Oakland 1987, "Theory of Public Goods," in *Handbook of Public Economics*, vol. 2, ed. by Alan J. Auerbach and Martin Feldstein (Amsterdam: Elsevier Science, 1987), p. 530.

51. Gordon Adams, *The Iron Triangle: The Politics of Defense Contracting* (New York: Council on Economic Priorities, 1981).

52. Ann Markusen, and Joel Yudken, *Dismantling the Cold War Economy* (New York: Basic Books, 1992), pp. 91–2.

53. Oakland, "Theory of public goods," p. 530.

54. Terry M. Moe, "The politics of bureaucratic structure," in *Can the Government Govern?* ed. by John E. Chubb and Paul E. Peterson (Washington, DC: The Brookings Institution, 1989), pp. 267–329.

55. William Greider, *Who Will Tell the People: The Betrayal of American Democracy* (New York: Simon and Schuster, 1992), pp. 113–4.

56. Ibid.

57. Philip J. Powlick, "The attitudinal bases for responsiveness to public opinion among American foreign policy officials," *The Journal of Conflict Resolution*, *35*, 4 (December 1991), p. 637.

58. Thomas R. Cusack, "On the domestic political-economic sources of American military spending," *The Political Economy of Military Spending in the*

United States, ed. by Alex Mintz (New York: Routledge, 1992), pp. 103–31.

59. Gregory Hooks, *Forging the Military-Industrial Complex: World War II's Battle of the Potomac* (Urbana: University of Illinois Press, 1991).

60. Mancur Olson, Comment, in *The Measurement of Economic and Social Performance*, ed. by Milton Moss (New York: National Bureau of Economic Research, 1973), p. 405.

61. Oden, *Military Spending*, p. 113.

62. Miroslav Nincic, *Democracy and Foreign Policy: The Fallacy of Political Realism* (New York: Columbia University Press, 1992), p. 14.

63. Theodore J. Lowi, *The Personal President: Power Invested, Promise Unfulfilled* (Ithaca, NY: Cornell University Press, 1985).

64. Nincic, *Democracy and Foreign Policy*, p. 17.

65. Bruno Frey and Lawrence J. Lau, "Towards a mathematical model of government behavior," *Zeitschrift fur Nationalokonomie*, 28, 3 (December): 355–80.

66. Brace and Hinckley, *Follow the Leader*, pp. 97–8.

67. Miroslav Nincic, "New perspectives on popular opinion and foreign policy," *Journal of Conflict Resolution*, 36, 4 (December 1992): 782.

68. Benjamin Page, Robert Y. Shapiro, and Glenn R. Dempsey, "What moves public opinion?" *American Political Science Review*, 81, 1 (March 1982): 23–43.

69. Michael Wines, "$8 Billion directed to wheat farmers and arms workers," *The New York Times*, September 3, 1992, pp. A1, A20.

70. Brace and Hinckley, *Follow the Leader*, p. 158.

71. Sidney Blumenthal, "All the president's wars," *The New Yorker* (December 28-January 4, 1992–93), p. 66–7.

72. Brace and Hinckley, *Follow the Leader*, pp. 146–7.

73. Ibid., p. 158.

74. Blumenthal, "All the president's wars," p. 63.

75. Robert Borosage, "All dollars, no sense: The Cold War is over, but the Pentagon is still spending like there's no tomorrow," *Mother Jones* (September–October 1993), p. 44.

76. Public choice theory does not explain why certain voting groups' utilities for the military social good vary greatly by ethnic group, gender, and race. For example, an analysis of opinions on military spending from 1973 to 1985 found the following proportions felt the United States was spending too much on the military (the average for the sample was 30 percent): 37 percent of those under thirty but 25 percent sixty and over; whites 30 percent but nonwhites 35 percent; Protestants 26 percent but Jews 51 percent; police and armed forces 22 percent, but engineers, scientists, and technicians 35 percent and education and social service workers 43 percent (Goertzel, "Public opinion concerning military spending," p. 67). There is reason to suspect that opinions on military spending levels are shaped by such social differences rather than abstract utility functions for public goods. More recent polling data showed that African Americans frequently opposed the Persian Gulf War in greater percentages than white Americans.

77. Walter Lippmann, *The Essential Lippmann: A Political Philosophy for Liberal Democracy*, ed. by Clinton Rossiter and James Lare (Cambridge, MA: Harvard University Press, 1982). pp. 106–7.

78. David W. Moore and Frank Newport, "Confidence in institutions: Military still tops the list," *The Gallup Poll Monthly*, no. 33 (April 1993): 22–3.

79. Joseph, *Peace Politics*, p. 115.

80. Haynes Johnson and Richard Morin, "Spoils of war victors gain public confidence," *The Washington Post,* March 10, 1991, pp. A21, A26.

81. Alan F. Kay, Stanley B. Greenberg, Frederick T. Steeper, and Hazel Henderson, "Global Uncertainties: Final survey of the four survey series on global issues" (Washington, DC, and St. Augustine, FL: Americans Talk Issues, May 10, 1993), p. 19.

82. Joseph, *Peace Politics*, p. 151.

83. Seymour Melman, *The Demilitarized Society: Disarmament and Conversion* (Montreal: Harvest House, 1988), p. 37.

84. Thomas R. Rochon and Daniel A. Mazmanian, "Social Movements and the policy process," *The Annals of the American Academy of Political and Social Science, 528* (July 1993), p. 80.

85. Edward S. Edward S. and Noam Chomsky, *Manufacturing Consent: The Political Economy of the Mass Media* (New York: Pantheon Books, 1988), p. 20.

86. Rochon and Mazmanian, "Social movements and the policy process," p. 82.

87. *ABC News,* "State of the union address: President Clinton's address to Congress," broadcast January 25. See also "Excerpts from President Clinton's state of the union message," *New York Times*, January 26, 1994.

88. Andre Modigliani and Franco Modigliani, "The growth of the federal deficit and the role of public attitudes," *Public Opinion Quarterly, 51,* 4 (Winter 1987): 473.

89. Robert P. Inman, "Markets, governments, and the 'new' political economy," in *Handbook of Public Economics*, Vol. 2, ed. by Alan J. Auerbach and Martin Feldstein (Amsterdam: Elsevier Science, 1987), pp. 705–10.

90. Lloyd J. Dumas, *The Overburdened Economy* (Berkeley: University of California Press, 1986), pp. 139–40.

91. Cohen and Rogers, " 'Reaganism' after Reagan," p. 402.

92. David C. Morrison, "Boom times for the arms trade," *National Journal, 23,* 50 (December 14, 1991): 3025.

93. Lawrence J. Haas, "Behind the times," *National Journal, 23,* 13 (March 30, 1991): 723.

94. Hooks, *Forging the Military-Industrial Complex*, p. 275.

Part IV

Conversion in the Former Socialist Countries

10

MICHAEL ODEN

Turning Swords into Washing Machines: Converting Russian Military Firms to Consumer Durable Production

If one views the success of reform in Russia as the most important national security concern of the 1990s, one must honestly look at the past years of half-measures and missed opportunities with dismay and to the future with a degree of trepidation. The failure of energy and imagination by all parties is nowhere more evident than in the area of military conversion. Yet, despite the drastic fall in output and chaos in economic policy, there are bright spots in the Russian economy. Now that the more naive programs of radical reform have withdrawn, an opening exists to carry out a national restructuring of industry anchored by the expansion of nonmilitary production at former military-oriented enterprises. Seizing this opportunity will require bravery and imagination on the part of the Russian government and the advanced market countries.

Military enterprises formed an important part of the manufacturing base in each former Warsaw Pact (WTO) country. The former Soviet Union, especially the Russian Republic, was the core of a more or less integrated military production network stretching across Central and Eastern Europe. In Russia, the military organized and participated in all branches of modern industry and dominated the nation's science and technology activities.

Fundamental changes in security policies and military requirements, together with the economic stresses of the transition, have led to the collapse of military demand across the region. Substantial cuts have been made in the military forces and budgets of each former WTO country since 1989, and, due to a number of factors, their military export sales have also plummeted. Enterprises producing military-related goods are coming under extreme financial pressure and a wholesale restructuring is underway. Many enterprises are expanding civilian output as military orders disappear. But the process of enterprise restructuring and conversion has been completely haphazard, unguided by de facto planning, clearly designed new technology or industrial policies, or an emerging operation of market forces.

The inability of the Russian central government to overcome entrenched institutional interests, particularly established managers of military and other large enterprises, has yielded a damaging policy of indirect subsidies without any requirement that enterprises improve their performance. For observers of the U.S. military complex, this phenomenon has a somewhat familiar ring. But the situation in Russia is much more dire. At a crucial time, substantial resources are being wasted as technologies, know-how, and badly needed products remain bottled up under the control of military enterprise managers with few incentives to convert resources to productive pursuits. In Russia, this excessive resource loss is exacerbated by the failure of central policy makers to devise and implement a broader set of consistent transition policies and sell them to the public. On top of this, assistance from the OECD countries[1] to stimulate conversion has been shockingly inadequate. It is a tragic irony that the United States plans to spend roughly six times more to maintain military forces in Western Europe than it will spend on all aid programs in Eastern Europe.[2] Moreover, the approach of OECD countries to the conversion challenge has been based on tired nostrums about conversion that are generally irrelevant to the situation in Central and Eastern Europe.

The transition to a new market-oriented economy in the Russian Republic may well founder without the successful transformation of military-oriented enterprises into civilian firms supplying essential capital, infrastructure, and consumer goods to the internal market. Many enterprises once under the military ministries represent potential leaders in their respective sectors, possessing the most modern plant and equipment and the most capable workers, technical personnel, and managers. The dearth of foreign investment combined with effective foreign-exchange limits on imports means that the domestic market for most goods and services will be satisfied largely by the development of competent domestic enterprises rather than external investment or imports. Unless the microfoundations of the Russian economy are rebuilt, there is little prospect for macroeconomic stability and growth. If more military-serving enterprises are rehabilitated and restructured to expand output of civilian products of adequate (if not world-class) quality, competition will be increased in near-monopoly sectors, and complementary development of new supply and demand backed by income will be stimulated.

To establish this proposition, the first section of this analysis outlines the dimensions of the military conversion problem across the former WTO area. Then, a description of the nature and current status of the military complex in Russia is followed by an analysis of the characteristics that distinguish the conversion problem in Russia (at both the macro and the micro level) from the problem in OECD countries such as the United States. Recent Russian government conversion policies are then reviewed and compared with certain prerequisites for a successful conversion process. Finally, a set of practical policy options is outlined—options aimed at improving the essential microeconomic performance of Russian military enterprises and stimulating the growth of new businesses in new economic sectors.

The Russian Hub: The Military Division of Labor in the Former Warsaw Pact

If the WTO military production system were viewed as a single industrial conglomerate, facilities in the Czech and Slovak Federal Republic (CSFR), Hungary, Poland, and other WTO members would be minor branch operations highly dependent on the Russian center for technology, product, and sales. The former Soviet Union (FSU) accounted for an estimated 85 to 90 percent of total WTO military spending.[3] Total defense-related employment in Slovakia—an area with a high concentration of military production—is estimated to be 80,000, while the Leninets military communications production combine in St. Petersburg alone employs over 50,000.[4]

These countries of the Warsaw Pact were tied into a more or less integrated military command, research, and production complex. Yet within this system, the military forces and production base of each country developed along distinct lines. A particular specialization and division of labor emerged among the WTO partners. The character of this specialization was sometimes determined by natural comparative advantage, but was more often the outcome of the specific political and security concerns of the Soviet Union. As a result, the aggregate scope of the conversion problem in terms of the macroeconomy, the manufacturing sector, and the labor force varies considerably among the former WTO countries.

Table 10.1 offers some very rough parameters on the size and distribution of military burdens among the former Warsaw Pact countries before the revolutions of 1989 and 1991. If we take 1987 as a reasonable base year to evaluate the previous structure, the share of military output in Soviet GNP was estimated by major Western organizations such as the Stockholm International Peace Research Institute (SIPRI) and the U.S. Arms Control and Disarmament Agency (ACDA) as over 12 percent. This is not a particularly meaningful estimate. SIPRI, an organization that traditionally offered low-end estimates of Soviet military spending, now admits that when all indirect subsidies, real resource costs, and indirect spending are accounted for, the share of military spending in Soviet GNP was in the neighborhood of 20 percent.[5] Estimates of the Soviet military burden depend on what is included and excluded in budgetary allocations to military ministries, how much of this allocation went to military versus civilian activities, highly speculative estimates of real relative prices of inputs and components to final systems, and exchange rate estimates. Whatever the actual number, it is agreed that the military burden of the Soviet Union was among the highest in the world. Broadly speaking, Bulgaria, the CSFR, and Poland could be said to have been minor but significant partners in the WTO military system in terms of the share of their national output dedicated to military purposes. Hungary and Rumania, on the other hand, were more marginal players.

Arms exports of WTO countries were also an important feature of the military division of labor. Total annual arms exports from the former Soviet Union averaged roughly $20 billion per year in the 1980s (in constant 1987$) and constituted nearly 20 percent of total exports in value terms. Arms exports became a major source of hard currency earnings in the 1970s, and by the mid-1980s, less than 40 percent of Soviet exports were to other WTO countries.[6] It has been estimated that roughly 17 percent of total Soviet weapons production output was for export markets.[7]

Table,10.1

Military Indicators of Former Warsaw Pact Countries

	USSR	Russian Republic	Bulgaria	CSFR	Hungary	Poland	Rumania
Military spending/GDP	12.5%	13.2%	7.2%	5.1%	4.1%	5.1%	3.2%
Military exports/total exports	19.7%	*	2.8%	5.6%	1.2%	2.5%	2.4%
Armed forces (1,000s)	4,400	*	191	215	116	440	248
Military-related industry employment (1,000s)	9,700	7,200	*	250	50	200	90
Direct arms production and R&D employment (1,000s)	5,190	3,900	*	133	30	125	45
Direct arms production employment/total manufacturing employment	15%	17.8%	*	5.3%	1.9%	3%	1.2%

Sources: U.S. Arms Control and Disarmament Agency, *World Military Expenditures and Arms Transfers* 1988 (Washington DC: U.S. Government Printing Office: June 1989) tables I and II; *SIPRI Yearbook 1992* (Stockholm: SIPRI: 1992) Appendix 7A; Julian Cooper, "Defense industry conversion in the East: The relevance of Western experience," paper presented to the NATO C&EE Defense Conversion Conference, May 1992; Ministry of Defense, Republic of Bulgaria, "Problems and trends in the realization of defense industry conversion within the military repair factories in Bulgaria" (1992); Federal Ministry of the Economy of the Czech and Slovak Republic, "Defense conversion and armament production in the Czech and Slovak Republic," paper presented to the NATO C&EE Defense Conversion Conference, May 1992; Experts Group Hungarian Minister for Foreign Affairs, "Defense conversion and economic transformation in Hungary, paper presented to the NATO C&EE Defense Conversion Conference, May 1992; Katarzyna Zukrowska, "The dilemmas of Polish arms industries in the period of systems changes" (Berlin: 1992); Berghof Stiftung für Konflictforschung, "Present condition, principal problems and prospects of Polish defense industry and opportunities for foreign cooperation," paper presented to the NATO C&EE Defense Conversion Conference, May 1992; "Some considerations on the conversion of the defense industry in Rumania," paper presented to the NATO C&EE Defense Conversion Conference, May 1992.

The CSFR was the second largest arms exporter and an important actor in the world arms market. Estimates of CSFR arms export activity vary considerably. According to SIPRI and ACDA, total arms exports were high over the 1980s, averaging between $600 million and $1 billion per year in the 1980s, well over 5 percent of total exports in value terms. Some estimates have suggested that more than one-third of total export earnings were from arms-related transactions.[8] According to CSFR government estimates, over 65 percent of total arms production output was for export and only about one-third for equipping domestic forces, indicating that military industry employment was more dependent on export than on domestic demand. Between 60 and 80 percent of arms exports were to other Warsaw Pact countries, the remainder going mostly to the Middle East.[9] Estimates of average annual Polish arms exports over the 1980s vary wildly, from $300 million to over $1 billion per year.[10]

The size of each country's armed forces also indicates a certain division of labor in terms of the provision of overall WTO military capability. Again, the former Soviet Union dominates, accounting for nearly 80 percent of total troop strength. Soviet armed forces were in the neighborhood of 4.4 million in 1987. Poland, because of its large population, had the second largest armed forces and was a major provider of ground force strength for the Warsaw Pact. This is reflected in the share of its domestic defense budget allocated to personnel and operations and maintenance spending, which equaled 67 percent of the total budget.[11]

The final set of figures presented in Table 10.1 is estimates of total military-related employment and direct employment in arms production facilities. Interpreting these estimates is difficult since they do not correspond to conventional approaches to measuring military-related employment used in OECD countries.

Total WTO military-related employment is often equated with total employment at enterprises under defense-oriented ministries, or total employment at enterprises that have some military work. For instance, in the case of the former Soviet Union, close to 10 million production workers are employed by enterprises under the eight or nine ministries that constitute the core of the defense complex. However, approximately half of the output of these enterprises is actual weapons or military equipment, while the other half is civilian goods or services. Some of these civilian products served as inputs into military equipment production or the army, but most were produced for general consumption or capital goods for purely civilian enterprises. Direct military employment, by contrast, is a measure of those engaged in the R&D and production of purely military products.

In the other countries, total military-related employment often measures all those employed at enterprises that have some military contracts, even if, for example, only 20 percent of total enterprise output was sustained directly by military orders. Direct military employment, on the other hand, often measures only those employees directly producing military equipment and may exclude workers producing generic products under military contract. But for most former WTO countries, this measure may capture personnel employed producing weapons for export.

Keeping these caveats in mind, the figures show that the total and direct military R&D and production work force in the former USSR was very large. Nearly 10 million workers were employed under the ministries that constituted the core of the military-industrial complex. According to Cooper, of this total, 8 million were labeled industrial production personnel, and 5.7 million of these were employed in the Russian Republic.[12] In addition, an estimated 1.7 million personnel are engaged in R&D activities directly or indirectly related to military work.[13] This R&D work force was highly concentrated in the Russian Republic, with about 1.5 million of the total.

Perhaps only 50 percent of this production work force and 70 percent of the R&D work force were directly engaged in the development or production of weapons systems or other military technology or equipment in the mid- to late 1980s. The direct military work force (excluding workers in the civilian category) constituted roughly 15 percent of total manufacturing employment in the former USSR and nearly 18 percent in the Russian Republic. The higher figures often reported include all employees of enterprises under the defense-oriented ministries; the military-related, as opposed to direct military work force, is put in the numerator. If this figure were used, total military-related employment would equal over 33 percent of total manufacturing employment. *By any measure, the military labor force was a major segment of overall manufacturing employment and a dominant segment of the research and development establishment.*

In sum, these very speculative aggregate data indicate that, before the dramatic changes of the past three and a half years, the military "division of labor" among former WTO countries accorded three countries a significant role. The former USSR, and especially the Russian Republic, dominated the system on every level. Military production was a main drive shaft of Russia's entire industrial system. The CSFR was an important player, with significant military production and employment, and was an important exporter of military equipment. Poland was responsible for providing troop strength and had a significant but more limited role in the realm of weapons production and arms export. The other countries, with the possible exception of Bulgaria, were minor players in the overall military system; their production was oriented more to providing inputs and components to end-use weapons makers in the other WTO countries.

The Defense Economy of the Former USSR

The research and production complex of the former Soviet Union was capable of producing the full range of weapons systems and military equipment necessary to support its huge military effort. Virtually every industrial sector had some role in military production. Western analysts have been surprised that central authorities apparently kept no systematic inventory of the military production complex—and this was not simply a matter of secrecy. There was evidently no disaggregated data on military production by industrial sector, no detailed data on the characteristics of the military-related production work force, and little data on the regional distribution of military production and employment. Data are remarkably sketchy. Most information has been compiled by Western analysts.

In terms of industrial organization, the arms sectors operated under nine "production" ministries. Analysts have emphasized that enterprises under these defense ministries had the highest priority in the planning system. They received the best capital equipment, paid higher wages and benefits than civilian enterprise, and had priority in commandeering supplies, often creating separate supply industries under their control.[14] It has been estimated that between 2,000 and 3,000 plants in the former Soviet Union were engaged in some form of military-related production.[15] It has also been noted that, because of the relative autonomy of defense-oriented ministries, enterprises or enterprise groups have a high degree of vertical integration—"make" rather than "buy" was for a number of reasons the order of the day. As a result, many military enterprises were gigantic, employing over 50,000 workers in single production locations.

Calculations of the industrial distribution of military production based upon international standard industrial classifications (ISIC) have not been compiled. However, the major industry groups in which military-related employment and output were concentrated can be sketched by analyzing the end-use weapons systems and equipment produced. Six core military industry groups can be identified:

1. Aerospace: including guided missile, airframe and aero-engine manufacturing industries;
2. Ground equipment: including transportation equipment industries (tanks, personnel carriers, jeeps, road equipment, etc.), engine production industries, structural metal industries (mobile bridging, other structural equipment);
3. Electronics and communications equipment: including radar, command and control electronics and telecommunications, aero-astronautical communications, computer and information system industries;
4. Nuclear materials: including nuclear materials industries, warhead fabrication and production, and the like;
5. Shipbuilding;
6. Ordnance-ammunition: including elements of the chemical industries.

This industry mix highlights groups that have been most affected by recent military cutbacks and in which conversion and diversification pressures are becoming most intense. However, in the former Soviet Union, the analysis is complicated by the fact that enterprises classified in these various groupings typically produce civilian products in completely different industry and product groups. For example, the Votkinsk Engineering Plant, which produced the SS–20 missile, was also principal producer of the "FEYA" washing machine, while the Leninets avionics and communications equipment enterprise produces most Russian vacuum cleaners.[16] In terms of industrial employment, the International Labour Office estimates that defense workers are concentrated in the broad ISIC category 38 (fabricated metal products, machinery, and equipment) constituting over 25 percent of employment in these industries.[17]

The military production system in the former Soviet Union was completely supported by an indigenous complex of scientific, research, and design bureaus and institutions. Basic science and weapons design were generally performed outside the production enterprise at large design centers such as Tupolev, Yakovlev, and Raduga. The balance of the military R&D effort occurs outside the enterprise; hence most technical personnel are attached to design bureaus rather than production enterprises.[18] Nearly 1.2 million engineers, scientists, and technicians were estimated to be engaged in military-related R&D in the FSU as late as 1988.[19]

In addition, most enterprises heavily engaged in systems production employ a significant number of such personnel to evaluate and test prototypes received from the design bureaus as they enter production. Very crude estimates of occupational employment within defense-related enterprises suggest that 77 percent of the military-related work force is in production occupations, 14 percent in scientific and technical occupations, 7 percent in management, and 1.4 percent in clerical.[20]

The lion's share of both the military research and the military production complex is contained within the borders of the Russian Republic. Roughly 70 to 75 percent of military production occurred in Russia and perhaps 85 percent of the R&D effort. Ukraine accounted for about 15 to 17 percent of FSU military production, and Belarus in the neighborhood of 2 to 3 percent of the total. The other republics have a much smaller military manufacturing base, with their defense output accounting for less than 2 percent of the FSU total.[21]

Within the Russian Republic there are a number of highly military-dependent regions where the conversion problem is particularly acute. Table 10.2 provides a rough breakdown of major regional-industrial agglomerations in the Russian Republic. The largest are: the Moscow region, which dominates R&D, aerospace, and electronics and communications production; the St. Petersburg region, with its huge military shipbuilding, electronics, and ground equipment production; and the Urals region, which holds a dominant position in the production of military ground equipment and also has a large military aerospace sector.

In terms of measuring the military dependency of particular regions, it is important to view military production relative to the region's overall employment and industrial base. Cooper has devised a measure based on the number of defense industry enterprises per capita. This measure shows that the Vladimir, St. Petersburg, and Urals regions have the highest levels of military dependency, yet even with its large population, the Moscow region ranks in the top ten.[22] Clearly, the

Table 10.2

Regional Distribution of Russian Defense Enterprises by Branch of Industry (in percent)

Region	Aerospace	Ground Equipment	Ship-building	Electronics and Communications
Moscow	22.1	9.4	1.2	12.0
Tula	—	6.2	1.2	0.6
Vladimir	2.3	3.1	4.7	3.5
St. Petersburg	3.5	9.4	20.0	8.5
Volgo-Vyatka	8.1	7.8	8.2	4.6
North Caucasis	4.7	1.6	4.7	4.0
Volga	12.8	9.4	8.2	6.9
Urals	12.8	28.1	2.4	6.3
West Siberia	4.7	9.4	1.2	6.3
Far Eastern	2.3	—	10.6	0.6

Sources: Julian Cooper, "Defense industry conversion in the East: The relevance of Western experience," paper presented to the NATO C&EE Defense Conversion Conference, May 1992; and "The Soviet defense industry and conversion: The regional dimension," in *Defense Expenditure, Industrial Conversion and Local Employment*, ed. by Richards and Paukert (Geneva: ILO 1991) p. 167.

possible effects of military-industry restructuring and employment losses will be severe in these specific regions. Moreover, this breakdown does not highlight the extreme military dependence of the many so-called special cities.

These facts underscore that, in the Russian Republic, the military sectors account for a substantial part of the work force, and of the R&D and manufacturing base. The huge regional military production agglomerations pose enormous challenges in terms of sectoral and regional adjustment. The notion proffered by some Western experts that a large segment of the military manufacturing base be scrapped is rendered impractical simply by the enormous size and regional concentration of military production.

The Collapse of Military Spending and Export Demand since 1989

Weapons procurement, R&D and nuclear weapons production fell dramatically in the former Soviet Union over the 1989–91 period. After the failed 1991 coup, military spending began to fall rapidly. This is likely to continue in the short term. Total military spending in the FSU fell by more than 20 percent, and military procurement by over 30 percent between 1988 and 1991. In 1992, military spending was slashed. Procurement spending is now roughly 80 percent lower in real terms than it was in 1989. Military R&D spending stands at roughly 50 percent of its real 1989 level, and spending for nuclear weapons is also approximately 50 percent of the 1989 level.[23]

It is also reported that indirect subsidies from the general budget to organizations in the defense complex have been significantly reduced. One estimate puts the cut in wage subsidies and subsidies for material inputs to defense enterprises over the last two years at 35 percent.[24] On top of these formidable pressures, managers of military enterprises have been coping with high general inflation and rapid changes in relative input prices resulting from the 1992 round of price liberalization.

Moreover, military-oriented enterprises have little inkling of future demand. A new security and military policy for the Russian Republic has been advanced, yet it is unclear whether the money is available to fund it. Despite concerted efforts of military suppliers, export demand has also been falling. Since over 50 percent of Soviet arms exports were to the Middle East (principally Iraq) and other WTO countries, the major arms exports markets of the past have severely contracted. New arms export markets such as Iran have not been sufficient to sustain export demand at previous levels. While more sophisticated forays to secure new foreign customers for top-line weapons systems have had some success, with, for example, a significant MIG–29 sale to Malaysia, the growth in weapons systems exports is likely to be quite modest. Russian arms sales agreements fell to a paltry $1.3 billion in 1992, and recent agreements will not lead to anywhere near the $25 billion in sales achieved as late as 1987.[25] In this environment enterprises find it impossible to forecast and plan future military production.

Finally, although the former Soviet Union was self-sufficient in military production, with its massive and integrated R&D, production, and supply network, the breakup of the WTO and the Soviet Union has caused havoc for Soviet military enterprises. The testy financial and political relations among the republics, most notably between the Russian Republic and Ukraine, are causing significant technical and supply problems for military production enterprises in each republic.

In light of these extreme conditions, a large number of enterprises—

perhaps as much as 50 percent—are close to bankruptcy.[26] They are currently being sustained in large measure by credits issued through the banks and supported by central bank money printing. Pumping short-term credits into the system has apparently allowed military enterprises the liquidity to avoid immediate mass layoffs of personnel: they are not producing but are still employing. However, it is hard to see how this approach can be sustained even over the short term, given the immediate danger of hyperinflation. If the expansion of money and credit to enterprises is curtailed, severe work force reductions will occur, and regions and local areas will be seriously affected. Add to this the ongoing reductions in the uniformed armed forces, which have amounted to about 1.5 million over the last three years, and the unraveling of the military system emerges as an economic and political problem of the first order.

General Features of the Military Conversion Problem in the Russian Republic

Conversion at the Macro Level

In the West, the issue of conversion at the macro level usually boils down to what else happens once defense outlays are reduced. As a first-order effect, military spending cuts reduce aggregate demand. But they almost invariably trigger policy changes in the form of tax cuts, government debt reductions, or increases in nonmilitary government activity. Each change has direct implications for the composition of industrial demand and hence the pattern of industrial, occupational, and regional employment. As many have noted, macroconversion does not generally imply preserving the preexisting structure of industrial demand or employment.[27]

With Russia experiencing a free fall in recorded output estimated at 38 percent since the beginning of 1990, the macro dimension of conversion is more complicated.[28] Military cuts are being used to plug gaping holes in government budgets and to service mounting debts of large state enterprises. But if military enterprises receive credits to stay open and pay wages even as their actual output of military and other products falls, this results in a deadly kind of budget reallocation. Payments are being channeled to military enterprises and no extra marketable output is generated in return. This equates to a special social-welfare program for politically powerful military enterprises and their work forces, and a clear trigger for hyperinflation. On balance, massive military cuts are going to sustain consumption in a period of falling aggregate output.[29]

The implications of the macroenvironment for the behavior and prospects of military-oriented enterprises in Russia are grave. From the demand side, new markets for civilian public or private capital goods are contracting due to falling real income, cuts in the government nonmilitary capital budget, and the collapse of demand from military enterprises to suppliers. For example, some enterprises producing tanks and military ground equipment have attempted to move into farm and large road-building equipment only to find no demand from government or private sources. From the supply side, there are no incentives and few assistance programs to stimulate increased output of marketable commercial products. Some enterprises still produce tractors with design parameters dictated to allow easy switchover to tank production in case of war (a legacy of the crazy Soviet policy of high defense surge capacity), making the tractors so large and heavy that they are unsuitable for farm use. In this environment, many enterprise managers are collecting subsidies, selling off inventories of final goods and raw materials, and spending a lot of time in Moscow to keep the cash flowing. They have no incentive to produce much of anything.

Enterprise Conversion—The Untapped Potential

Despite the dark picture painted above, a host of military-serving enterprises in Russia have made great strides in expanding commercial output. Indeed, a select number of military enterprises are among the most dramatic success stories in the Russian transition. This should not be surprising once the nature and position of military enterprises in the former planning system are understood.

The discussion of the military conversion problem in the OECD area has highlighted a large number of factors that distinguish military-oriented firms from firms producing for civilian markets. The structure, conduct, and performance of military firms or military divisions of corporate conglomerates are quite distinct. Military-oriented firms operate under fundamentally different market, efficiency, and pricing conditions than do civilian enterprises. It is argued that military firms operate under such unique conditions that the barriers to directly converting defense plants and their work forces to civilian production are often insurmountable.

At first glance, many unique characteristics are shared between military enterprises East and West. The structure, conduct, and performance of these firms deviate significantly from the benchmarks of competitive civilian firms in a market economy. Yet, for several important reasons, the general impulse of Western analysts to discount the desirability of converting military enterprises in Russia misses the mark.

First, in the Russian Republic and other WTO countries, military-oriented enterprises had many similar attributes in terms of structure and conduct to those of purely civilian-oriented enterprises. There are no civilian firms operating under competitive market conditions. All enterprises operated under instructions from a state monopsonist; all had unusual degrees of vertical integration; all were relatively cost-"unconscious"; and distribution and pricing for all enterprises were strictly administered. Hence, *while defense firms in OECD countries are islands of highly regulated, quasi-planned economic activity, in Russia they were simply part of the sea of centrally planned production.*

The second, most striking difference from OECD defense firms is that many defense enterprises in Russia have a long history of producing less specialized capital goods and consumer durable goods. This civil/military production often occurred within a single enterprise. Unlike their Western counterparts, there is no "wall of separation" between military and civilian production.[30] These enterprises at least know how to produce civilian goods and have the capability in place to do so.

There are in fact key attributes of military enterprises and their work forces that make them equal, and in certain senses superior, to civilian enterprises in terms of their potential contribution to new civilian economic activities. For instance, military-serving firms have greater experience with quality-control and inspection procedures when compared with many purely civilian state-owned enterprises emerging out of the planning system. Many military-oriented firms have more modern, higher-quality capital equipment and more experience with advanced manufacturing technology. Finally, in the case of the Russian Republic, military enterprises still have access to more steady and qualitatively superior supply sources than do purely civilian enterprises.

It will likely take several years before opportunities for conversion at the macro level emerge in the form of new public goods markets and major civilian R&D projects. In the meantime, the crazy system of providing working capital with no strings attached will sooner or later have to be scrapped. At a minimum, if firms continue to receive credits, they must be required to restructure and expand civilian activities. *Certain* military firms, particularly those with long experience producing civilian goods, have clear opportunities to expand their civilian activities and convert part of their capital and labor resources.

This would serve two immensely important purposes. First, it would open up internally generated supply and demand in a range of industries and product areas where severe shortages prevail. Second, it would create internal competition in a number of consumer and capital goods markets, which would contribute to efficiency gains and price stability. *Competition rather than privatization is the first prerequisite of efficiency gains in light of the starting point for market reform in Russia.*[31] Given that foreign direct investment will be limited and foreign-exchange constraints will continue to restrain imports, there may be a period during which enterprises can restructure without brutal competition from foreign producers. Yet, a vigorous expansion of civilian output by military enterprises can lead to the beginnings of real domestic competition. Over the short term, some firms will simply close down, others will diversify into civilian production (often locating separate facilities at the same production complex), and some enterprises will convert all or part of their plant and work forces to civilian production. Over time, a high-profile commitment by central and regional authorities to restructure and convert would substantially reduce resource and fiscal costs compared with the current program of extending credits.

Conversion of Human Resources

As the unsteady subsidy approach reaches its limits, there will be significant unemployment at military enterprises, even if a strong conversion policy is developed. Large-scale military cuts hence require mechanisms to rechannel unemployed military production personnel into civilian work more efficiently. Because of the unique attributes of military-serving firms, the defense production work force itself is quite different from the labor force in the civilian economy.

The unique characteristics of the military production work force are very similar in both OECD countries and Russia. There are higher number of skilled technical personnel and production workers. A privileged (high-wage) status prevails for military managers and production workers. But in OECD countries, the special skills of this work force have at least some chance of being preserved and redirected under the edicts of demand for skilled labor in the labor markets. In the Russian Republic, there is no short-term means to transfer the special, and in some cases scarce, skills embodied especially in the military labor force.

This problem is exacerbated because housing and other services have traditionally been provided by the enterprise rather than by government institutions or individuals. The chronic shortage of housing, the continued prevalence of company housing, and the absence of a developed private housing market currently act as a severe constraint on labor mobility.

Yet, even more than in the West, the Russian economy desperately needs to preserve and to utilize the skills and know-how embodied in the military work force. Again, in terms of developing the civilian economy, employees of military enterprises and institutions have valuable skills and competencies relative to their civilian counterparts. In the case of management occupations, the management culture of both military and civilian enterprises has been shaped by the experience of central planning. Such skills as cost accounting and control, marketing, and human resource management are grossly underdeveloped in both military and civilian enterprises. On the other hand, military enterprise managers do have experience with quality control, strict inspection, and more advanced production methods and technologies. Hence, they may have certain advantages over managers in purely civilian sectors in terms of being able to produce civilian goods at higher levels of efficiency and quality.

Military scientists, engineers, and technicians are recognized as being more specialized and in many cases more advanced than their counterparts in civilian industry. But again, the benchmark, at least in the case of Russia, is completely different. There are really no separate or independent civilian high-technology sectors or industries. If civilian telecommunications, computer, electronics, environmental, and medical equipment sectors are going to emerge and grow, they will be forced to draw on the huge technical labor force engaged in military-related activities.

Finally, the skill and culture mix of military-oriented production workers is also distinct from that found in civilian enterprises. But here also certain skills may be more advanced than civilian production workers within the Russian Republic. Segments of the military production work force may be more experienced with automated numerically controlled machining, and more sophisticated materials handling, quality control, and assembly techniques. These skills may prove quite useful as civilian manufacturing is upgraded and modernized.

In OECD countries, training options, labor market measures, and employment initiatives are typically geared to provide bridges to job opportunities in high-growth civilian sectors. In the United States, at least, this approach has had very limited success. In Russia the problem is more profound. Civilian sector job growth within existing enterprises is nil, and labor mobility is highly constricted. The only means to utilize the labor and know-how of military workers is through the creation of new economic activity through new business formation. In the short to medium term, employment policies must focus on training and support mechanisms to increase the birth and survival rate of new small businesses within military-dependent regions.

Government Decision Making: Unraveling of Central Authority and Military Sector Restructuring

In the case of transitional economies such as Russia, the overall re-alignment of the economic system, not just the military complex, is contingent on how the state redefines its role in the economy. For economic reform to progress, the state must advance a clear and generally consistent exit strategy from direct administration over economic production and price setting. It can try to extract itself from production through rapid privatization, or it can carry out a slower, more organized exit through slow privatization and restructuring of enterprises remaining under state control. Either approach requires some move toward freeing up of prices. But, as the experience of Central Europe shows, the central government either by action or by default necessarily continues to play a major role in the restructuring of large state-owned enterprises. Even if privatization builds momentum, a quick withdrawal of the public sector from these enterprises is impossible for both political and economic reasons.

In Russia, prices have been partially freed up, significant privatization has occurred, but a clear policy stance to reshape large enterprises and change the industrial structure has not been agreed upon or sold to the public. To date, restructuring has moved in three directions: significant privatization and new business creation in the retail, service, and other small-scale enterprise sectors; very limited restructuring and/or spontaneous privatization of some leading large-scale enterprises in the natural resource, aviation, and consumer goods sectors; and a broader freezing of the large-enterprise industrial structure through the disorganized granting of state credits.

Within the overall restructuring process, military activity is by its nature more directly determined by government decisions than by emerging market forces or profit opportunities. Both military domestic and export demand depend on government foreign and military policies. The process of military restructuring is contingent on a number of connected decisions by central and local governments. The degree to which clear and coherent government decisions are taken determines whether military resources are reallocated with relative efficiency, or whether the process remains chaotic, wasteful, and politically volatile.

Broadly speaking, the restructuring of military sectors is contingent on many types or levels of government decision making. It depends in the first instance on how the Russian government defines and funds national security policies and longer-term defense needs. It also depends on arms export policies and on how arms exports are regulated and controlled. Related decisions have to be made on the degree to which foreign firms are allowed to participate in segments of the military-related industries and how this participation will be managed. The role of the military in national science and technology policies has to be redefined, and truly civilian industrial and government R&D activities have to be created and funded.

Diversification and conversion require alternative spending priorities and industrial policies. Sooner or later, some consensus will have to be fashioned on which industries represent potential growth drivers and which can be cut loose to fend for themselves. An industrial policy incorporating industry and enterprise restructuring decisions, the allocation of state subsidies, and selective trade protection must be hammered out by central and regional authorities. This is true whether shock therapy or a more deliberate overall policy is implemented.

Decisions also have to be made about how to manage enterprise restructuring in military-oriented sectors (the privatization process, level of state participation, incentives to enterprises, and how to finance restructuring). Labor market adjustment policies in general need to be developed, along with specific training and retraining policies targeted to the special needs of workers made redundant at military enterprises. The housing and social support services formerly provided directly by military enterprises must now be provided through some other public or private mechanism. And central and local governments have to decide what types of specific regional adjustment support should be given to areas strongly affected by military reductions.

The ideal process in which these decisions form a seamless strategy for reallocating military resources does not operate in practice in any country, East or West. It has always been a more haphazard process involving the mediation of conflicting goals and interest group pressures. It is unfortunate, but not surprising, that under the difficult circumstances currently being experienced in Russia, many of these decisions have not yet been made. Policies for restructuring military sectors are emerging on paper, but they have failed to gain the attention or broad-based backing necessary to move forward. The law on conversion (described below) is an example of the failure of determined and consistent decision making toward the military complex.

Policies for Military Restructuring in the Russian Republic

Prior to the 1991 coup attempt, several ministries of civilian industry were actually transferred into the Soviet defense complex. The rationale for this plan was that management and technical capabilities in the military sector were superior and could help revitalize key civilian sectors. The production units of the Ministry of Machine Building for Light and Food Industry and certain production units in the medical equipment and computer and information technology area were transferred to the defense complex in 1989.[32] One goal of the 1989 plan was to convert six hundred plants from military to civilian production. Only six of these plants were completely converted by 1991. However, according to some reports, defense-oriented industries output of consumer goods increased by 5 percent in 1989 and by 10 percent in 1990—yet this was below the planned targets.[33] This earlier conversion initiative hinged on classic planning from above. It consisted mainly of new orders being sent from Moscow for civilian goods, and resulted in some rather humorous conversion directives. The Ilyushin aircraft enterprise supposedly received an order for spaghetti-making machines, heating and drying equipment for footwear and hide production, and potato-peeling equipment. After the failed coup in 1991, this plan was apparently abandoned. Various transitional measures for restructuring the defense complex and privatizing a significant share of military enterprises have been under consideration: none made it past the talking stage.

The most concrete legislative framework to emerge is "The Law of the Russian Federation Concerning Conversion of the Defense Industry in the Russian Federation," passed in late March of 1992. This legislation did offer a blueprint of a conversion strategy incorporating many elements of the decision-making steps alluded to above. Key elements of this legislation include:

1. *Some attempt to base decisions on an appraisal of long-term security and defense needs.* According to the law, "Military enterprises will be restructured based on the military requirements of the Russian Republic." A process to define long-term defense needs and projects was developed by the Ministry of Defense and was released in December of 1993. On this basis, enterprises will be notified two years in advance about reductions in defense orders and long-term contracts with arms producers will be negotiated. The government will presumably compensate enterprises that do not receive the two-year prenotification of cuts in defense orders. The problem is that the funds to support the new force structure and defense requirements are not available.[34]

2. *An outline of parameters regulating foreign investment in military-oriented enterprises.* Enterprises or parts of enterprises that cease military production can be privatized. Foreign investors can participate in these privatizations. However, a large mobilization capacity is retained, which inhibits conversion of enterprise subunits.

3. *Guidelines were also established on how the arms sector is to be restructured.* The emphasis in the legislation is on a bottom-up process involving eventual privatization of civilian activities. In light of defense needs and military production requirements, each enterprise will be responsible for the transfer of excess capacity to civilian research or production. A special conversion fund is being established to assist

enterprises. The European Bank for Reconstruction and Development reports that 41.5 billion rubles (about $120 million at January 1994 exchange rates) were allocated to this fund in 1992.[35] Special tax incentives are granted to military enterprises for civilian R&D and product development. Accelerated depreciation allowances also apply to enterprises undergoing conversion. Unfortunately, the money for conversion has apparently been exhausted in the general subsidization program and has not been channeled into real conversion activities.

4. *Very vague elements of labor policies for unemployed defense workers.* Workers unemployed due to conversion will be eligible for unemployment benefits for up to two years and have rights to all social protection measures. Workers who have been employed in military enterprises for fifteen years or more shall have use of health benefits and will retain existing housing rights.

5. *Some policy guidelines for impacted regions.* Localities where 20 percent or more of the population become unemployed due to military conversion receive the status of priority development territories. To date, it is unclear whether military-serving regions have benefited from anything except central government subsidies and credits to their defense enterprises.

This legislation provides some framework for the future but, at this writing, few concrete measures in the legislation have actually been implemented by the central government. Overall direction from the central government has been grossly inadequate. Uncertainty from the lack of clear policies has left many military enterprises in a state of limbo. They do not know what the domestic or export demand for their existing military products will be over the medium term, exactly how the privatization process will affect them, or what the prospects are in alternative civilian markets. They fight for subsidies and adopt a wait-and-see attitude. In light of all these difficulties, the fact that a number of conversion success stories have emerged underscores the tremendous potential in the military complex and provides insights for the formulation of specific policies that could pay off.

Scattered Success Stories

The military collapse has stimulated some energetic responses by individual enterprises and at the level of local and regional government. In most cases, the presence of real incentives to convert was crucial, and in a few cases innovative initiatives were the result of energetic Western assistance projects. A number of Russian aerospace enterprises and design bureaus have entered into joint ventures and development programs with Western and East Asian companies. An *Aviation Week* survey at the time of the mid-1993 Moscow air show revealed about sixty significant cooperative ventures between Russian and Western aerospace and airline companies.[36] From the Western side, these have been stimulated by the formidable technology assets in Russian aerospace and by the longer-term potential of the Russian civilian aerospace market. From the Russian side, strong interest from the West, together with the real potential for expansion into both domestic and foreign areas, has motivated managers to launch commercial forays and to develop military and civilian aerospace technology jointly. Despite the high level of activity in these sectors, there has been consolidation among the big aerospace groups (Mikoyan, Tupolev, Ilyushin, Sukhoi) and design bureaus (Myasischev, Yakovlev, Raduga, Kamov). Activity and conversion in aerospace show that the high-technology assets in the Russian military complex have the immediate, short- and long-term potential to support conversion and diversification. As such, enterprise managers can reap direct benefits by pursuing these ventures without losing access to heavy state subsidies. A policy of slowly weaning the more successful groups from open credit access over a specified period of time could stimulate even more activism on the part of managers of large aerospace enterprises.

The Leninets enterprise association provides a more specific case of restructuring and conversion of a military-oriented enterprise. Located in St. Petersburg, Leninets was heavily involved in production of military avionics, electronics, and communication equipment. Characteristically, it also produced a range of civilian products, such as vacuum cleaners. Over the last three years, management has worked closely with a Western consulting firm (expenses subsidized by the European Commission) to restructure the operations of this huge enterprise. The keystone of the restructuring strategy was splitting military and civilian work into separate operating units. The overall restructuring strategy had three basic components: to remain active in military electronics and pursue export opportunities; to spin off civilian high-technology applications in dual-use areas from military work; and to improve and expand civilian durable and consumer goods operations for the domestic market. This restructuring effort has apparently had some success. In 1989, the firm relied on military contracts for 60 percent of its work; military work accounted for only 30 percent of turnover at the end of 1992. Civilian production had expanded about 30 percent in real terms as of the end of 1992. It is not known to what degree Leninets is shedding labor to achieve its strategy, but the firm has avoided mass layoffs.

Local and regional initiatives to support military enterprise restructuring, conversion, and broader diversification are also taking hold in several cities. In St. Petersburg, regional authorities are mobilizing the area's technical institutes to provide technical assistance and sometimes repair and supply services to troubled local enterprises.

Nizhny-Novgorod, formerly Gorky, a region highly dependent on military industries, has embarked on an independent, rapid privatization drive in the retail and service sectors to encourage small-business formation. It is thought that rapid small-business growth will absorb job losses at military production facilities and, as a consequence, make it easier for these enterprises to restructure and shed labor. It also has used tax revenues to set up a regional "conversion bank" that is beginning to fund small pilot projects to convert military production to civilian use.[37] The region has also been active in promoting more aggressive conversion of larger military-oriented enterprises, with significant conversion projects under way at the Uljanov Works (shipbuilding components to kitchen appliances and heating equipment), Sverdlovsk Ammunition (ammunition to synthetic fiber spinning machinery, NN-Television (radar to television) sets. These cases underscore the need for innovative regional approaches.[38] Since labor mobility will continue to be severely constrained, labor retention through conversion, as well as stimulating the growth of new businesses, is crucial.

Success in conversion of large military enterprises has also been achieved in Perm in the western Urals, where three large enterprises have converted by increasing or commencing production of metal castings, minitractors, washing machines, and alternative energy equipment. The Votkinsk combine, which formerly produced SS–20 missiles, is now actively increasing output of large refrigeration units, microwave ovens, and machine tools.[39] And in Moscow, the Krasny Proletary plant has moved from warhead fabrication to the production of a range of machined products, including lathes and a hot-selling brick-making machine that is yielding high profits.[40]

These initiatives show that the potential for military conversion in Russia often lies in low- to mid-tech consumer and capital goods markets unserved by domestic and foreign sellers. With honest management, rational incentives, and in some cases a dose of Western technical assistance, conversion can and will happen. But the military restructuring problem will require a much more concerted and organized response by the central government of the Russian Republic and by organizations in OECD countries if a social and political crisis rooted in the military complex is to be averted. Even though military spending has been slashed, the other shoe has yet to fall. The subsidy policy encourages firms to operate at very low capacity levels without equivalent reductions in their work force—labor productivity plummets, prices rise. Faster progress in commercialization of military enterprises requires the elimination of passive credit generation. To move forward means not just stimulating new activity and employment through new business formation, but sharply improving the performance of large enterprises that have been privatized or remain under public control. A central emphasis in a new phase of reform must be achievement of broad productivity and quality improvement in a low-investment environment.

From Subsidy to Conversion: Improving Enterprise Performance in a Low-Investment Environment

Restructuring Military Enterprises

Many have pointed to the Marshall plan as a valuable precedent for the current transition process, yet few seem willing really to examine this experience and to apply the valuable lessons. What is striking about postwar reconstruction is that improvement of productivity and quality across all industrial and service sectors was a matter of high national priority in Western Europe and Japan:

> The vehicle for the TA [technical assistance] program of the Marshall plan in each Western European country was a high priority national productivity drive: a strategic effort undertaken with full support at the highest levels of government. . . . This drive was overseen by a high-level productivity commission composed of top level representatives of

government, business, labor, and executed by productivity centers located in each country. The staff of these centers were experienced managers and engineers, committed to reducing the gap in productivity with the U.S., and well acquainted with local industry.[41]

This priority commitment to improve productivity and quality was perhaps even more intensive in Japan, where it included a massive public campaign, the holding of seminars and courses for all levels of industrial personnel, and steady emphasis on productivity and quality improvement in exhibitions, the press, and other media. In both cases, impressive improvements were achieved in a low-investment environment through training large numbers in new work cultures and skills.

Russia lacks the historic legacy of private economic institutions which helped the Marshall Plan technical assistance program succeed. It is sometimes suggested that the transfer of technology and management expertise can only be achieved through traditional market mechanisms—joint ventures, direct foreign investment, importation of Western-trained managers.[42] While these mechanisms are crucial, they are unlikely to bring about the widespread gains in quality and performance required to stabilize output and employment in enterprises throughout the economy. They affect only a few enterprises and sectors and cannot provide the "snowball effect" of a broad-based, organized effort.[43] At the same time, wholesale restructuring and liquidation of inefficient enterprises are neither politically nor economically feasible. Privatization can change incentives, but a new, competent management class will not spring fully formed from the head of Zeus. Existing managers of both newly privatized enterprises and those that remain under state control have to be retrained to turn enterprises around. To create new competition and effectively reallocate resources from overdeveloped sectors, such as military production and heavy primary industry, to consumer goods and underdeveloped service and transportation industries requires a focused drive to improve enterprise performance.

Broad-based management and worker retraining within existing enterprises can play an important role in productivity and quality improvements. And military enterprises currently producing civilian goods are ideal candidates for turnaround. As previously noted, perhaps 50 percent of total output in the enterprises organized under the defense ministries has traditionally been civilian goods and services.

Due simply to the sudden collapse of defense orders, this total rose to nearly 70 percent. Furthermore, this civilian segment within the complex is not a new phenomenon. These enterprises have a long history producing civilian-oriented goods in both the consumer durable and capital goods areas. In some cases, production occurs within plants that also produce military hardware; in other cases, plants concentrate solely on civilian production. Key consumer and capital goods produced by military enterprises include washing machines, refrigerators, televisions, radios, personal computers, cameras, videocassette recorders, motorcycles, machine tools (including numerically controlled machines), tractors and farm implements, irrigation equipment, medical equipment, and rail freight cars.

Many experts from OECD countries simply shake their heads when they look at this civilian production under military auspices. This system makes little sense by the standards of the advanced market economies where independent competitive firms concentrate on these consumer and capital goods markets. In the short term, however, we are not considering ideal or even second-best solutions. Given the pressures of the transition, maximum benefits must be derived from existing assets.

New domestic or foreign investment will not be adequate to stimulate significant new supply of consumer durable or capital goods in the short term. Imports and direct competition from OECD country firms will be a minor factor in these sectors due to foreign-exchange and currency constraints. Hence, while Western standards are certainly a goal to work toward, new supplies of consumer durable and capital goods, either imported or produced domestically, will be severely limited. Yet, domestic demand for these goods will be relatively robust; domestic sales of three consumer durable categories—refrigerators, televisions, and cars—grew or remained stable in 1993, even as overall output plummeted.[44]

Even if these civilian production activities may not be optimal in the long run, efforts to improve the capability of these units over the next few years could yield substantial payoffs. Making improvements in the quality and price performance of these civilian production lines could get more and better consumer and capital goods into the domestic market in the short term. Intensive and broad-based retraining of managers similar to the Marshall Plan technical assistance program can play an important role in achieving productivity and quality improvements in these sectors in a low- or zero-investment environment. *Advances in these enterprises must come as returns from improved organization, not new investment.* Quick changes in the organization of production and the work culture of the enterprise must be implemented. This can be accomplished through exposure to new ways of looking at problems and training in new skills that can be quickly incorporated in the enterprise and in the behavior of the work force.

Improvement in the civilian operations of the military complex cannot work without a change in policies and incentives. Some relatively coherent system of incentives must emerge to encourage management change. A willingness to remove across-the-board credits slowly and even to scrap certain highly inefficient production must be present. Where there is joint production of military and civilian products under one management, efforts should be made to put military and civilian lines under separate management structures. And where there is joint production, the military should amend its sometimes bizarre policy of maintaining huge mobilization or surge capacity. This would allow the redeployment of high-quality capital and labor resources to expand civilian capacity. Without at least some of these measures, it makes little sense to try to use technical assistance to improve short-term performance in these sectors.

Assuming some commitment to improve performance, Western technical assistance in the area of management training could yield a substantial payoff. Quick changes must be implemented in the organization of production and the work culture of the enterprise. This can be accomplished by exposing Russian managers to new ways of looking at problems and training them in appropriate new skills. Western experts and consultants have identified a set of management skills and practices that are underdeveloped due to the legacy of central planning. These constitute the areas upon which management retraining needs to focus:

Cost control and cost accounting
- Energy conservation
- Plant layout
- Materials storage and handling
- Maintenance and repair
- Environmental cost accounting
- Inventory control

Quality control
- Statistical quality control techniques
- Creating clean work environments
- Handling, packaging, and storage
- Inspection
- Creating customer service capabilities
- Incorporating customer information into incremental quality improvements

Marketing, sales, and distribution
- Simple customer surveys
- Improving speed of delivery
- Incorporating customer information into design changes

Managing human resources
- Communication
- Inculcating new organizational goals in the work force
- Participation and information exchange
- Team working

Improving management capabilities in these areas through Western assistance would have high returns in terms of reducing costs, improving quality, and creating the beginnings of a real orientation toward the customer. *Significant cost reductions could be achieved, particularly in the areas of energy conservation and material use and handling, without major inputs of capital. Productivity improvements could be gained by changing the plant layout and improving the conditions on the shop floor.* Important quality improvements would occur by implementing basic quality control procedures and improving handling, packaging, and storage.

Over a somewhat longer time frame, an orientation toward the consumer could be created. Simple survey methods could be developed to gauge consumer satisfaction and incorporate information about defects and overall product satisfaction into product improvement and redesign. Establishing service and repair networks would add substantially to the overall usefulness of products and create new employment opportunities. If these organizational changes could be accelerated through Western training and assistance and some significant improvements result, this would clearly represent an important gain for the Russian economy and for the Russian consumer.

How can such training and assistance be delivered most efficiently to enterprise management? The needs for improvements in these civilian-oriented military enterprises are immediate. In these circumstances, experiential learning within the enterprise—"learning by doing"—promises to achieve results most efficiently. The performance of these enterprises can best be improved by Western consultants and manager volunteers working together with Russian managers in their plants. Equally important is bringing large numbers of Russian enterprise managers to the United States, East Asia, and Europe to work in high-performance civilian operations. Such a process allows managers to identify the specific problems and opportunities in individual enterprises based on a world standard of manufacturing practice. The new management skills are effectively transferred when a plan is implemented back in the Russian work environment.

As noted in the Leninets case, consultant firms have been quite active over the last years in developing restructuring plans and in conducting specific management retraining programs in military-related enterprises. Some of these consulting activities have been partially funded by international organizations and the European Economic Community. This approach should be continued and strengthened. However, these efforts are often costly, take a relatively long time, and are simply too few in number, given the vast needs in the military complex.

A cheaper and more effective way is to implement a broad-based conversion and productivity drive, retraining thousands of Russian managers and workers. Technical assistance programs to help restructure enterprises are already operational, but are tiny compared with the vastness of need. Under the Marshall Plan technical assistance program, about 19,000 managers, technicians, and workers traveled from Western Europe to the United States between 1949 and 1957. Silberman and Weiss estimate that a full Marshall Plan–type productivity program for the Russian Republic would cost about $42 million per year once established. This would finance in the neighborhood of 95 Russian productivity teams of 20 individuals in 57 industrial sectors, 33 agricultural sectors, and 5 distribution/marketing sectors.[45]

The objective of intensive technical assistance should be to build a viable set of civilian enterprises out of the military complex. The creation of such enterprises across Russia would begin to bring supply to the market, would improve quality and price, and would foster competition to create a trajectory of longer-term improvement in quality and productivity. Creating such a trajectory will require significant reallocation of labor resources—increasing unemployment. It is naive to believe that this process can occur through a massive one-time shock. It is equally naive to believe that increasing unemployment can be avoided. The creation of new businesses in the sectors underdeveloped in the planning system is the primary mechanism to absorb the labor released from the large enterprise sector.

Training and Support of Military Sector Personnel for Small-Business Startups

Changing the sectoral distortions in the Russian economy inherited from central planning will involve creating new businesses in underdeveloped sectors and the vertical disintegration of many large enterprises. Huge vertically integrated military production facilities are likely to contain subunits that are attractive and competitive, and others that are in poor condition and not capable of surviving without military contracts. A key challenge is to restructure these large facilities. This will involve converting the more viable parts of the facility to civilian production, shutting down the nonviable parts, and redeploying individual work force skills to other economic establishments. Opportunities exist to create new small businesses providing research and development, manufacturing services, and a range of more conventional services.

There has been a lot of emphasis on how training and support services can stimulate the growth and survival rate of new, small, privately owned firms in Central and Eastern Europe. The Nizhny-Novgorod initiative includes this element. U.S. experience, however, shows there are certain ways that entrepreneurial training and small-business support services could be specifically designed to help military managers, technical personnel, and production workers start and grow small businesses.

One useful focus is on training and support services that encourage enterprise management, as well as scientists and engineers, to spin off small commercial businesses from military enterprises. This might be so-called high-technology spin-off—using some specific product or process technology to produce new products for civilian markets. Or it might be a more mundane effort to encourage some groups within enterprises to set up independent private firms in the industrial service or supply area.

A second area would involve specific training and support for military production workers to set up retail, transportation, and service and repair franchises to market and service the civilian goods and equipment produced by military enterprises. These service networks are an important part of modern market economies, but are often missing in the Russian Republic.

To start businesses in these areas, unemployed military enterprise personnel need training and support services. Moreover, because of the types of businesses best suited to the skill and expertise of former military enterprise personnel, this training and support must be more extensive than what is found in generic support programs. In particular, training needs to be linked more closely to the specific areas of technology and product development most closely associated with particular types of military enterprises. At the same time, these individuals need help in establishing the feasibility of their concepts or ideas in price-sensitive civilian markets. Because military production is technology-driven rather than market-driven, the development of a business plan is an especially important exercise for former military-oriented personnel attempting to start a business. Stories of military engineers proposing technologically sophisticated but totally unmarketable products are common in both Russia and OECD countries.

The literature on entrepreneurial training suggests that the most effective training is "learning by doing." The best mechanisms are those that teach essential business and management skills to the aspiring entrepreneur in the process of starting a new business. Two types of training and support have proved particularly effective in increasing the survival rate of small manufacturing-type businesses in the OECD countries. And these seem most appropriate to provide the intensive training and support required to stimulate business spin-offs by military-oriented personnel.

The first type is the business incubator, offering ongoing training and counseling for new entrepreneurs. But business incubators also offer work and laboratory space at reasonable and sometimes subsidized rents. They also may provide centralized services such as secretaries, personal computer access, and marketing information and services. These support services reduce individual overhead costs. In

OECD countries, the sponsorship and financing for business incubators usually come from enterprises that may provide space and some financing, as well as from local and regional governments and development agencies. The specific design of the incubator must be based on the particular type of business formation that is most compatible with local technologies, local resources, and local markets. For example, if a community is dominated by military electronics firms, the incubator might be designed to provide technology support and marketing information for small electronics supply or assembly businesses.

Business incubators may be particularly suitable for delivering training and support to new businesses in Russia. By providing space, counseling, and training, and support services in one location, they overcome several serious constraints faced by new entrepreneurs in the Russian Republic. In the United States, abandoned military bases and arsenals have often been used to set up business incubator centers. These types of facilities are now also available in Russia. OECD country assistance programs have provided some financial and technical support to set up business incubators in Central and Eastern Europe. This assistance should be vastly expanded and more incubator projects should be started.

A second, less intensive training and support mechanism is counseling and advisory services for small-business startups. These training and service networks primarily aim to provide one-to-one counseling to individuals who are attempting to create a business. Sometimes in OECD countries these services are attached to business or technical schools. In some cases, they include classroom training in general skills such as accounting and marketing for groups of aspiring business people. This type of on-the-job training and support also seems well suited to generate successful startups by former military technical or production personnel. Again, a modest level of OECD country technical and financial assistance could be very helpful in setting up projects of this type.

Conclusion

The military complex has a central place in the Russian economy in terms of industrial capacity and technological capability. The recovery of output and eventual growth of the economy are contingent on a more efficient reallocation of human and capital resources to civilian activities. At this stage, this must involve the allocation of idle capacity to existing civilian production units in the military complex. In the present environment, unless unique pressures or opportunities affect the enterprise, managers have no incentive to make crucial changes. Neither sudden removal nor continued granting of credits to large enterprises is a viable policy in the short to medium term. Large enterprises must be encouraged to make substantial changes in their organization, management, and production practices in order to stand on their own feet. This will take time, yet the process must involve a consistent and disciplined drive to force improved performance; it will not be painless.

Sadly, the Russian government has provided no vision about how to move from the current situation to a new path of economic development. This task is crucial. A key lesson of the Marshall Plan is that economic turnaround can be accelerated by an energetic and high-profile national effort to improve productivity and quality performance in enterprises. Because of the distorted structure of the Russian economy, improved macroeconomic performance depends even more on changing the composition of output and improving the performance of enterprises. A crucial missing link is a strong conversion program positioned at the top of the national reform agenda. If military enterprises must be subsidized for political reasons, they should in return be given strong incentives to increase production of civilian products for the Russian market.

The two policy initiatives outlined here involve a more coherent and concentrated commitment on the part of both the Russian government and OECD governments and organizations. On the one hand, a big dose of technical assistance directed at civilian segments of military industry could yield rapid improvement and growth in consumer durable and capital goods production in the military complex. On the other hand, a vigorous program to stimulate regional growth and survival of small business could not only absorb unemployed military workers but also provide new higher-quality goods and services to industries and consumers. These initiatives could form two complementary parts of a larger national productivity drive. Obviously, these ideas represent only general propositions. It is a massive task and the needs are great. What is most urgently needed is movement and action. Concerted, determined action—informed by some specific strategy about where policy initiatives could have the biggest short-term payoffs—can achieve real, measurable results, even in this difficult context.

Notes

1. The Organization for Economic Cooperation and Development (OECD) consists mainly of the developed countries of Western Europe, North America, and the Pacific, specifically: Australia, Austria, Belgium, Canada, Denmark, Finland, France, Germany, Iceland, Ireland, Italy, Japan, Luxembourg, Netherlands, New Zealand, Norway, Spain, Sweden, Switzerland, United Kingdom, United States.

2. See Robert Borosage, "Inventing the threat: Clinton's defense budget," *World Policy Journal, 10,* 4 (Winter 1993–94): 9.

3. See U.S. Arms Control and Disarmament Agency, *World Military Expenditures and Arms Transfers 1988* (Washington, DC: U.S. Government Printing Office, June 1989), table 1; and Katarzyna Zukrowska, *From Adjustments to Conversion of the Military Industry in East Central Europe* (Warsaw: Polish Institute of International Affairs 1991), p. 10.

4. Julian Cooper, "Defense industry conversion in the East: The relevance of Western Experience," NATO and C&EE Conversion Seminar, Brussels, May 1992, p. 9.

5. *SIPRI Yearbook 1992: World Armaments and Disarmament* (Stockholm: SIPRI, 1992), pp. 224–5.

6. David Holloway, *The Soviet Union and the Arms Race* (New Haven, CT: Yale University Press, 1983), pp. 123–5.

7. U.S. Arms Control and Disarmament Agency, p. 61, table 1; p. 112, table 3.

8. See Peter Rutland, *Oxford Analytica* (June 24, 1992).

9. CSFR Ministry of Economy, "Defense conversion and armament production in the Czech and Slovak Republic," NATO and C&EE Conversion Seminar, Brussels, May 1992.

10. Katerzyna Zukrowska, "The dilemmas of Polish arms industries in the period of systems changes," NATO and C&EE Conversion Seminar, Brussels, May, 1992.

11. See *SIPRI Yearbook 1992*, p. 238.

12. Cooper, "Defense industry conversion in the East."

13. Ibid., p. 6.

14. Holloway, *The Soviet Union and the Arms Race*, pp. 119–20.

15. Julian Cooper, "Developments in industry," The Soviet Economy under Gorbachev, NATO Colloquium 1991 (Brussels: NATO Economics Directorate, March 1991).

16. G.K. Khromov, "Conversion from military to civilian production: The Votkinsk plant," in *Defense Expenditure, Industrial Conversion and Local Employment*, ed. by Liba Paukert and Peter Richards (Geneva: International Labor Office, 1991), p. 185.

17. Peter Richards, "Of arms and the man: Possible employment consequences of disarmament," *International Labour Review, 130*, 3 (1991): 284.

18. Holloway, *The Soviet Union and the Arms Race*, pp. 142–5.

19. See Julian Cooper, "Military cuts and conversion in the defense industry," *Soviet Economy*, 1991, 7, 2, 121–42; and Cooper, "Defense industry conversion in the East," p. 6.

20. Richards, "Of arms and the man," p. 285.

21. Cooper, "Defense industry conversion in the East," pp. 31–2.

22. Cooper, "The Soviet defense industry and conversion: The regional dimension," in *Defense Expenditures, Industrial Conversion and Local Employment*, ed. by Liba Paukert and Peter Richards (Geneva: International Labour Office, 1991), p. 170.

23. Cooper, "Defense industry conversion in the East," p. 3.

24. Ibid., p. 15.

25. John Morrocco, "U.S. arms dominate shrinking market," *Aviation Week* (July 26, 1993): 59.

26. Cooper, "Defense industry conversion in the East," pp. 15–16.

27. See, for example, Stephen Chan, "The impact of defense spending on economic performance: A survey of evidence and problems," *ORBIS, 29* (1985): 403–34.

28. "Carry on comrade," *The Economist* (January 15–21, 1994): 67.

29. T. Palankai, "Conversion problems of Hungary," International Conference on Conversion, International Institute for Peace, Vienna, January 25–28, 1992, pp. 2–3.

30. For a definition of the wall of separation between military-serving and civilian firms, see Ann Markusen and Joel Yudken, *Dismantling the Cold War Economy* (New York: Basic Books, 1992), pp. 90–100.

31. See Stephen Cohen and Andrew Schwartz, "The tunnel at the light: Privatization in Eastern Europe," Working Paper no. 56, The Berkeley Round Table on the International Economy, U.C. Berkeley, 1992.

32. Cooper, "Defense industry conversion in the East: The relevance of Western experience," 1992, pp. 4–6.

33. Ibid., p. 5.

34. See "Lack of funds may stymie Russian arms development," *Defense News* (January 31, 1994): 12.

35. See European Bank for Reconstruction and Development, "Privatization, restructuring, and defense conversion," London, EBRD discussion paper, vol. 1, 1992.

36. See Boris Rybak, "Russian shows attract broad participation," *Aviation Week* (August 23, 1993): 49–59.

37. *The Economist* (December 5, 1992): 25.

38. Dominick Bertelli and J.T. Marlin, *Defense Conversion in Russia* (New York: Council on Economic Priorities, 1993): 17–18.

39. Ibid., pp. 18–20.

40. Steven Erlanger, "To Russia, with good ol' American know-how," *New York Times* (June 13, 1993): 5.

41. J. Silberman and C. Weiss *Restructuring for Productivity* (Washington, DC: World Bank—Energy and Industry Department, February 1992).

42. See, for example, Jeffrey Sachs, *Accelerating Privatization in Eastern Europe: The Case of Poland*, World Bank Annual Conference on Development Economics, April 1991, pp. 1–5.

43. Ibid., pp. viii–ix.

44. "Carry on comrade," *The Economist*, p. 67.

45. Silberman and Weiss, *Restructuring for Productivity*, pp. 38–39.

11

JOHN E. ULLMANN

Conversion Problems in the Changing Economies

I wasted time and now doth time waste me.
Shakespeare, *Richard II*

Conversion is a process with a large technical and scientific component. In that respect, the conversion problems of the changing economies of Eastern Europe and the former Soviet Union are not materially different from those of other industrial countries. The profound and, in many respects, daunting differences arise in their socioeconomic setting, which in turn affects the urgency of the whole process, the way it has fared so far, and its prospects.

With few exceptions, conversion has been handled badly everywhere. The need for it should have been clear to all countries long ago, as the evidence mounted for the depletion that an oversized military sector visits on all economies that have one. As the Cold War wound down, the need for conversion should have been elevated to the highest possible priority. The reason was not merely to find people in the military sector something else to do, but a need to restore the countries affected to industrial, scientific, and technical health. Now it is a matter of pulling the world economy out of what amounts to an almost global recession.

In this process, the role of government action is all-important. Since governments are, in effect, the only customers for military products, they should have shouldered the principal responsibility for effective conversion in the wake of the severe cuts in their military requirements. This need, however, became clear exactly at a time when a conservative political ascendancy has called virtually any government enterprise or nonmilitary investment initiative into question.

This is so not only in the West, notably in the United States, where candidates for high office have developed a habit of running against "government" as such—that is, against the enterprise that they presumably want to manage. It is also felt in the changing economies whose peoples have been so traumatized by their governments that a true hatred has developed between them and their masters, whoever they are. After so drastic and complete a change in the political picture, almost any concerted action becomes difficult. Inevitably, remedies there have also become entangled in the whole privatization issue, the general political and social turmoil, and ongoing economic collapse.

Clearly, decisive steps should have been taken all along in the awareness that time was a powerful constraint, not to say a major enemy. It should have been obvious that almost any industrial change is time-consuming and raises the urgent social and political problem of how the people affected will find new work and how they will keep body and soul together in the interim. Yet, this virtual tautology was generally ignored, even after the widespread initial refusal in the West to believe that the Cold War was over had given way to acceptance, or the Communist regimes had actually collapsed.

Just about the only detailed analysis of the time problem in a conversion setting is in a 1964 study directed by the writer in which James E. Baird developed a PERT (Program Evaluation and Review Technique) analysis for a conversion project.[1] The result is a diagram in which all tasks are set forth, together with the minimum time that can be expected for traveling through the maze. This minimum time is based on the realization that most tasks require the completion of one or more previous tasks: it turns out to be about two years. In Baird's model, substantial research was required on the product. That may not always be necessary. On the other hand, the analysis started with the assumption that the company had already chosen a product in a general way, and that may be a complex and potentially time-consuming problem in its own right.

So far, some enterprises in the changing economies have struck successful deals with foreign firms, though not enough to mitigate the overall impoverishment of consumers. They did have time working for them, or rather timing; they got there first and therefore were like people in an auditorium who first smell smoke and head for the exits before the stampede. For the rest, conversion in the changing economies is deeply entangled in their other unsolved transition problems.

The Scale of Conversion

As in other industrial countries, the role and importance of conversion in the changing economies depend on the relative size of their military sectors. Japan and Germany, for instance, have fewer problems than the United States, Britain, and France, with their relatively much greater military establishments. In the same way, Russia's problems are much greater than those of the other successor states, since Russia had 80 percent of the Soviet Union's military industries. The Ukraine and Belarus had 15 percent more between them, leaving them their share of problems too (especially the former).

As discussed in more detail later, the general problems are exacerbated by sharp local ones which, in at least one case, have already led to a significant international change. The fact that the technical industries of Slovakia were mainly military, while those of the Czech Republic were not, created such conversion-related differences in industrial needs that it was a major, if not the principal, factor in the breakup of Czechoslovakia.

The Centrality of Conversion

That there would be a severe conversion problem in the Soviet Union had long been clear to at least some elements of the Soviet government; it was certainly so in the first conference on the subject between U.S. and Soviet experts in June 1984. While some of the Soviet participants recognized the scope and complexity of the problem, others, amidst Marxist-Leninist clichés, averred that if it ever came to a large cutback in military needs, Gosplan would see to a quick transition, and that having such a command economy was a source of strength for them. Even in a century much given to political self-deception, such sentiments stand out as gross examples.

By the time President Gorbachev came to power in March 1985, the Soviet Union's economic and industrial troubles had clearly multiplied enormously. Realizing the central responsibility of the military sector for most of them, Gorbachev first proclaimed the critical importance of conversion in a speech in December 1987. It was the first official recognition of the price paid by the Soviet Union for its military excess.

In March 1989, the National Conversion Commission was set up by the Soviet Academy of Sciences and the All Union Central Council of Trade Unions (AUCCTU), under the chairmanship of Academician V.A. Avduyevsky. In November of that year, the commission convened an international conference on conversion in which the writer also participated and sought to set forth some of its basic requirements.

At a conference in Vienna in January 1992 on "Conversion: National Case Studies," Avduyevsky gave a gloomy report on what had happened in the meantime. Essentially,

> [N]o results were achieved . . . because conversion was to be implemented under the conditions of centralized economic planning and an administrative-command system of managing the national economy on the basis of state orders. The program . . . was condemned to failure because it was developed by a military-industrial complex that did not wish to scale down defense production.[2]

As matters stood, much Russian production of civilian goods with technical content took place as a byproduct of military production, the arrangement consuming over 25 percent of national income. This turned out to be a disaster that is still at the center of the industrial problems of the succession states, just as it was in the Soviet Union. Materials went to military production first, and neither the military nor the civilian goods produced in military enterprises were economically viable. As Avduyevsky makes clear,

> [A]ny increase of the output of civilian goods at defense plants was planned to be achieved by additional investments and creation of new production capacities which meant an extra burden for an [already] weak civilian economy.[3]

Conversion, in fact, was supposed to be associated with secret increases in military capacities. Production of civilian goods like TV sets, refrigerators, radios, and vacuum cleaners continued, but prices were high and quality was poor. In 1989, portable stereos cost 380 rubles, or 1.7 times the average monthly wage. Television sets cost 700 rubles to produce; on the basis of average monthly earnings in the

United States, that would be about $5,000. In June 1993, after much inflation, a 19-inch black and white set cost 70,000 rubles, or about 2.7 months' earnings for a skilled worker.

This organization of the technical industries had two fatal defects. First, in both quantity and quality of goods, managers had to please their bosses in Gosplan and the defense-related ministries rather than their customers. Second, they brought to civilian production the endemic waste and bureaucracy that afflict military sectors everywhere and result in grotesquely inflated costs.

One of the perennial jokes about the Communist regime was that it had two governing principles: (1) nothing is produced but all quotas are fulfilled; and (2) everybody steals but nothing is missing. It was easy to add a third: Everything is centrally controlled but nobody knows what is going on. As the failure of the system accelerated, it became clear that, as so often, life was imitating art.

Meanwhile, attempts to get conversion legislation through the Supreme Soviet were stymied by the same kind of military-industrial– trade union alliance that has always been a potent and fatal lobby against similar initiatives in the United States. The military-industrial nomenklatura desired above all to preserve its privileges in a society that belied its claims of equality at every turn. So did the trade unions. At the 1989 meeting, a representative of the trade union of defense workers asserted that their jobs were more prestigious than others and that therefore they were paid more (300 rubles a month, compared with 225 for factory workers). He insisted that this differential would have to be maintained, together with any bonuses for living in the remote and often awful places where their factories were located. Apart from anything else, this served to introduce the locational problems in conversion in a Soviet context, a point to which we will return.

Also, while conversion was traditionally opposed in the United States as counter to the ideology of free enterprise, Gosplan resisted it in the Soviet Union with equal fervor. Conversion was seen as conflicting with the command structure of the Soviet planning system, because, properly done, conversion initiatives would come from the bottom up rather than from the top down. Thus, conversion turned into a macroeconomic variant of the "antagonistic cooperation" by which the military-industrial complexes of the Soviet Union and the United States had both used overblown assessments of each other's weaponry and menace to scare their respective governments into letting them take ever larger and more dangerous bites out of their respective societies.

The years since the first serious interest in conversion were thus largely wasted. Except for a few cases, there was a failure to create viable producers for *domestic* civilian markets out of the converted resources of the military-industrial complex. The first two years should have been spent decentralizing the overall control structure and paving the way for privatization. With some overlaps, the next two years should have been used to switch individual enterprises from military to civilian production.

Markets and New Products

A good textbook definition of marketing is "the anticipation, management and satisfaction of demand through the exchange process."[4] Anticipation of demand requires a firm to do consumer research to develop and introduce products desired by consumers, as well as to identify those consumers, whether public or private. The management of demand involves making it convenient to buy the product by establishing marketing and distribution channels. It also includes advertising and promotion. The satisfaction of demand means having a product to do the job, making it available, and providing services to maintain the product (if required) after purchase. Merely stating the elements of marketing in this way shows the difficulties in doing them well in *any* kind of enterprise or economy, let alone in one that seeks to reshape itself after having, so to speak, rewritten the book on what economic failure can mean.

Once a market is created (or discovered), it is not a steady state even if the term perhaps connotes something existing, something static. Rather, it must be constantly sustained by successful applications of commercial product development and marketing. It is skill in those areas that has proved most elusive in the changing economies. Much of the redevelopment of the changing economies has so far consisted of small-scale, almost fringe enterprises not based on commitment or significant investment. It has produced what one Russian economist described as a "flea market economy." There are also larger enterprises that mainly seek to perpetuate the old ways and especially the old managers, if necessary by deals with large multinational firms. While a few of those deals have good potential, whether a combination of self-perpetuating military-industrial complexes (with their own agenda) and small semi–black market deals is the way to build a functioning industrial society is questionable.

The first task in conversion—picking suitable new products—is complicated by the internal inefficiencies and waste of military firms and general lack of marketing skills for nonmilitary products. Any new products must meet three essential conditions:

First, *they must be functionally viable*—that is, they should fulfill a new function or do better than existing products at fulfilling a current one. In a sense, this stage of the analysis asks what arguments could be used to persuade potential customers to buy the product. In economies with pervasive shortages, this is not the problem it is in the more saturated West, but it is still a factor. Even in the old regime, there was plenty of unsold junk.

The second requirement is customers who *can afford to buy* the product—that is, there must be "effective demand" from consumers, the emerging private business sector, the nonmilitary part of the public sector, or some combination of these. Mere need is not enough. This is the most difficult factor in the changing economies; the impoverishment of the population continues to the point where an estimated 90 percent is in distress. In 1992, there was an estimated drop of 30 percent in production, but only 20 percent in GNP. People use up what they have and there is a huge underground economy that lets much of production disappear into the black market. On top of that, the official data are not fully reliable because nobody really knows what is going on.

The effectiveness of the public sector's demand depends on its having extra funds, which, in practical terms, can only come from substantial cuts in the military budget, as well as from extra tax collections if these are politically feasible. Whatever the details, public funds are certain to be involved in the most important alternate markets for conversion, as direct investments, tax incentives, employment subsidies, or other indirect public support.

Consumers in the changing economies clearly need just about everything, but their personal resources are nowhere near sufficient to sustain such markets. The market for the capital equipment that would be essential for the success of the new private business sector depends in turn on the economic health of other businesses. Some takeoff of these economies must therefore take place before they become viable markets in the above sense. In the United States, by contrast, the market for most major consumer products is saturated and a large share is dominated by imports, but there would be opportunities in the replacement market if more of the products involved could be made in the United States.

For both public and private consumers, "effective demand" refers to the ability as well as the inclination to buy the product. Beyond its utility and perceived quality, that is determined by two main factors. The first is its price, which in turn must be higher than its costs in order for the product to be economically viable. Here, as noted in more detail in the next section, making the design and production systems more efficient strongly influences the outcome.

The second factor is the confidence of consumers, which depends on their perception of their future prospects. These can fairly be described as abysmal in most of the changing economies, even though consumer confidence is also down in much of the rest of the industrialized world, as in the United States, Western Europe, and even Japan.

The last requirement for good prospects of new products is that *they are not now being adequately supplied by anyone else.* Because there is no money for major imports, the CIS and other changing economies are clearly well placed with respect to this criterion. A new supply of goods, if it comes, will not initially meet the kind of competition faced by the other industrial countries, but the current poverty makes this issue almost moot.

Even so, one of the lessons that the new business sector will have to learn is that, however tempting it is to produce junk for quick sale in their "flea market economy," in the longer run, superior quality and design are essential. One of the most dangerous illusions in this respect has always been the belief that military products "have to work, no matter what," whereas commercial products can be held to a lower standard. "No matter what" then became an invitation to military waste and there were enough weapons failures to turn this notion into a combination of pious wish and bad joke. Meanwhile, many consumer products, especially electronic ones, gave high quality at competitive prices. This was the key ingredient of the success of Japan and the other Asian countries that came to establish themselves in those fields.

Production Systems

The current reality of most of the production facilities in the changing economies is that they are, for the most part, obsolete. Even such elementary tools as power screwdrivers are rare; hand work rules where machinery is standard everywhere else. While a few of the most sophisticated arms factories are of world-class quality in that industry, most of the industrial complexes are nightmares of antiquated machinery and poor organization.

This is hardly surprising in what are in effect offshoots of the military industries and thus oblivious to cost constraints. This has led to grave problems in the former East Germany, where Western firms have taken over Eastern factories only to close them down. While it was charged that in some cases, they did this in order to stifle competition, there were also no doubt many other cases where the new owners found their acquisitions beyond remedy.

One factor in the present state of arms factories is that weapons have changed. In World War II, many weapons could be made in mass-production facilities, even aircraft. All belligerents did this to some degree, including Russian firms like Mikoyan, Ilyushin, Sukhoi, and others. Today's heavy weapons are made in much smaller quantities and put together by what are virtual handicraft methods. This makes the facilities in their current state quite useless for a competitive market economy; not even the prevalent very low wages, especially in Russia, are much of an advantage.

The dangers of ignoring the criteria of cost-effectiveness in conversion products were well illustrated when, in April 1990, the Soviet Union mounted an exhibition in Munich of commercial products turned out by Soviet military industry. It was a creditable first effort, even though the products were, for the most part, imitations of Western products or prototypes or models of problematic products.[5] Aside from two of the firms that saw fit to present a plastic sex shop product, there were such concepts as cranes or freight carriers mounted on tank chassis for roadless country. Such problems as weight limits, fuel consumption, or chewing up the ecologically fragile terrain of the north had clearly not been addressed. Other products, such as an extraordinarily heavy bicycle, appeared woefully behind the times.

The senior managers present included the then-chairman of the defense committee of the Supreme Soviet who also was the director of a large aircraft consortium. In a public lecture, he made clear that, in his view, anything that could be technically turned out in the same factories with the same equipment, personnel, and management would be a viable commercial product.

The director's colleagues at lower levels were much more realistic and conceded that, while many of the products shown were not of "world class," they offered possible parts and subsystems for joint ventures. While this has already resulted in CIS industries providing castings, structures, and other components to foreign customers, the results have been limited.

It was clear at the show that the firms were wedded to the concept of "dual use"—making military and commercial products in the same factory at the same time with the same equipment, workers, and management. Dual use is an equally durable illusion in Western countries, but in the changing economies, it rests on the hope that the dire need for almost everything would make up for any shortcomings in quality, design, costs, service, and the like. Yet, it was exactly such a set of beliefs that bore major responsibility for the industrial collapse, and the above-mentioned penury of the private sector makes it even more problematic now.

It is the basis of a successful business, and not some radical notion, that regardless of the economic system, technical products for consumers or the civilian sector generally can only be made by firms where managers and workers have a true commitment to that line of work. Under dual use, however, commercial work is often treated as only a temporary embarrassment, with managers mainly hoping that sometime, somehow, the military machine will be cranked up again. One often notes palpable nostalgia for the old easy life when money poured into operations where costs did not matter and product failures and poor quality did not exact penalties from the marketplace. The managers would prefer to operate once more by an industrial version of Gresham's Law: Bad practice drives out good, and protected incompetence drives out industrial strength.

Thus, if a tank factory starts making baby carriages as an afterthought to its product line, they may not look like tanks, but they will surely cost like tanks. In order that people can buy them, the government must then subsidize them, just as it does with weaponry, where it offers, in effect, a 100 percent subsidy. There are, however, clear limits to this: the often painful shifts from subsidized to real prices are among the worst problems of the changing economies. They are the main component of the so-called "market shock."

Another such show was held in Birmingham, England, in May 1993. As reported in the press, it seemed similar to the earlier one in Munich, with the difference that the Russian products now competed primarily on price, determined by the almost worthless ruble.[6] That is not a strategy that augurs well for a better life for the Russian people.

Worse still, there as elsewhere, there are military-industrial dreams of survival, if not prosperity, through arms exports. When this idea was mentioned at the conference in 1989 by the above-mentioned union leader who had insisted on maintaining the privileges of his members, it was treated as a bad joke by many of those present, even though it was presented as a way to raise capital for conversion.

The idea was still there at another conference on conversion hosted by the General Confederation of Trade Unions (GCTU) in Moscow in June 1993. This way out of trouble was mentioned by several speakers, despite the enormous glut of second-hand weaponry, new players like China and North Korea, and the military uselessness of most of the products. Shortly before the conference, there had been a show in Abu Dhabi to drum up weapons business for Russia. Its sponsors found out, however, that the Arab countries can also go broke—even Saudi Arabia. Worse still for them, while peace in the region is still to be achieved, developments since then are hardly favorable to the kinds of arms potlatches for which they had hoped.

In an even farther reach, one speaker at the 1993 GCTU conference proposed a new generation of nuclear missiles to destroy the asteroids which, he said, threatened the earth. Such ideas had originally surfaced at the fringes of the American space fraternity, but had soon been relegated to the UFO tabloids and their ilk. One can, of course, note that U.S. plans to "save jobs" by speeding up military spending to stimulate the economy are hardly more rational.

Rebuilding Production Capacity

The requirements for making a military factory useful for competitive commercial manufacture have long been defined. In assessing them, a first step is to take inventory and determine how much of the existing machinery and buildings can be used in modern commercial production, or adapted with minimum cost. While it may often be tempting to start anew, capital is likely to be short enough to require careful balancing here.

Note, however, that *the only way to be competitive and avoid a permanent, hopelessly low-wage economy, is to have good equipment.* While the internationalization of manufacturing can help with markets for certain products or components, continued reliance on low wages as the main sales argument forecloses any chance for prosperity. Good products and equipment and high productivity can make up for higher costs. The process can work both ways. During decades of rising productivity, American workers could be paid more than those in other industrial countries, while American industries remained competitive. Beginning in the 1960s, as military excess led to industrial decline, higher costs could no longer be compensated for by higher productivity, and so had to be passed along in higher prices and inflation, in lower real wages of workers, and in declining U.S. competitiveness.[7]

Location Issues

Location has always been a potent complicating factor in the conversion process, in that past policies of regional favoritism in the location of military industries and facilities quickly became major issues in regional rivalries. This was so in the United States where contracts and bases often followed locally powerful politicians. In the changing economies, this quickly led to the nationalistic destabilization of federal and would-be federal structures.

In several of those countries, military installations, industries, and contracts were concentrated in regions that might otherwise consider themselves aggrieved, or discriminated against, or unjustly poor in relation to richer ones. Dubious "strategic" considerations, often based essentially on refighting past wars, played a part as well. Except where natural resources are being directly exploited, industrial location in general allows wide choices. It therefore becomes possible for central governments to favor such regions for a variety of reasons. Nowhere is this easier to do than in manufacture of arms, where criteria of cost-effectiveness are typically ignored.

One such controversy probably was the main cause for the breakup of Czechoslovakia. Slovakia, its eastern part, had disproportionate troubles when the Warsaw Pact regimes disintegrated because its durable manufacturing was largely military; it had large tank factories and most of the other arms makers that had made Czechoslovakia the eighth largest arms producer in the world.

During the second Czechoslovak Republic, the Czechs had to contend with constant Slovak demands for industrial investment. They took these demands seriously, because Slovakia had defected from the first republic and become a loyal satellite of Nazi Germany. It was easiest for the central government to move the arms factories there, at the expense of Bohemia and Moravia, the two Czech provinces. Rival nationalisms also played their part; though speaking very similar languages, historically, Czechs and Slovaks had not been united in the same country since medieval times.

One result of the above industrial imbalance was that Zbrojovka in the Moravian capital of Brno, once one of the most sophisticated makers of small arms, converted to tools and agricultural machinery, leaving only a small operation that made hunting rifles. Most important, Skoda in Pilsen, once one of Europe's greatest arms complexes (ranking with Krupp or Schneider-Creusot) abandoned armaments altogether, and turned instead to its car and electric and diesel locomotive business and other industrial equipment. It had good products and so, when the Communist regime ended, it received multibillion-dollar investments from Siemens and Volkswagen; like much of the rest of the Czech Republic, it is doing quite well. Together with others whose involvement with arms manufacture was limited, the above two firms could thus weather the enormous dislocations that followed the "Velvet Revolution" far better than the Slovak arms factories whose markets virtually dried up almost overnight.

Unable to convert quickly, Slovakia again demanded more money, as well as a slowdown in the reform measures that the central government was trying to pass. Not to trivialize a very serious matter, the result was much like somebody asking the boss for a raise and threatening to quit if it is not granted, only to have the boss say "bon voyage." Thus, divorce, fortunately nonviolent, was the result, with the Czech Republic hoping to become another Austria or Switzerland, and Slovakia likely to become a small version of Poland.

Serious problems have also beset Russia, which, as noted, had about 80 percent of the defense industries of the Soviet Union. Within it, the southern end of the Urals and western Siberia had seen much industrial development, in large part for security reasons. In so large a country, any big factory soon comes to dominate the economic life of a community that is far enough from any other to preclude commuting to other jobs.

For reasons known mainly to Gosplan, moreover, it was precisely the large complexes that became the preferred form of industrial development. As a result, any industrial enterprise became something like a lottery prize for the community that finally got it. As the Supreme Soviet acquired more power by the late 1980s, geographic log-rolling for industrial development became public, where previously such issues had been private bureaucratic battles in Gosplan, and between and within the various ministries.

An especially acute problem is presented by the so-called "secret cities" where the most sensitive and secret weapons were made, and which probably qualify as the world's ultimate company towns. Everything in these cities came from the "company" that owned them, including food stores, clinics, transportation, and housing. These have all had to be cut back greatly and, in fact, there have been many cases where the central government failed to make the payments still due. The living conditions for the million people who live in those places have therefore deteriorated sharply. Most secret cities are in remote regions, so nearby alternatives are virtually nonexistent.

One particular problem concerns the erstwhile nuclear facilities. What will obviously be an enormous job in environmental cleanups and dismantling of weapons has barely started and may employ many of those affected. Especially given the enormous nuclear armaments the Soviet Union had accumulated, the alternative of displaced workers in that industry spreading their talents elsewhere in the world is a danger that does not really need further elaboration.[8]

The problems of at least one center of arms manufacture also had nationalistic overtones. In January 1992, the Russian government proposed that Udmurtia, one of its autonomous republics and the original home of the ever-popular AK–47 rifle, turn its arms skills into becoming a world center for the industry in order to earn dollars in the arms export trade.[9] The Udmurts are a non-Russian people related to the Finns and Estonians.

The prevalent large industrial complexes also meant that, in all too many cases, a given plant or two made all of the product concerned for the whole country. This put an extra load on an already overloaded transport system and opened the door to other political pressures. It has also given the managers of such establishments a taste for monopoly and a distaste for competition—yet other mindsets that stand in the way of a functioning, competitive economy.

Even in places where conditions are less daunting, those managers of large complexes who would take kindly to conversion tend to think in terms of converting the complex as a unit. This is hardly the way to go, however; in many new activities it would mean taking economy of scale to quite spectacular excess. It is well established that expecting industrial progress and efficiency mainly from economy of scale has drastic and definable limits.[10] What makes more sense is to take the often undifferentiated open bay space of the factory buildings and turn them into instant "industrial parks."[11] Polaroid's quite successful Russian operations make use of a small part of a larger factory sixty miles south of Moscow. It has followed what are good precepts anywhere: "Start small, test the waters, get to know the territory and be ready to expand when the economy turns around which could be a long time coming."[12]

Human Resources

That the employment structure in military industries is distorted, and that much of it does easily dispensable work, is hardly news. In the United States, it is responsible for the fact that the ratio of indirect to direct expenses is about 1.5 : 1 or 2 : 1 in commercial work, and 5 : 1 or 6 : 1 in military industries; in many military enterprises, there are equal numbers of production workers, engineers, and administrative/clerical workers. For many of the engineers and scientists, the constant pressure to write progress reports and follow other bureaucratic routines has attenuated the real technical or scientific content of their work almost to the vanishing point.

There is every indication from contact with Russian military enterprises and employees that the situation is exactly similar there, but it goes further. Not only was the military preemption of technical industries worse than in the United States, but all the old Soviet economy was grossly overstaffed in ways that actually were disguised unemployment. One nonindustrial example, now gone, which was familiar to visitors, was that of the women who did nothing but preside over the room keys on every floor of every hotel. One more directly related to the topic at hand was the manifest rank creep in the Soviet armed forces, easily observable in the streets of central Moscow by anyone familiar with rank insignia. Again, there had been signs of this in the United States as well.[13] Retraining on a very large scale is clearly necessary, and it is frustrating to find this a major problem, especially when the changing economies are now short of just about everything.

There are four general areas within retraining: The first is product studies—that is, bringing people up to the state of commercial art in the product itself. The second is commercial development, especially value analysis—that is, introducing efficiency in design by making the product's function realizable at minimum cost. Third, there would have to be production system studies, bringing students up to date in modern machinery and the new methods of production management and controls and the physical details of manufacturing. A major subtask would be training in the computer systems associated with this.

Finally, especially at the managerial level, there would have to be training in financial and related operations management. The last of these is especially crucial and likely to prove the most radical departure from past practice. If there is one thing that distinguishes military industry from the rest, it is its cost-plus mentality. Decision making independent of former superiors in the command economy, cost consciousness, and financial viability are the key to ultimate success in industrial conversion.

There appears to be very little systematic effort along anything like these lines. Certainly, there has been no attempt to assess in some way how much actual training individuals would need, and therefore how big an effort would be needed in a given locality. Instead, there have been widespread layoffs and dislocations. The problem is less only in plants which, although in a communist system, focused on supplying their customers by normal commercial criteria under international competition. These are found almost exclusively in the less militarized parts of the old communist bloc, as in Hungary and the Czech Republic.

A major retraining effort in the changing economies would run into constraints of its own. The most serious would be a lack of study material and of suitable faculty. Study materials specifically related to conversion will have to be newly created even in the West. But in the changing economies, in many respects, the new materials would run exactly counter to what practitioners had been taught and how they had worked throughout their careers. This problem applies even more to instructors than to educational materials *per se*. In effect, the instructors would have to be trained first. That takes time.

The Broader Purpose of Conversion

For the changing economies, the conversion problem is an inextricable, if not central, part of becoming market-oriented and developing a substantial private business sector. The worst damage by the communist command economies was done in the former Soviet Union, where most technical industry became an appendage of the military-industrial complex, neglected by its managers, undercapitalized, and starved for innovation. While their conversion is not faced with trying to enter alternative civilian markets already saturated by imports or domestic civilian producers as in the West, they have a population whose purchasing power has been largely destroyed. By any competitive standard, most of their industrial plants are obsolete for commercial products and would be unable to compete except by low wages. Wages have in fact fallen to grotesquely low levels, as measured not only by exchange rates, but by how much work time is needed to pay for many of the simplest things.

This raises the most urgent question of how this vicious circle is to be broken. There is no business sector to do it; there is a small, new, moneyed elite, but it is not a group likely at this time to make much in the way of long-term investments in industrial renewal. Some of it consists of members of the old nomenklatura who, by virtue of having access to natural resources, try to secure places in the new regime and enrich themselves in the meantime. Beyond the extra risks in what are quite often transactions of questionable legality, there must still also be a serious question in their minds about how secure private property is under the new governments, and whether it can again (as in the past) be expropriated by the stroke of a pen.

The notion of limits to the power of government flourishes to the greatest extent in only a very few countries, mostly those hewing to the Anglo-Saxon political tradition. Whatever the image they project today, the countries in most of Western Europe and Asia have more authoritarian proclivities, and those are the countries that are also held up as role models to the changing economies. Yet, surely, limited government powers would have to be at the center of any new "democratic" order deserving of the name.

At the same time, however, the public sector in the changing economies is still the only sector that has the power to muster enough effort to restart the economies. Gradualism in such efforts would not have been easy either. But the "market shock" approach (that is, changes without much government direction), as advocated by Jeffrey Sachs and other Western advisers, has performed poorly.[14]

In the best cases (e.g., of the Czech Republic, Slovenia, Hungary, and Poland), rapid inflation was avoided, and in some cases, the decline of production appears to have come to a halt. In all cases, unemployment continues to rise. And, most important, not a single economy has so far proved that shock therapy is leading to an increase in productive investment.

One might note that hyperinflation in Poland had taken place in earlier years, though it has abated. Polish elections in September 1993, however, showed a resurgence of former Communists. This presaged the far more disastrous results of the December 1993 elections in Russia, which made fascism, potentially combined with born-again Communism, a new global threat. Ultranationalist Vladimir Zhirinovsky had made the failure of conversion efforts a major issue in his campaign.

At the center of these continuing troubles is a still-deficient industrial structure that can only be remedied by conversion. And that in turn can only take place if there is effective demand for products. In the short or medium run, that can only come from governmental action, and, specifically, from a Keynesian injection of public funds. Public works projects are key. In the changing economies, only converted military industries can provide the resources necessary to carry them out. The Russian government's continuation of subsidies to military centers, to keep them and their political representatives in Moscow quiet, is just the wrong policy.

Constructive investment is now a necessity in many countries, most assuredly including the United States and the countries of Western Europe, both of which have been struggling with unemployment problems. In many of those countries, the problem is not only conversion to repair industrial decay, but that large corporations (including major multinationals) have their own profound troubles arising from the kinds of market misjudgments and bureaucratic overhead that are found in military enterprises. The result has been huge layoffs. Their recent troubles are a useful reminder that capitalism has its own dysfunctions and limitations.

As in the United States (where this is also an issue, especially on the federal level), it is essential to revise the budget practices to distinguish between investment and current consumption. Productive *investment*, not consumption expenditure, is key to effective economic renewal. A second element in the prescription, related to these accounting changes, would have to be an end to deficit hysteria as it relates to those investments, on the part of both domestic budgeters and international lending agencies. To be sure, the resources of the latter are also limited. However, such projects as making the neglected transportation systems and infrastructures work properly would not only improve the efficiency of the changing economies, but would get money to the people and thus help them toward a functioning society.

An important effect of such projects, particularly in the CIS countries, would be to help farming. Contrary to earlier periods of history, Russian agriculture now relies on electricity, motor fuel, and machinery and its spare parts, as well as on good transportation for its products. Any failure in those areas quickly impairs the food supply. Present food problems, in fact, are largely due to just such failures and mismanagement in recent decades.

One alternative sometimes proposed is that of using the changeover to create yet other export-driven economies, poor themselves and producing for richer customers abroad. But that way lies disaster; some misguided business leaders looking for acquisitions and some governments might favor this, but it would quickly lead to a downward auction in social and working conditions and a backlash in the putative recipients that would only exacerbate the already strong and rising opposition to free trade.

This is hardly what the world needs. The global economy is now much like a grievously ill patient whose condition is made worse by internal bleeding that promptly overcomes any therapy. Some of its causes, like overpopulation, are hard to remedy in the short run, but the military excess that is a principal cause of the decline of one industrial society after another can be changed by a simple act of political will. Its military sector, after all, is a country's ultimate discretionary expenditure.

In this respect, as in so many other proposals, including those related to conversion in the United States, the choice is not between making the new investments required and spending money on the one hand, and not doing them and saving money on the other. The choice is between turning the former Communist countries into functioning societies that can take part in the world economy, and having them as permanent international relief clients that stumble from one crisis to another and constitute a potentially disastrous threat to world peace. The second alternative would be infinitely more costly. That so much time has been wasted everywhere is a disgrace. But, as in so many other instances of economic dysfunction, nowhere is this more true than in the changing economies. For them, conversion is the key, the only one, to the industrial renewal which, in turn, is indispensable to their prospects for a better life.

Notes

1. J.E. Baird, "A network model of the conversion process," in *Conversion Prospects of the Defense Electronics Industry*, ed. by J.E. Ullmann (Hempstead, NY: Hofstra Yearbooks of Business, 1965), pp. 429–70.

2. Y.A. Avduyevsky, "Conversion and economic reforms: The experience of Russia." Proceedings of the Conference on "Conversion: National Case Studies," *Peace and the Sciences* (Vienna: International Institute for Peace, March 1992), p. 7.

3. Ibid.

4. J. Evans and B. Berman, *Marketing*, 5th ed. (New York: Macmillan, 1992), p. 9.

5. G. Richter and D. Straeter, *Conversion '90: Struktur-wandel durch Abruestung—Perspektiven fuer die 90er Jahre* (Munich: IMU-Institut, 1991).

6. R.W. Stevenson, "Russia's technology tag sale," *New York Times* (May 26, 1993).

7. B.Y. Hong, *Inflation under Cost Pass-Along Management* (New York: Praeger, 1979). See also J.E. Ullmann, "Economic conversion: Indispensable for America's economic recovery," Briefing Paper 3 (Washington, DC: National Commission for Economic Conversion and Disarmament, 1989).

8. W.J. Broad, "Russian says Soviet atom arsenal was larger than was estimated," *New York Times* (September 26, 1993).

9. C. Bohlen, "Arms factories can make bricks, but, Russia asks, is that smart?" *New York Times* (February 24, 1992).

10. J.E. Ullmann, *The Improvement of Productivity* (New York: Praeger, 1980).

11. J.E. Ullmann, "Building a peacetime economy," *Technology Review* (August–September 1991): 56–63.

12. S. Greenhouse, "Polaroid's Russian success story," *New York Times* (November 24, 1991).

13. J.E. Reilly, "The Armed Forces," in *Problems in the Growth and Efficiency of Administrative and Service Functions*, ed. by J.E. Ullmann (Hempstead, NY: Hofstra Yearbooks of Business, 1978), pp. 175–208.

14. J. Kregel, A. Lushin, E. Matzner, and L. Specht, *The Post-Shock Agenda* (Vienna: Austrian Academy of Sciences, Research Unit for Socio-Economics, 1993).

Index

Contributors

Domenick Bertelli is associate director for economic conversion programs at the Work and Technology Institute in Washington, DC, and program coordinator for the Workplace Economic Conversion Action Network. Formerly, he was director of the Conversion Information Center at the Council on Economic Priorities in New York City.

Gregory A. Bischak is executive director of the National Commission on Economic Conversion and Disarmament in Washington, DC. He is editor of and contributing author to *Towards a Peace Economy in the United States*, and former economic research analyst at Employment Research Associates of Lansing, Michigan.

Lloyd (Jeff) Dumas is professor of political economy and economics at the University of Texas at Dallas. His work on conversion and related matters includes *Reversing Economic Decay: The Political Economy of Arms Reduction, The Overburdened Economy: Uncovering the Causes of Chronic Unemployment, Inflation and National Decline*, and *Making Peace Possible: The Promise of Economic Conversion*. From 1991 to 1993, he served as vice chair of the Texas Taskforce on Economic Transition, under Governor Ann Richards.

Dana L. Dunn is associate professor of sociology and director of women's studies at the University of Texas at Arlington. Her teaching and research interests focus on the sociology of work, gender issues, and social inequality. In addition to numerous research publications, she is coauthor of forthcoming texts in sociological research methods and in social problems.

Amitai Etzioni is University Professor at George Washington University in Washington, DC. He is currently president of the American Sociological Association.

Jonathan M. Feldman is research associate at the Project on Regional and Industrial Economics at Rutgers University. He was previously program director and senior fellow at the National Commission for Economic Conversion and Disarmament in Washington, DC.

George Mehring is a consultant in personal and organizational change at Clinical Hypnotherapy, Inc., of Baltimore, specializing in communications-based interventions that result in new learning systems. He is a Certified Rehabilitation Counselor and an instructor in the Applied Behavioral Sciences Program at Johns Hopkins University.

Elizabeth Mueller is assistant professor at the Graduate School of Management and Urban Policy and Senior Researcher at the Community Development Research Center of the New School for Social Research in New York City. Her current research involves community-based strategies for urban revitalization and displaced/disadvantaged worker retraining programs.

Michael Oden is a postdoctoral research fellow at the Project on Regional and Industrial economics at Rutgers University, where he coordinates the defense Adjustment and Conversion Research Program. He previously worked with local development authorities in Central and Eastern Europe for the Organization of Economic Cooperation and Development in Paris.

James Raffel is a doctoral candidate in the Department of Urban Planning and Policy Development at Rutgers University and is a researcher for the Project on Regional and Industrial Economics at Rutgers University. From 1990 to 1994, he was research and legislative analyst at the National Commission for Economic Conversion and Disarmament in Washington, DC.

Fred Rose is assistant professor of urban and environmental policy at Tufts University in Medford, Massachusetts. He is an activist, currently helping to organize the Military Conversion Accountability

Project in Massachusetts. He completed his doctoral dissertation, *Peace, Labor and Environmental Coalitions: Social Process and Democratic Change* at Cornell University in 1994.

John Ullmann is professor of management and quantitative methods in the School of Business at Hofstra University. An industrial engineer, he has written on conversion and related problems for thirty years. His books include *The Anatomy of Industrial Decline, Prospects of American Industrial Recovery, Social Costs in Modern Society,* and *The Improvement of Productivity.*

DI